Even the Women Must Fight

Militiawoman, painting by Nguyen Ngoc Tuan, 1974.

Even the Women Must Fight

Memories of War from North Vietnam

Karen Gottschang Turner

with Phan Thanh Hao

John Wiley & Sons, Inc.

New York • Chichester • Weinheim • Brisbane • Singapore • Toronto

Library of Congress Cataloging-in-Publication Data

Turner, Karen Gottschang
    Even the women must fight : memories of war from North Vietnam /
Karen G. Turner with Phan Thanh Hao.
        p.   cm.
    Includes bibliographical references and index.
    ISBN 0-471-14689-7 (cloth : alk. paper)
        1. Vietnamese Conflict, 1961–1975—Women—Interviews.
    2. Vietnamese Conflict, 1961–1975—Personal narratives, North
    Vietnamese. 3. Women—Vietnam (Democratic Republic)—Interviews.
    I. Phan, Thanh Hao. II. Title.
    DS559.8.W6T87   1998
    959.704′30922—dc21   97-30281

To our mothers,
Veronica Walsh Niewerth and Vo Bang Thanh,
and our daughters,
Ngo Bich Hanh, Suzanne Zhang Gottschang,
and Kelley Gottschang

CONTENTS

ACKNOWLEDGMENTS

UNLIKE MY ONGOING PROJECTS ON CHINESE LAW, this book has a discrete beginning and ending, and so the list of people who deserve my thanks should be limited. But because I ventured into a new area of study to write the book, the debts I have incurred are in fact many. It all began with a call from an agent, Theresa Park, who had read about my Vietnam trip in 1993 in the East Asian Legal Studies Newsletter circulated by the Harvard Law School. She was convinced even before I was that the story of Vietnamese women in war was worth telling. Hana Lane, my editor at John Wiley & Sons, took the next great leap of faith. To both of these literary woman warriors, thank you. Phan Thanh Hao: my debt to you is obvious to everyone who reads this book. Less obvious is your family's support. I want here to thank your husband, Nguyen Quang Hien, whose delicious meals and kindness warmed my stays in Hanoi; your mother, Vo Bang Thanh, son, Nguyen Phan Quang Binh, daughter-in-law, Ngo Bich Hanh, and granddaughters, Nguyen Phan Thao Dan and Nguyen Phan Linh Dan, for letting me borrow you to work on this book.

William Alford, Director of Harvard's East Asian Legal Studies Program, has offered generous moral and financial support, in part from a Henry Luce Foundation grant, and the Research and Publication Committee at Holy Cross College has also funded travel and research time to complete the work. The William Joiner Center for the Study of War and Social Consequences at the University of Massachusetts in Boston, directed by Kevin Bowen, provided library and archival support and good advice. Phan Chan at Harvard's Yenching Library also helped with materials.

In Vietnam, Professor Phan Huy Le, Director of the Center for Cooperation in Vietnamese Studies, provided me with library access and arranged for a very useful briefing with Professor Nguyen Quoc Dung, Vice-Director of the Vietnam Institute of Military History. To Professor Le and his student and colleague in the History Department at Hanoi University, Nguyen Van Kim, I owe an interesting and productive trip to Thanh Hoa Province in early 1997. Ngo Thao, literary critic and Deputy Secretary of the Vietnam Theatrical Association, inspired me with his deep sympathy for women veterans. The students in the UJPCP Program in Hanoi represent a fine example of a new generation of scholars and leaders for Vietnam; my time working with them was one of the high points of my life in Hanoi. I want especially to mention Nguyen Minh Thu for her ongoing dedication to this project, and Hoang Nga and Hong Hanh for their help in 1996.

Families usually come last in these formal lists but mine deserves a place closer to the top. To my husband, Tom Gottschang, thank you for getting me to Hanoi in the first place, and for the meals, the long talks, the solid academic support, and unquestioning belief that this book was worth it all. To my daughters, Suzanne Zhang Gottschang and Kelley Gottschang, thanks for reminding me of my audience as I wrote and for helping me think through the meanings of these wonderful stories from Vietnam. To my mother, Veronica Walsh Niewerth, my sister, Judith Beth, and my brother, Thomas Niewerth, thank you for showing me early in life the power of quiet strength. To my father, Leland Wright Niewerth, thank you for giving me good history books as soon as I could read.

I owe a great deal to the many experts in the field of Southeast Asian and Vietnamese Studies who generously guided me, an academic interloper from Chinese Studies, as I entered a new research area. In particular, I thank Tai Van Ta and Ho Hue Tam Tai. Marilyn Young and John Whitmore deserve a special thanks for reading the manuscript in its early form and Ngo Vinh Long for checking it as it was going to press. Cynthia Enloe has encouraged and inspired me since we first met in Worcester years ago.

Many colleagues, Vietnamese and foreign, in Hanoi during 1993, 1996, and 1997, and back home in Massachusetts, helped me in various ways. Long talks with Le Thi Quy during the year she taught as a Fulbright Scholar at Clark University took me beyond the realm of the interview and into friendship and collegiality. In addition, I take special note of help given by Nguyen Ngoc Tuan, Duc Hoan, Luong Anh, Le Thi Hoai Phuong, Doan Quach, Le Trong Tam, and Andrea Esser. To Nguyen Thuy Mau and the members of Volunteer Youth Team C814, I will never forget the times we spent together and I hope this book conveys to readers your courage and resilience.

Our roommate on Le Ngoc Han Street, Dan Westbrook, as much a brother as a friend to Hao and me, helped us and our families on many occasions, grand and ordinary. Others who helped along the way with moral support, good talk, and information are: Le Minh Khue, Vu Thu Giang, Nguyen Thi Hong Nhung, Phan Ngoc Anh, Vu Thi Bich Loc, Edie Shillue, Mary Woodward, Ronnie Wynn, Jerry Hembd, Elizabeth Mock, Duong Thi Thanh Mai, Catherine Laswell, Jenny Jaensch, Le Thi Nham Tuyet, Nguyen Kim Cuc, Van Tao, Nguyen Ba Chung, Nguyen Tuyet Mai, Nguyen Thi Minh Ngoc, Selma Botman, Susan Rodgers, Christine Greenway, Joanne Baldine, Joel Popkin, Kandice Hauf, John Prados, Miriam Corneli, Nguyen Van Ngoc, Mark Sidel, John Cruickshank, Ngo Thi Minh, Dermott Morley, Robert Brigham, Ann Marie Leshkowich, Beth Popich, Michelle Meisner, Zhang

Xiaodang, Harriet Phinney, and Vu Kim Dung. To a pioneer in Vietnamese-American friendship, Lady Borton: At this writing, we have not yet met. But your sterling reputation and friendships in Vietnam continue to help pave the way for other American women.

Technical support, library help, and sheer good will at Holy Cross came from Pat Chalifoux, Joel Villa, John Buckingham, and Gudrun Krueger, at Wiley from Joanne Palmer, and in Hanoi from the staff at the UNDP Library.

Lastly, to my own cats, and the humans, birds, cats, and other creatures, past and present, at the Worcester Cat Hospital and Bird Clinic where I have worked as a volunteer, thank you for helping me keep my perspective when I had been too long at my computer.

Despite all the help I received, I must take full responsibility for the interpretations in this book.

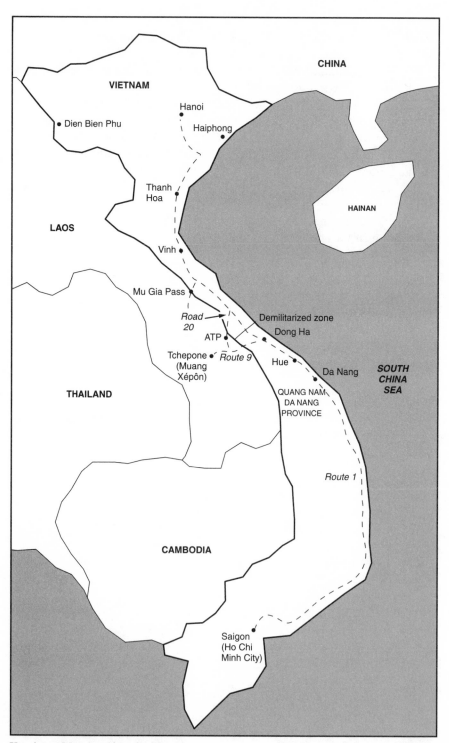

Key Areas Mentioned in the Text

CHRONOLOGY

40	Trung Sisters raise a revolt against the Chinese and set up an independent court.
43	Chinese general Ma Yuan subjugates the rebellions and the Trung Sisters die. Chinese domination of North Vietnam consolidated.
248	Ba Trieu (Lady Trieu Thi Trinh) rallies Vietnamese rebels against the Chinese.
939	Chinese driven out and an era of Vietnamese independence begins.
1117	Queen Mother Linh Nhan manages the realm in her husband's absence and advocates better treatment for slave girls.
1765– 1820	Life of Nguyen Du, author of the *Tale of Kieu*.
1802	Woman general, Bui Thi Xuan, commands a unit of Tay-son rebels against the ruling Vietnamese Nguyen dynasty.
1858	French attack Vietnam at Danang.
1873	French attack Hanoi.
1884	French colonial era begins.
1926	Mme. Nguyen Khoa Tung and other women form a Women's Labor Study Association near Hue. Influential male writer Phan Boi Chau takes up women's issues.
1929	*Phu Nu Tan Van* [Women's News] published in Saigon.
1930	Ho Chi Minh establishes Indochinese Communist Party; Vietnam Women's Union Founded. Women participate in uprisings against the French in Nghe An and Ha Tinh Provinces.
1935	A woman, Nguyen Thi Minh Khai, represents the Indochinese Communist Party at the Seventh International Congress in Moscow.

1938   Women organize and speak out at a May Day rally in Hanoi.

1940   Uprisings against the French in the South spearheaded by women resistance fighters.

1941   Viet Minh Nationalist Front—a coalition of nationalistic Vietnamese forces—created; Nguyen Thi Minh Khai captured and executed by French.

1945   Ho Chi Minh declares Vietnam an independent nation, the Democratic Republic of Vietnam (DRV); French troops return to Vietnam; Madame Nguyen Thi Dinh leads uprising against the French in Ben Tre Province.

1946   Constitution of North Vietnam proclaims economic and political equality for women and women suffrage. Women vote for first time and send ten women to the new Chamber of Deputies; War of resistance against the French begins.

1950   United States gives military and economic assistance to French in Indochina.

1954   French defeated at the battle of Dienbienphu. Thousands of women transport materiel to support the Vietnamese armies at Dienbienphu. Geneva Accords divide Vietnam at the 17th Parallel with elections to be held in two years. North Vietnam independent under a socialist government. South Vietnam governed as a Republic (RVN) under Ngo Dinh Diem, supported by U.S. aid. Viet Minh resistance forces in the South regroup to the North, where radical socialist land reform begins.

1955   RVN President Diem announces elections will not take place; United States begins program of direct aid to South Vietnamese government.

1957   Uprising in Nghe An Province to protest harsh land reform policies of the socialist government.

1959   Line 559 set up as a military unit by DRV to handle logistics for the Ho Chi Minh Trail; "trail" to the sea established.

1960   Uprising in South against Diem regime, led by Nguyen Thi Dinh. National Liberation Front (NLF) established; Law on Marriage and Family promulgated in DRV.

1963   Diem and brother killed in a military coup. U.S. military personnel in Vietnam numbers 16,300.

1964   Military coup puts Major general Nguyen Khanh at head of RVN in the South; first air strikes against targets in the North; U.S. embargo against Vietnam.

1965   NLF attacks military base at Pleiku. United States steps up bombing of North. April 3–4, United States begins bombing of the Thanh Hoa (Dragon's Jaw) Bridge where Ngo Thi Tuyen performs heroic actions. U.S. military personnel now at 385,000; Nguyen Thi Dinh appointed Deputy Commander of NLF; "Three Responsibilities Movement" to mobilize women announced by DRV.

1966   B-52s bomb North. Ho Chi Minh calls for all-out people's support. Women enter volunteer youth corps.

1967   Bombing of Hanoi area.

1968   January 30, TET offensives by NVA and PLAF armies begin against major targets in the South; November, United States halts bombing of North, but concentrates on Ho Chi Minh Trail.

1969   September 3, Ho Chi Minh dies.

1971   February, ARVN launches attacks on the Ho Chi Minh Trail in Laos; United States resumes bombing of DRV.

1972   Peace talks continue. April 15, bombing of Haiphong; December 18–30, bombing of Hanoi and Haiphong areas; second wave of volunteer youth called up.

1973   January 27, peace agreement signed; U.S. ground troops withdraw from Vietnam. Bombing of Indochina halted by order of United States; war between North and South continues.

1974   People's Army of Vietnam (PAVN) begins all-out offensive against the South.

1975   April 30, PAVN troops enter Saigon; Americans leave; civil war ends and Vietnam is unified. Re-education campaigns begin in the South.

1977   Vietnam admitted to United Nations.

1978   Khmer Rouge invade South Vietnam.

1979   Sino-Vietnamese border war.

1986   Law on protecting the rights of children without fathers promulgated.

1986   Renovation (*doi moi*) of economic structure from a centrally planned to a controlled market system initiated. Open-door policy announced.

1990   Vietnamese troops withdraw from Cambodia. First period of peace since 1945.

1991   Labor law to protect the safety and welfare of women workers promulgated.

1993   Vietnamese government policies to control prostitution and AIDS introduced.

1994   U.S. embargo against Vietnam ends.

1995   Civil Code promulgated.

1997   Full diplomatic relations and exchanges of ambassadors between United States and Vietnam.

INTRODUCTION

Lucky Distance

Every book tells stories, some intended, some not.

Lila Abu-Lughod, *Writing Women's Worlds:
Bedouin Stories,* 1993.

A woman is like a drop of rain, which can fall into a palace or muddy rice fields.

Vietnamese proverb.

AS I REFLECT ON THE HISTORY OF THIS BOOK, I am struck by the irony that it all began with a kitchen talk in Hanoi in 1993. It took me three years, listening to women tell their war stories, reading Vietnamese diaries and poetry, and watching the films that represent a lifetime of experiences by a female director and veteran of two wars before I began to understand how the American War affected the Vietnamese women who lived through it. For me, safe in a nation untouched by the direct brutality of war, the decade between 1965 and 1975 brought new opportunities to free myself from domestic definitions of the ideal woman. For women in Vietnam, those years brought so much death and destruction that dreams of returning home to normal family life sustained them. What I have come to see as my lucky distance from war might well have blinded me to the meanings of war, family, and the good life for Vietnamese women. Until one night in May 1993, when two Vietnamese friends let down their guard to talk about what the war meant to them.

We sat in the kitchen not because a Vietnamese kitchen is a cozy spot designed for conversation, but because it was the only place with good light and chairs. My husband, Tom Gottschang, and his colleague, Dan Westbrook, in Vietnam to teach economics at Hanoi's National Economics University, had rented a house on a busy market street in the center of the city. I was there to begin a comparative project on the legal status of women in China and Vietnam.

Our neighbor, Phan Thanh Hao, had brought us together to examine a series of paintings of the Ho Chi Minh Trail. The artist, Nguyen Ngoc Tuan, a film studio set designer at the time, had carried his water colors as he

1

Women fording a stream on the Ho Chi Minh Trail, painting by Nguyen Ngoc Tuan, 1974.

walked down the Trail in 1974 to paint scenes for a film he wanted to produce. It was to be called "The Song of the Ho Chi Minh Trail," to celebrate one of the most potent symbols of Vietnamese resistance to the United States. Funds for the film never materialized, and twenty years later his paintings had become important historical pieces, for they preserved the artist's first-hand responses to wartime life. As we turned the paintings over one by one, to the clatter of tired ceiling fans and the hum of an ancient Russian refrigerator, we were surprised to find women in some of the pictures, engaged in the danger, the drudgery, and the camaraderie that make up any war. We asked whether the heavily burdened women crossing a mountain stream, the exhausted women shoveling gravel to fill a bomb crater, or the teenagers relaxing together in a secluded jungle station represented reality or the artist's imagination.

Tuan told us that these women were real indeed, that their presence on the Trail had moved him deeply. "They had a deep spirit, a love of life, even as they did the hardest work. And there were so many of them on the roads." For him the Ho Chi Minh Trail was more than a maze of footpaths and roads, more than the main route for shipping supplies from the rear in the North to the regular army units and Viet Cong guerrillas south of the seventeenth parallel. It was a potent symbol of Vietnamese patriotism and determi-

Crossing a rope bridge on the Ho Chi Minh Trail, painting by Nguyen Ngoc Tuan, 1974.

nation in the face of a technologically superior enemy. "The Trail," he told us, "stays in my mind. It was the only road that would lead us to victory and everyone knew how hard it was to build it." The women who used primitive tools to open and maintain the Trail represented for him the best traits of Vietnam itself: they were small but tough, ill-equipped but effective, romantic but realistic.

Hao was equally intrigued with the lore of the Ho Chi Minh Trail but more troubled about the consequences of Vietnam's wars. A journalist in her mid-forties, a cosmopolitan person fluent in English and French, she was accustomed to dealing with foreigners who trekked to Hanoi in search of information and forgiveness. We didn't know until that night that she had volunteered as a teenager to collect and bury the dead during the 1966 and 1967 bombings in the Hanoi area. This intimate contact with the carnage of war haunted her—especially the death of the young, who, as she put it, "had never known love, had never really lived." For Hao, war meant nothing but suffering and sorrow.

How differently a woman and a man could interpret a common past, I thought at the time. As Tuan reminisced about the brave women who had inspired his paintings, Hao interrupted. Yes, she acknowledged, the women had been good soldiers. But they had paid dearly for their war service, in ways

Rural women at work, painting by Nguyen Ngoc Tuan, 1974.

that men had not. With apologies to the men in the room for talking frankly, she explained that many women had lost their sexual health after years in the jungles, returning to their villages barren, unmarriageable, condemned to life on the margins in a society that values family above all else. Stress, back-breaking labor, malnutrition, contact with death and blood had eventually robbed these young girls of the very future they sought to defend when they left home in the first place.

It was not just women's indomitable spirit that counted, she reminded us, but their physical labor that made the difference, and not just during wartime. "Look around you. Notice who balances the shoulder pole, who tends the markets and stalls all over the city. In the rice fields, along the roads throughout Vietnam, the main labor is done by women. They work with sim-ple tools, shoveling rocks, carrying goods in small baskets, bending over in the paddies to transplant, and then cooking, cleaning, and caring for the fam-ily when the outside work is done. During the war, women added men's work to their daily chores as they learned to shoot antiaircraft guns, bury the dead, plow the fields—all the while coping with air raids and the disruption and panic they brought."

Most troubling to Hao was that the state had neither properly recog-nized the dead nor repaid the living. Plagued by what she often referred to as "survivor's guilt," she lamented as well that people like herself, with decent jobs and children, had no way to make it up to the veterans who had returned home wounded in body and spirit. In particular, she feared that women's sacrifices might be overlooked, or their contributions trivialized, as Vietnam moves toward an open, market economy where youth and the competitive spirit will likely become more important than history, service, and community.

After that momentous talk, I began to comprehend how well Vietnam hides its war scars. Initially, I had been fooled—by Hanoi's old buildings and markets, seemingly untouched by bombs, by the welcoming smiles of people ready to move on to a pragmatic relationship with Americans—into thinking that the war was truly over, a distant memory. "Why do you want to talk about the war?" an interpreter in his thirties asked me. "We want to forget about it. It is only you Americans and the older people who think about it." And an elderly veteran, now a high-ranking member of the Ministry of Defense, presented the official line to me during a luncheon meeting with his delegation at Harvard in 1996: "Women in the war? Yes, I remember how my mother supported me. It was our mothers who kept our spirits high, you know. But now Vietnam is ready to prosper and develop. We don't want to dwell on the war." I knew by then, however, that there was much more to the war story than mothers who stayed home while their sons did the fighting. And not all Vietnamese people were ready to welcome a new era without reflecting on the past.

I looked at Hanoi differently after I began to see Vietnamese history through the eyes of the war generation. Despite the absence of visible signs of destruction from American bombs, Hanoi is a city whose public spaces are defined by war. Almost every major street is named for a hero who liberated Vietnam from outside invaders. Two of the streets I crossed on my bicycle every day bore the names of famous women warriors of the past. A temple to the sisters Trung, Vietnam's earliest national patriots, graced a nearby neighborhood. Near Hoan Kiem Lake, in the center of the city, a large statue of a woman with a gun over her shoulder and a baby in her arms reminds passersby that in Vietnam a woman can be both a warrior and a mother, that as the proverb of uncertain origin declares, "When war strikes close to home, even the women must fight." The tradition of the fighting woman and the experiences of women in the American War are not minor themes in Vietnam, but part and parcel of national and popular culture. Hao's concern for women veterans was not the product of an eccentric individual obsessed with memories, but emerges from a sense of history that defines an entire generation.

AFTER I RETURNED HOME IN JUNE 1993, I decided to put aside temporarily my work on comparative law. It seemed to me then and more so now that I could not assess the place of law in postwar women's lives in Vietnam without weighing first the link between women and war. Comparisons between China and Vietnam at first glance seem appropriate, for both have drawn from a common well of religious and cultural traditions and socialist ideologies as they have struggled to maintain political and cultural integrity in the face of outside forces.[1] But while China defines itself as a culture devoted to civil virtues, Vietnam's very identity as a nation has been molded by war. In the past fifty years alone, Vietnam has fought against the French from 1946 to 1954, the Americans from 1964 to 1973, and the Chinese and the Khmer Rouge on and off from 1979 until 1989. It is no surprise that these years of nearly constant disruption and violence have affected all aspects of Vietnamese culture, including attitudes toward women and women's own life histories.

WHEN I BEGAN TO THINK ABOUT WOMEN, WAR, AND VIETNAM, I had to face up to my own ignorance of Vietnam's postwar circumstances, to figure out why women warriors, so essential to Vietnam's long history and so important in the most photographed war in history, have remained invisible to most Americans. To be sure, like many American women who came of age during the Vietnam War, I was fascinated and inspired by wartime media portraits of militiawomen and stories of martial heroines. In my own case, cautioned by my studies of Chinese model women, who often represented the officials' dream girls rather than real people, such superpatriots seemed to represent isolated cases or nationalistic propaganda. In the two images of women that did stick—Kim Phuc, the little girl running naked from a napalm attack, and a small militiawoman pointing a big gun at a downed American pilot—it was the link with our guilt and failures that left their mark. Women soldiers competently going about their business away from the American cameras never found a place in my memory.

Once the war was over and the embargo in place, like most Americans I lost touch with ongoing life in Vietnam. The image of the militiawoman faded away, as passive, inert female accessories to the American story—prostitutes, war brides, and displaced refugees—filtered through a media and literary world dominated by male veterans and filmmakers. This is not surprising, for "authentic" war stories are traditionally regarded as the exclusive domain of the men who experience combat firsthand. The women who supposedly linger on the sidelines, away from the real violence, stay in the shadows when the stories are retold.[2] Anyone who reads the few accounts by American nurses who served in Vietnam feels their pain not only for the tragedies they witnessed but for their second-class status in the military and then the civilian worlds.

Vietnamese women too disappeared from their country's record of struggle and victory, both in the United States and in Vietnam itself. Critic Kali Tal points out that Asian women have all too often been defined largely by their

"The small guerrilla woman holds high her gun and the tall American walks with bowed head." (*Caption and photo courtesy of the Vietnam Women's Museum*)

relationships with American men: "These fictional relationships with Asian women, whether mistresses or prostitutes, do not indicate any feeling *on the part of either character or author* that women are human beings deserving of respect."[3] She argues that the flat female characters in the Vietnam war stories produced in the United States reflect the reluctance of veteran male writers to come to terms with the dehumanizing effects of war. But I think that many of us accepted portraits of women as victims because they were less troubling than real life accounts of women's all too human anger and daily struggles to survive. I sympathize with Susan Brownmiller, a television reporter during the war, as she recalls her reactions to the war era: "The truth was, I'd checked out of Vietnam emotionally a long time ago. I had ceased to follow its fortunes sometime after the 1968 Tet Offensive, had renewed my interest during the 1973 Paris peace talks, then dropped it again until those awesome shots on TV of the last helicopters leaving Saigon. We need our defense mechanisms, and mine had been to disengage from the horror by skipping the news stories, by turning the page."[4]

In Vietnam, as hundreds of thousands of wounded men returned to their families and communities, as male veterans and reporters began to write about the war, public pity focused on the male veteran. Hao told me that "everyone felt sorry for the men. There were so many veterans and they had so clearly suffered so much. Everyone could see it. No one thought about the women then." The few writings from Vietnam available in English portray the "people's" war as one fought by men alone.[5] Recently, the fiction of Vietnamese women veterans has started to appear in English. But most women veterans are not skilled with the pen, or have no access to the publication industry, and so ordinary women's remembrances can be preserved only through oral histories.

AS I PLUMBED MY OWN MEMORY, it came back to me that I had once been impressed when as a student of early Chinese history I had read about Chinese armies encountering women rebels in Vietnam. In 1993, as I talked about this current book with my husband Tom, a veteran who was drafted and served in Vietnam from 1970 to 1971, he reminded me that years ago he had described to me the Bravo 8/3 Female Mortar Platoon, a group of very young women—named for March 8, International Women's Day. A combat platoon, they had all been killed and their diaries forwarded to Army intelligence, where he had read them with deep sadness and respect. At the time he told the story, I was reluctant to bring up my feelings about his role in the war, or the anger I felt on behalf of these dead women, who were about the same age as my daughters. The memory of that conversation slipped away—until I began to talk with women in Vietnam.

Early in life I had learned that war is not a topic men and women discuss with ease. My father and uncles had served during World War II, and although they were not scorned after the war, neither did all of them fully recover. The haunted look on one uncle's face when he returned from Pearl Harbor, or the silence from another uncle about the Battle at Iwo Jima, stay with me. My mother did get stronger during the war—that I knew intuitively as a child. She changed worn-out tires with ease, drove herself from the farm to the city hospital to give birth to my brother, and hunted for game when the coffers were low. When the men returned there was no vocabulary to help families understand how to cope with war-scarred veterans. They weren't the same men who went off to war. A taste of freedom from everyday family worries, exotic travel as well as brushes with death and destruction, had changed them. Once home, they faced an uncertain economic future. It was no time for my mother and her female relatives to fight for their equality within the household. Harmony in the home became a priority and women acted as the peacemakers.[6]

AS I READ, REMEMBERED, AND WROTE from summer 1993 to early 1996, pretty much in isolation from ongoing life in Hanoi, I became committed to presenting a picture of Vietnamese women as active agents of their own lives rather than as hapless victims. Not only have I been influenced by the work of feminist anthropologists,[7] but I have learned to respect the strength of Asian women in the years I have worked in the region. I owe my late-blooming feminism to a year in China in 1979, when in a Beijing student dormitory with a reticent Chinese roommate, few creature comforts, and anti-American foreign students from all over the world, I finally had the time and the distance to reflect on my life and America's place in the world order. There, I learned simply from living with and observing women that despite its emancipatory rhetoric, China is still a patriarchal society. More importantly, I saw how women teachers, students, and workers had developed strategies to manipulate the system as they schemed to improve life for their families and maybe for themselves, once everyone else was cared for. That true grit is not always displayed in obvious ways, and that quiet resistance in the home and workplace can be just as effective as direct confrontation, are some of the lessons I took home from China. In my academic work on Chinese law, I began to focus on the "resistance of the weak," the hidden paths that individuals take to fight against stronger external forces that threaten their individual needs.[8]

China's history of heroic women, and what I knew about women's efforts to parlay war service into rights after nationalist revolutions in other countries, led me to assume that similar forces were at work in Vietnam. Surely, I thought, the Vietnamese women who fought alongside men must have made up a powerful political voice when the war ended; they must have asserted their historical and moral claims to full citizenship in the nation. Again, firsthand encounters brought home to me how complicated and culturally specific women's resistance can be.

WHEN I RETURNED TO VIETNAM in early 1996 to interview veterans, I found Hanoians generally more cautious about dealings with outsiders than they had been three years earlier and Hao even more sober about the costs of the war for ordinary people. The lifting of the American embargo in 1994 promised an influx of trade dollars and philanthropic aid, but these new opportunities seemed to create apprehension, in both popular and official circles, about the long-term repercussions of accommodating yet more foreigners, their culture, and their money. A major Party Congress loomed in June to decide the path of market reforms (*doi moi*) and the open door policy that began in earnest in 1986. Newly declassified military documents and the twentieth anniversary of reunification celebrated in 1995 generated media coverage that brought to light new stories of sacrifice, vivid reminders that nearly every family in Vietnam had been touched by war and death.

During the three years that I was in the United States boning up on the history of Vietnamese women warriors, filling my head with notions of glorious heroes of the revolution, Hao was living through a collective grieving that challenged the very legitimacy of the heroic mode.

Despite the cool political climate in Hanoi, as friends and colleagues both Vietnamese and foreign heard about my interest in women veterans' stories, help came in serendipitous ways. A phone call from an acquaintance with good news, "I know someone and I'll see if she wants to talk to you," would often lead to a trip on the back of a motorcycle with a young student guide and interpreter to meet women whose names in some cases I never learned. There was no overarching plan guiding my interviews, but eventually I was able to meet a good cross section of female veterans, from the city and countryside, the professional class, workers, and farmers. At first I had hoped to write this book entirely from oral histories, to record how these women remembered the war, how they placed themselves in the history of their nation. But as patterns emerged out of conversations, I could see that some topics never came up directly.

Different avenues to understanding Vietnamese women in war emerged from creative literature and archival materials. For example, letters, diaries, poetry, and Party and army reports that American soldiers took from captured Vietnamese and sent on to Saigon to be preserved in the Combined Document Exploitation Center (CDEC) contain some women's records. After the materials were analyzed by U.S. intelligence officers, they were microfilmed and sent to the National Archives. Today, ninety-four reels of film are available at the University of Massachussetts in Boston. Rich as these materials are for the historian, they have been virtually ignored.[9]

Wartime writings from Vietnam reveal that women's matter-of-fact determination in the face of terrible danger and daily hardship did not go unnoticed by the men who worked with them, as I learned after gaining access to a valuable unpublished manuscript containing copies of military records kept by men on the Ho Chi Minh Trail as well as memoirs by Vietnamese male soldiers and journalists who recorded their impressions of women they observed. These materials reveal how women's presence in war affected male visions of heroism, service, and gender relations. In addition, novels, short stories, television programs, and films produced in Vietnam in the past decade present alternative expressions of common experiences.

This book is limited to a study of women in war in North Vietnam. The situation in the South is better known in the United States through refugee accounts,[10] oral histories from Vietnam,[11] and two recent women's books, Le

Ly Hayslip's autobiography of her life in wartime South Vietnam and her journey to America,[12] and Lady Borton's moving reports of her experiences in Vietnam in the last two decades.[13] Far less is known about women's war service in North Vietnam, even by citizens there. More than one Hanoian recalled learning about the true hardships of the women volunteer youth teams during the war only after seeing a documentary produced in Vietnam in the 1990s. "We cried when we saw the films about the young women on the Trail, running from bombs, carrying heavy burdens, their eyes dark with tiredness and sickness," a good friend told me.

A dilemma faced by anthropologists in their work but one that is new to me as a text-based historian continues to trouble me. I want to offer as much detail as I can to bring these women's personal stories to life, but I do not wish to compromise or endanger them. Some women met me in neutral places and asked not to be named. Some wanted to be in the book and asked for a copy when it is published. Some were proud that an outsider was interested in their personal history and at times, as we talked, I would find husbands and sons circling us in amazement when they realized that it was Mom who had the story worth telling. I have changed names and situations in cases where anyone could be harmed by the information given me, but I have tried to retain the integrity of the voices and memories of all those who talked to me because they don't want to be forgotten.

Aware that much ink has been spilled over the limits and rewards of using oral histories, particularly when they involve a charged historical event, I knew that some veterans presented testimonials, which were directed at educating me and through me my American audience.[14] These carefully crafted accounts often drew from a common reservoir of experience and myth. For example, several women recalled that they had pricked their fingers to draw blood to use as ink when they wrote letters to local authorities, begging them to overlook the fact that they were not yet old enough to serve in the youth corps. Most women did not wish to disengage their personal histories from the story of the national struggle, precisely because their individual lives took on meaning through their links with larger events.

It was from ongoing conversations, as women who became my friends retold their stories, filling in gaps as we came to know each other better, that details and differences in personal experiences emerged most clearly. These exchanges did not end when I left Vietnam. Not only with Hao, my co-author, but with other women, e-mail and fax machines made possible a virtual dialogue, as I sent drafts to Vietnam to be read and critiqued. I was able to stay in touch with some of the veterans of a volunteer youth troop, C814, through friends. In July 1997, Thu, one of the young women who had worked with me to interview the veterans of this troop, went to their annual reunion and read them passages from the sections of this book devoted to their memories. She wrote to tell me about it: "When I finished reading, you

Author (*right*) with Phan Thanh Hao (*left*) and Duc Hoan, Hanoi, 1996.

know, the troop leader shook my hand and said this was the first time he had listened to a real, moving story written by an American. I wish you had been there on that day."[15]

I wish I had been there too, to ask the questions I didn't know enough to ask the first times we met, to hear for myself their responses, to observe firsthand their reactions to a foreign woman's version of events that still trouble both sides.

IN 1996, HAO AND I BEGAN TO WORK TOGETHER, aided by English-speaking students from the University Job Placement and Consulting Program that she supervises. We were both cautious. I knew from nearly two decades of work in China that involving a colleague from a country suspicious of foreigners in even the most benign research project can be harmful to both parties. She had reason to be wary of outsiders whose proposals had at times spun off in directions she never anticipated. At the outset, we tried to be clear about how we would work together but maintain our separate voices. We decided that I would write the book and she would help me collect information and comment in writing on my presentations of interpretations and facts. This give and take was at times painful, and sometimes we could not honestly see eye-to-eye and simply agreed to disagree. As we discussed hard issues—what is true, whose stories carry more authentic information than others, what materials should be included, how the stories might be focused—

we were learning more from each other than any book on discourse theory could offer. And I was hearing in the best way, through daily conversations, how nuanced one woman's views of history and postwar culture could be.

The self-confident woman I first met in 1993, dressed in jeans and high heels, carried her hard past and present difficulties lightly, as did so many of the middle-aged women I met. One had to look carefully to discover their histories and troubles. Once I began to know Hao as a friend, I noticed things I had ignored before. In 1993, impressed by her modern house with its art-filled walls, our American household had fantasized that she was so powerful a force in the neighborhood that she had actually halted the early morning slaughter of pigs outside our bedroom window after I confessed that I plugged my ears against the inevitable morning screams. Later I discovered that it wasn't Hao who chased the butchers away. She too felt vulnerable in the neighborhood as she negotiated constantly with the street vendors, who blocked her front door and then used her house as a hiding place when the police came around to check their licenses.

I learned, too, how Hao herself viewed us, the foreigners, when we first moved into the neighborhood. She told me that she had not known when we looked at the paintings of the Ho Chi Minh Trail together in 1993 that Tom had served in the U.S. army during the war: "So that night when we talked about the paintings in your house, I just thought that Tom's sympathy was for the plight of the painter. Only later, when I knew Karen better, did I discover why Tom had been so somber when we looked at the paintings of the Trail—because they brought up his bad feelings about the past."

We, the guilty Americans, were not the center of our Vietnamese friends' universe. They had other matters on their minds: family dramas, friends who needed money, sick children, and jobs.

I found out over time that Hao's life history was similar to mine only in that we had both married and become mothers at a very young age and had fought hard to gain an education. Socialist political campaigns had disrupted her childhood almost as much as war. She was the daughter of a famous poet and activist during the anti-French resistance and a woman from one of the old Hue mandarin families, and her family paid for its bourgeois background most dearly in 1954, when her paternal grandparents were killed in the radical land reforms. In 1965, as North Vietnam's leaders geared up for an all-out war to reunify the South and to respond to an escalation of the air war against the North, her father was arrested on vague charges that he had too many foreign ideas and possible counterrevolutionary sympathies. Her mother and siblings were treated at once as social and political outcasts, denied access to education, decent jobs, adequate food, and housing. But by the war's end, by dint of hard work and a talent for languages, Hao had earned a place as a journalist and an interpreter.

I saw her as a prime exemplar of a woman who had made the best of her life through diligence and careful decisions. She felt that pure luck lurked behind any woman's success, and that good fortune could all disappear in a flash, just as homes and people had disintegrated even before the noise of the B-52s could be heard over the skies of Hanoi during the war. As she and I talked about a title for this book, our differences came to the fore. I wanted a title that bespoke heroism, courage. She argued for something that pointed to victims, sorrow. I believed that Vietnamese women had for too long been dismissed in the United States precisely because we never saw their anger and their survival strategies.

As Hao and I talked over these thorny issues, the caution of a Vietnamese scholar now in the U.S. came back to me: "If the Vietnamese people are treated only as a bunch of overgrown children, Vietnamese women are often described as perfect models of femininity—submissive to the authority of their fathers and husbands, passive, dependent and domesticated." Professor Long goes on to argue that when the Vietnamese people are regarded as passive puppets, then it follows that they cannot act as the agents of their fates and have no business governing themselves. "The Vietnamese revolution, therefore, is a search for a new authoritarian master and a new security. This explanation not only denies the Vietnamese any real and rational grounds for having a revolution, but justifies the American intervention and its failure to install democracy in Vietnam."[16]

Moreover, the very point of bringing women's voices into the war story is to empower them, I told Hao, and so I wanted to write against the grain of the standard male war story by giving women an active role. She agreed that after the war, male veterans' experiences dominated the literature and media and that women had been neglected. But she continued to show me how our different personal experiences had to be kept in mind, how she had learned firsthand that when destruction comes from the bombs of distant airplanes, everyone, even the most powerful of men, becomes frozen with fear, and victimized.

> It is much easier if you didn't have to go through the period of seeing thousands of youth volunteering to leave from the railway stations, and knowing they might never return, and if ten years after the war you didn't have long interviews with so many survivors, men and women, telling their painful memories, choking, with tears in their eyes. You didn't have to hear about food shortages, people eating barks of trees, parents feeding starving children food they knew was contaminated with toxic chemicals. No one could imagine the hunger, the water shortages, the pain of mothers with children dead or wounded from "baby" bombs. It was hard for me to keep myself from feeling guilty for having a family, a son, when the wounded volunteers back from the Ho Chi Minh Trail in their wheelchairs at the rehabilitation centers asked me to tell them about my son.

❖   ❖   ❖

IT WAS NOT ONLY WITH HAO that my American identity created barriers. Some women were reluctant or embarrassed to tell me how much they hated the Americans who bombed their homes, and others wanted me to face up to the hard realities. At times, the simple fact that we were middle-aged women eased the gap as we checked each other out to see if we should use the form of address for older or younger sister and compared notes about health, work, and families in our respective lives.

The men and women I interviewed knew full well that memory can be tricky, and they often expressed a responsibility to get it right. I knew that I was hearing certain themes repeated because they had become part of the national story[17] and they knew that there were certain truths they could never reveal to a foreigner. There were almost always tears and anger in the retellings, especially when women faced me and talked about American bombs that killed family and friends. Often people would warn me during our conversations that I had to be careful in my reporting so that people in America would believe their stories. At one point, my own sense of objectivity became blurred when I became so engrossed in the Vietnamese perspective that I called the Americans "the enemy"; Hao gently reminded me that there were two sides, that war is always complicated, and that all points of view must be considered.

Hao, like others of her generation, couldn't come to terms with her survival: "Why did I live when the bomb hit my neighbor's house just a few feet away and killed the whole family?" she asked. Guilt was always present in the room when I talked seriously about war in Vietnam. But it played out in sometimes surprising ways. One night in May 1996, I found a student waiting for me at our guest house, excited because a veteran had consented to meet me at the last minute. As we darted through the evening traffic on a motorbike too small to haul a largish foreign woman, I found out that this veteran did not want me to know her name and was not enthusiastic about Americans. When we reached the fairly modern apartment and settled in, a dignified, middle-aged woman came into the room and looked at me long and hard. The guard dog at the door growled at her, so I knew we must be in a borrowed space.

We were all tense at first, but then she began her story, which she told in a slow, deliberate way, with a full sense of history and her place in it.

> I was born in Thai Binh Province. My family were farmers. In 1948 my father was killed in the French War. My mother was with child when he died and she raised us four children alone. In 1968 I volunteered to be a people's soldier, *bo doi,* and I spent five years in the field during the most terrible time of the war. Why? Four people in my family died when the Americans bombed the Hanoi suburbs. I was angry and I believed that what men could do, I could do too.

Life was hard. In the jungle, we kept the telephone lines open, and at first I was homesick and afraid. But I wanted to avenge my family, to kill Americans for what they did.

I survived and when the war was over, my spirits soared. But life was still not easy. My husband is a career military man, who served in the South during the American War and then in Cambodia. He carries a bullet in his body and he is not well after sixteen years in the battlefields. We are lucky because we have two children, a boy and a girl.

She held both of my hands in hers, even as she told me her story of anger and bombs and death. And then she turned to me to ask about my life. Fair enough, I thought, and recounted my own small-scale tale of heroism, of my divorce and struggle to get an education as a single parent. After all, as a good socialist woman she must have some feminist leanings and would understand if not honor such a decision. I was wrong. She pulled away, became distant and cold. "A woman must always put her husband and children first. It is a woman's duty to sacrifice her own needs to help her family."

How ironic, I thought, stunned. I had gone into the interview mired in deep guilt about American bombs, the weapons that killed her family. I left feeling shamed about my personal life. The biggest barrier between us was not that my country had bombed hers but that we had different notions about family and individual responsibility. She could forgive me for the acts of my government, but not my decision to break up my family. She reminded me, as others would time and again, that as teenagers they fought for the future, to preserve their homeland as a safe place where they could one day live as whole human beings, raising children and grandchildren, worshipping the ancestors. When I asked her whether it had been hard to return to domestic life after having been on equal terms with men during the war, she stared at me with disbelief: "Why would I not treasure my home? Sure my family would never be the same again—some were dead, some wounded and sick. But the hope that I could raise children in a safe place one day kept me alive. It was what I was fighting for. And I was lucky. I survived when so many died. I have children when so many stay alone."

In the end, we talked about peace. "Only when women tell the truth about war can there ever be true peace. Please tell American women about our experiences so they can understand." I told her that I would try.[18]

PART ONE

Messages

CHAPTER ONE

Through a Hairnet: Mothers, Warriors, and the Nation

A rosy-cheeked woman, here I am fighting side by side with you men. The prison is my school, the sword my child, the gun my husband.

Attributed to Nguyen Thi Minh Khai, 1941.

The American pilots never knew that beneath them, our Vietnamese women had woven a fine hairnet of opposition.

Military historian Nguyen Quoc Dung, Hanoi, 1997.

The platoon of combat engineers from Battalion 33 commanded by Nguyen Thi Nha fought heroically at A-shaped bend and moved to Pakhe ("HTP"), west of a frontier post and road number 20. There Nha and four of her mates died heroically on January 4, 1968. Nha was replaced by her second-in-command, Mai Lien. This platoon has been fighting since the early days of building Road 20 and their determination to fight enhanced the morale of the men of Line 559.

Vietnamese field report submitted from the
Ho Chi Minh Trail, 1968.

ANY ACCOUNTING OF THE AMERICAN WAR in Vietnam that leaves out Vietnamese women tells only half the story. Professor Nguyen Quoc Dung, a military historian and veteran, asserts that women's collective service can never be forgotten, for their active participation after 1965 tipped the balance between victory and defeat.[1] "It was the simple, modest activities of Vietnamese women, armed only with small-bore 12.7 mm antiaircraft guns, that won out against the well-fed American pilots in their big heavy planes. Women used their small guns to shoot and their delicate hands to defuse bombs. We had to counter every U.S. plane and pilot with nine of our own people and most of the defense against the air strikes was carried out by women.

"Yes, their lives were hard. But many women learned to read in the jungles. Their teachers used raincoats as blackboards and forest plants for ink. Most women went home more confident and better educated, for the war liberated them from the bamboo gate of the village."

Despite their undeniable significance in the victory over the superior technology of the American air force, few women have been singled out for their courage and service. From the Vietnamese perspective, the war with America was a people's war. Individual heroism in such a collective endeavor counts only when it inspires others to strive for even greater acts of sacrifice. Most of the women who fought on the Ho Chi Minh Trail, in the jungles, in the militias and local forces, remain unnamed, remembered only for the collective sacrifice demanded by a people's war. As one bitter male veteran told me, "Out there in the villages so many women who served with courage put down their guns and were never heard from again."

The few individuals who have been remembered publicly are almost always associated with particular sites that were hotly contested during the air war and now serve as locations of collective memory and mourning.[2] Road 20, where Nguyen Thi Nha and her sisters died in 1968, claimed so many young girls that by the end of that year, reporters and soldiers who travelled the Trail made a point to visit their graves, scattered along the roads these teenagers died to maintain. At Dong Loc in October 1968, bombs buried ten young girls from the Fifty-Fifth Volunteer Youth Corps as they filled craters to keep the road open. Today one of the survivors, La Thi Tam, appears regularly on television programs and documentaries as she tends the graves of her dead comrades. The story of one of North Vietnam's most beloved heroines, Ngo Thi Tuyen, is linked with her hamlet's efforts to save the strategic Dragon Jaw Bridge after it became a prime American target in the air war after 1965. Against all odds, driven by a superhuman, patriotic spirit, this young militiawoman earned her place in history by hoisting on her back a load of ammunition over twice her body weight. Near the site, a small museum, its walls covered with plaques naming the dead, serves as a place of commemoration for the community and outside visitors.

These are exceptional cases. Most women's stories remain hidden. Yet military historian Dung estimates that the total number of women in the regular army of North Vietnam (NVA), the militia and local forces, and the professional teams added up to almost 1.5 million. Of these, sixty thousand women joined the regular forces and thousands of professional women were sent by government ministries, hospitals, and universities to lend their skills to the war effort. Least known, even to citizens in the North until the past decade, is the full story of the volunteer youth (*thanh nien xung phong*), the men and women who signed on through their local Ho Chi Minh youth unions after 1965 to serve in shock brigades at the most dangerous spots along the Ho Chi Minh Trail. How many young men and women worked in volunteer youth corps is a matter of dispute in Vietnam today. Conservative estimates state that between 1965 and 1975 at least 170,000 young people joined, and that between 70 and 80 percent were women.[3]

Better known, because they remained within their communities, are the militiawomen who learned to shoot at American planes from factory tops and village fields, carried supplies and treated the wounded, and all the while maintained agricultural and industrial production at prewar levels. Professor Dung estimates that almost a million women in the North carried out duties in local guerrilla and militia forces. That the armies and the civilian population continued to be fed and armed during the war was due in large part to women's work. Indeed, women eventually supplied food to much of Indochina, as a famous wartime saying indicates: "Every grain of rice was divided into four parts: One for A (the North), one for B (the southern battlefields), one for C (Laos), and one for K (Cambodia)." Women played a large role in making sure the goods were delivered as well. A male diarist writing in 1968 paints a feminine image of the Ho Chi Minh Trail, which he likens to the Vietnamese woman's long shoulder pole with a heavily laden basket on each end, one tipped toward the supplies in the north and the other toward the battlefields in the south.

IN RETELLING THE WAR AS A WOMAN'S STORY, I have kept three goals in mind. First, I want to bring to the foreground women's personal experiences during the American War, to showcase how they remember that time and how they place themselves in the history of a long-term national struggle. Oral histories coaxed from modest women veterans document individual women's stories of how violence and dislocation affected them when they were too young to think of the consequences and how they coped when they returned to homes that would never be the same again. As some of these women took the risk of going back in time with me to relive the most interesting and terrible years of their lives, they talked about why they volunteered—or their mixed emotions when they were called up to provide special skills to the war effort—who their heroes were, how they went about their daily lives in strange new territories, how they kept their spirits up as the war dragged on, what they hoped for when they dreamed of the future, and what actually awaited them when they returned to families scarred and scattered by war. Their experiences demonstrate that these were no "Rosie the Riveters" who stayed home, hoped for peace, and gained new skills doing men's work, while the men went off to take care of the dirty business of war. Sometimes for one year, usually for three, and sometimes for as long as ten years these Vietnamese teenagers shouldered "men's work" and suffered women's particular hardships.

By contrasting Vietnamese women's war service with American women's work during World War II, I do not mean to diminish the sufferings of the women who stayed home or the contributions of the thousands of women who served in the WAVES (Women Accepted for Volunteer Emergency Service), the WACS (Women's Army Corps), and to a lesser extent the air force auxiliary squadrons. But for Vietnamese women, the war came to them, to their homes, cities, and villages, and this difference must be kept in mind.

Second, I hope to show that when women enter Vietnam's military history, boundaries shift. Historical chronology looks different, for example, as dates that mark women's actions appear. The maps change too. As Tom and I constructed a map for this book, we identified places that had significance in Vietnam because women fought and died there. The name of a cave that was only a target for the U.S. military, for example, calls up for the Vietnamese the memory of the young girls buried by bombs inside. A road that was but one of many paths on the Ho Chi Minh Trail attracted Vietnamese journalists even before the end of the war because so many young girls had given their lives to keep it open.

Moreover, when direct contact with the normally male world of violence and death becomes a common experience for men and women, discourse about war changes. Women's oral histories reveal how they pitied the men's daily struggles to survive and their fears of death. Men noticed women's squeamishness about leeches and snakes, for example, and marvelled at their matter-of-fact determination to carry on in the face of real danger.

In the postwar era, male veterans can be counted among the strongest supporters of their female comrades-in-arms. Female writers are beginning to voice concerns on behalf of all the women who fought, but still the majority of writers and editors are men. Two groups of women have received attention in the media and literature: single veterans who returned home unable to marry and thus deprived of an opportunity to partake in normal family life, and mothers of martyrs whose loss of sons impoverishes and isolates them. How these women's sacrifices are interpreted offers one avenue for understanding the soul-searching, the anger, and the hope in Hanoi as the Vietnamese nation enters the international political and economic arena as a unified, independent nation for the first time in its modern history.

Third and finally, the Vietnamese case adds important insight into timeless moral and philosophical questions about war. How does the presence of women influence the fighting men's morale? Is a woman's relative physical weakness a liability in combat situations? Can women stand up to constant violence and danger as stoically as male soldiers? And the most difficult and troubling problem for feminist theorists: Is war a natural male realm and peacemaking the women's essential task? Is there in fact a contradiction between women as maternal thinkers and actors and women as patriotic avengers?[4]

The Vietnamese case is particularly intriguing because the image of the "moral mother" who tends the home and the "citizen-warrior" who must fight for the nation in times of emergency both hold great power in Vietnam's cultural and national history. Threading throughout this book, readers can detect that accounts by and about women in war in Vietnam during the war and even more in the postwar era is really about women's maternal duties to the family and the nation. But this focus on motherhood plays out in surprising ways. On the one hand, a culture that values a woman only for her reproductive role can oppress those women who do not fulfill their "natural" function. On the other, when motherhood is considered a right, an essential element of a woman's personhood, women can manipulate this belief to attain personal goals that might otherwise threaten the traditional family system. Women veterans whose war service rendered them unmarriageable and childless soldiers' widows bear children outside of marriage without the social ostracism one would expect because their peers believe that motherhood is their due. Some married women veterans ignore the two-child per family policy because others assume that they deserve to be repaid for their service. In other words, "maternal thinking" in Vietnam is a double-edged sword—it can be used as a weapon against women who don't fit but it can also be used by women to circumvent social norms.[5]

I HAVE OFTEN THOUGHT while working on this book that America's recent fascination with gender relations in the military emanates from our fortunate history. The U.S. military can be choosy about who carries the gun and flies the bomber because we have not been forced by circumstances to put lethal weapons into the hands of women. Other countries have had to be more flexible about their definition of the viable warrior. In modern times, women have served in resistance movements in France during World War II and Algeria after 1954, and in the Sandinista National Liberation Front in Nicaragua in 1961, to name a few instances.[6] Women were a visible presence in the Red Armies in China during the late 1940s and in India 1,500 Hindu women left the protection of *purdah* to fight in an all-female regiment of the Indian National Army between 1943 and 1945.[7] In terms of numbers of women in combat, however, only the Soviet Union during World War II comes close to the Vietnamese case. According to K. Jean Cottam, by 1943 8 percent of all Soviet military personnel were women, numbering about 800,000 to

1,000,000 soldiers. They achieved distinction as snipers, artillery and tank-women, communications workers, combat engineers, and machine gunners.[8]

Vietnamese women who had studied in Russia during the 1960s and 1970s told me that they had been deeply inspired by stories of Soviet heroines they heard about while there. But they also reminded me that they could look to their own long history of women warriors as a source of strength. Indeed, the Vietnamese case is unique not only because so many women went out to fight but because the tradition of the fighting woman is so integral to the Vietnamese national story that she cannot be easily overlooked once the wars come to an end and her proper place reverts to the home.

THERE IS NO BETTER PLACE TO EXPLORE current conceptions of the role of women in the nation than the Vietnam Women's Museum in Hanoi. Founded by state directive and funded by local women's unions, it houses a rich mix of official and popular images of women throughout history. The impressive stucco building in downtown Hanoi opened its doors to the public in 1995. "No one goes there because it's just about women," a male student told me. But in fact, it is a favorite destination for Hanoi women on holidays and special occasions.

A recent issue of *Women of Vietnam* describes the museum's mission: "This is the biggest cultural establishment of the Vietnam Women's Union, where the union preserves and displays documents and artifacts about the history of the Vietnamese women's movement and traditions, and at the same time an educational centre aimed at developing the fine traditions and improving the knowledge of women in all fields. . . . Throughout the display, the image of the Vietnamese mother stands out."[9]

The museum is indeed organized to celebrate the mother, but a close look reveals that the fierce fighting woman cannot be erased from the national story. A tour of its displays shows that the ideal Vietnamese woman is a juggler, who can raise and nurture soldier sons, fight like a man in times of war, and act as a peacemaker when combat ends.

A giant statue of a well-endowed Amazon with an infant perched on her shoulder looms over visitors in the museum's vestibule. She stands beneath a conical ceiling that represents a giant breast, according to the museum guide. "The lights hanging from the breast are like mother's milk, flowing over all of Vietnam." The young guide, employed by the Women's Union, makes a point of telling us that this great mother is a unifying force who places the entire nation—southerners, northerners, lowland farmers, and highland minorities—under her maternal power.

Women from National Economics University at the entrance to the Vietnam Women's Museum, Hanoi, 1996.

The theme of the great mother continues in the first layer of exhibits. The Princess Au Co, who gave birth to the one hundred children who were to become the first Vietnamese rulers, deserves special attention.[10] As the story goes, her husband the Dragon King took half of their children to the seacoast while the other half stayed with their mother in the mountains. The legend can be read in many ways. The Vietnamese people's common ancestry, despite their diverse geographical environments, could be considered a force for national unity and cultural tolerance. Yet Hao interprets the founding story as a negative portent: "The Dragon King and the Fairy Mother lived together for awhile, but then they had their differences and separated. When there was trouble, the children went to the sea to call for help from their daddy. That legend sticks in our hearts. In one way our sacred totem tells us that we are united in one country, the children of one family. But in my childhood, I always wondered why a family had to separate from each other. Why did our ancestors choose that legend to tell us about the foundation of our nation? Was it a fatal story?"

Some historians read the myth of the split first family as one indication that at a time in the distant past, inheritance rights could pass through both the maternal and paternal lines.[11] Perhaps a matriarchal society once existed, according to some scholars. In Vietnam today "two hundred and fifty of the one thousand sites of worship are dedicated to goddesses or deified female historical personages."[12] Interestingly, in light of women's roadbuilding labor during and after the American War, one female deity, Lady Nu Oa, is paired with a male god who joined her as a construction engineer to transport pieces of rock to patch up heaven and build mountains and dig rivers on earth.

Recorded history begins with the tale of two patriot sisters, the daughters of a local Vietnamese lord, Vietnam's equivalents to Patrick Henry and George Washington, who raised a rebellion against the Chinese in 40 C.E. Their property rights appear to have been threatened by Chinese policies, which placed land and ritual rights under the total control of men. Trung Trac, the elder sister, was the wife of a man in trouble with the Chinese legal officials. According to the Chinese records, this woman "of a brave and fearless disposition" talked her husband and other local notables into rebellion. After driving out the Chinese authorities, she and her sister set up court in their birthplace, and she was recognized as queen by other local Vietnamese elites. She abolished taxes and suspended Chinese law for the two years she held power, but eventually the Chinese returned in force. In 43 C.E. her followers were defeated and both sisters died. Some historians speculate that they failed because traditional local Vietnamese ideals that honored women had in fact been so eroded by the Chinese that a Vietnamese woman could not hold power for long.[13]

These patriotic women left their mark, however, and today throughout Vietnam city streets, temples, souvenirs, and a national holiday preserve their cult. Beliefs about their motives for fighting change as priorities in Vietnam shift. The Trung sisters' legend, for example, can conjure up the image of a filial woman who goes to war to avenge her husband or a patriotic woman who fights for a higher cause. In the early twentieth century, the reformer Phan Boi Chau (1867–1940) argued that the Trung sisters acted as patriotic fighters at a time when women's support for a nationalist revolution against the French was badly needed. In his writings, he did not rule out their womanly sentiments, however, and describes the elder sister as crying over her husband's body—but then he has Trung Nhi reprimand her: "Come now, we can't give way to ordinary female emotions. We've got to get out and take care of military matters."[14] When a more domestic model serves larger interests, the elder Trung sister's decision to fight is presented as the duty of a loyal wife to avenge her dead husband—even though the historical records belie this interpretation.

Another colorful woman from the past is remembered for her prowess in battle and her large-scale feminine attributes. Lady Trieu, according to an eighteenth-century account, was nine feet tall, with breasts three feet long. She was capable of killing a troublesome sister-in-law and strong enough to resist the entreaties of male relatives that she stay at home. Around 240 C.E. she rode into battle against the Chinese, perched on an elephant, her huge breasts slung over her shoulder. According to some stories she was as brave as a man in battle, but as weak as a woman when confronted with dirt and chaos. When her armies were defeated because the enemy offended her feminine sensibilities by sending unwashed ruffians into the field, she ran off and killed herself.

Even after her death men feared her. It is said that Lady Trieu so troubled the Chinese commander she fought that he blamed a pestilence on her and ordered woodcarvers to hang phallic images on doors to counteract her female potency. She could serve good causes as well: a Vietnamese rebel against the Chinese dreamed that she supported him. Today she is one of Vietnam's most beloved heroines. Her response to her brother's advice that she should stay home speaks to many a modern women who would do almost anything to escape domestic drudgery: "I want only to ride the waves, slay the big whale of the Eastern sea [China], clean up our frontiers and save the people from drowning. Why should I imitate others, bow my head, stoop over, and be a slave? Why resign myself to menial housework?"[15]

Lady Trieu was the last woman to lead a rebellion but not the last to join a just cause with courage and spirit. Bui Thi Xuan, for example, became a general in the Tay-son peasant rebellions of the late eighteenth century. The enemy was Vietnamese this time, the Sinicized Nguyen Dynasty (1802–1945). Trained from a young age in martial arts, she knew how to fight with simple weapons—sticks and bare hands. According to historian David Marr, her enemies considered her so dangerous that they executed her by having an elephant trample her. Then the enemy soldiers consumed her heart and liver.[16]

The theme that runs through Vietnam's traditional history, then, is this: Indigenous, pure Vietnamese culture allotted high status to women. When foreign influence muted these progressive forces, women suffered and so their revolts made sense—when fighting for the nation they were fighting for their rights. History bears out some of these beliefs. For example, the Le Dynasty that ruled Vietnam from 1428 to 1788 tempered Chinese influence, and the Le law codes offered women far greater property and inheritance rights than the Confucianized Chinese codes of the later regimes.[17]

In the end, however, brave as they were to try to free the nation from oppressive native rulers and outside invaders, Vietnam's fighting women never enjoyed for long the fruits of their struggles or challenged seriously the dominant patriarchal culture.

❖   ❖   ❖

IN THE VIETNAM WOMEN'S MUSEUM, the gentler side of Vietnam's traditional warrior women sets the stage. Lulled by imaginary depictions of gentle fertility goddesses and plump women riding elephants, visitors are jolted into recent Vietnamese history when confronted with stark black and white photos of real women, fierce, organized, and armed, and (to the embarrassment of my sensitive Vietnamese friend who tried to steer me past it) a large-scale painting of a woman shooting at an American plane.

After 1858, when French warships attacked the weakened Nguyen regime, women fell victim to a more organized force than the Chinese had ever mustered. A history of women in Vietnam produced in Hanoi in 1978 describes how the French colonial government with "their honeyed words—'preservation of old traditions, respect for Viet Nam's ancestral customs and usages' . . . prolonged feudalism, adding new forms of exploitation and oppression."[18]

Organized resistance against the French colonial regime in the 1940s brought the question of women and the family into debates about the effects of long-term colonial dominance. In Vietnam, as in China, male intellectuals who pondered the reasons for the nation's weakness against a European power looked to the weak elements of their own past, pointing to the Confucian family system as one source of backwardness. In 1922, Ho Chi Minh linked women's oppression with colonial domination[19]:

> Colonization is in itself an act of violence of the stronger against the weaker. This violence becomes still more odious when it is exercised upon women and children. It is bitterly ironic to find that [French] civilization—symbolized in its various forms, viz., liberty, justice, etc., by the gentle image of woman, and run by a category of men well known to be champions of gallantry—inflicts on its living emblem the most ignoble treatment and afflicts her shamefully in her manners, her modesty, and even her life.
>
> Colonial sadism is unbelievably widespread and cruel, but we shall confine ourselves here to recalling a few instances seen and described by witnesses unsuspected of partiality. These facts will allow our Western sisters to realize both the nature of the "civilizing mission" of capitalism, and the sufferings of their sisters in the colonies.

On the arrival of the soldiers, relates a colonel, the population fled; there only remained two old men and two women: one maiden and a mother suckling her baby and holding an eight-year-old girl by the hand. The soldiers asked for money, spirits, and opium.

As they could not make themselves understood, they became furious and knocked down one of the old men with their rifle butts. Later, two of them, already drunk when they arrived, amused themselves for many hours by roasting the other old man at a wood fire. Meanwhile, the others raped the two women and the eight-year-old girl. Then weary, they murdered the girl. The mother was then able to escape with her infant from a hundred yards off, hidden in a bush, she saw her companion tortured. She did not know why the murder was perpetrated, but she saw the young girl lying on her back, bound and gagged, and one of the men, many times, slowly thrust his bayonet into her stomach and, very slowly, draw it out again. Then he cut off the dead girl's finger to take a ring, and her head to steal a necklace.

Ho's nationalist revolution against the French of course included in its program the liberation of women and the anti-French wars produced heroines as colorful as the women warriors of old, and inspired by them. Latter-day Trung Queens appeared: In 1945, just before the First Indochina War (1946–1954) the patriotic Duong Thi An donned a uniform and rode her horse as part of a liberation army on its way to Hanoi. "Maybe women along the road didn't see a Trung sister on an elephant," she commented a quarter century later, "yet they were stunned and excited to see a woman handle a horse well."[20]

By this time non-elite women began to make a name for themselves as resistants. In 1930 the peasant girl Nguyen Thi Hung, about to be forced to marry a much younger man, ran off to a pagoda to be a nun. Her parents tracked her down but she left again and met a teacher who inspired her to join the newly formed Indochinese Communist Party with stories about the Trung sisters and Lady Trieu. Women organized strikes and demonstrations against French colonial policies, and set up rural base areas founded on ideals of gender equality and universal participation in political life. Nguyen Thi Minh Khai, the daughter of a trader and a railroad worker, used her father's station to hide revolutionary literature from the French and her mother's trading networks to spread her message. She travelled to Hong Kong and Shanghai, and in Moscow in 1935 addressed socialist comrades:

We wish to inform you that in Indochina, particularly during the years of the revolutionary upsurge [1930–1931], the contribution of women has been a worthy one: Women have taken part in demonstrations

"Women participating in the self-defense force during the Nghe-Tinh Movement, 1930." (*Caption and photo courtesy of the Vietnam Women's Museum*)

and shows of strength, standing in the front ranks. They have taken the floor in meetings. And we are glad to stress that in many cases, they have shown bravery in the struggle. They have headed demonstrations and not only forced soldiers to retreat, but also known how to convert them.[21]

She married and had a daughter, but her husband died from torture, never having seen the child, and Minh Khai was executed in 1941.

By the time of the August Revolution of 1945, when North Vietnam gained independence, women resistants had shared the world of jail, torture, and death with their male comrades. Ho Chi Minh's nationalist forces, the Viet Minh, had given ordinary women land, a voice in political meetings, and a stake in the revolution. Historian David Marr describes the spirited defiance women displayed during the Nghe-Tinh uprisings of the 1930s: "In one particular confrontation colonial soldiers tried to break up a demonstration by tearing off the clothes of one female activist in front of her peers. To show that they would not be cowed in this way, other women proceeded to strip off their clothing in solidarity, then marched to jail with the first activist, chanting Communist Party slogans en route."[22]

When Japanese armies occupied Vietnam during World War II, women organized against yet another enemy. As hatred flared up against the Japanese and their French collaborators for hoarding rice while ordinary people starved, some women took action. Nguyen Thi Hung, the young peasant woman who had joined the Indochinese Communist Party after running away from a forced marriage, led them. In her memoirs she demonstrates that these were not simply spontaneous eruptions carried out by rag-tag irregulars:

"South Vietnamese women guerrilla groups fighting the French aggressors."
(*Caption and photo courtesy of the Vietnam Women's Museum*)

Attacking a rice depot was a serious operation. We had to discuss in
detail the whole field of battle: the morale of the people, the strength
of the guard at the depot. . . . Then we prepared for the mobilization. A staff [member] took charge of the leadership of the struggle,
the organization of the people coming from adjacent villages and the
formation of specialized units for rice transportation, distribution
and defence. And finally, the watchword and the time of action and
the itinerary of the demonstrations were decided and the final battle
plan against the repression drawn up.[23]

The hard labor of ordinary women contributed to the demise of French
military control of Vietnam at the final battle at Dien Bien Phu in 1954. Of
the more than 260,000 laborers—some sources call them conscripts, others
volunteers—who hauled supplies, half were women. Men pushed pack bicycles, and women used the shoulder poles. A history of women in revolution
describes the transporters' contributions:

From North to South, from the plains to the mountain regions, from
the enemy-occupied zones to the free zones, as soon as night fell,
line upon line of *dan cong* resumed their long march, which they

"The long-haired army, pride of the Vietnamese people's rebellion against the French." (*Caption and photo courtesy of the Vietnam Women's Museum*)

interrupted during the day, following a labyrinth of invisible roads leading to the front. For nine years, goods and munitions were transported continuously to the front, to the hot spots of the resistance. [They] brought the wounded back to the rear, and removed the war booty. They took part in a series of offensives.

Women traveled great distances from their villages to supply the remote border fronts. Some were minorities from the mountainous areas who supported the Vietnamese cause. It is estimated that in one campaign in 1950 on the border with China, the *dan cong* contributed a million work days. A few stood out, such as the woman who braved enemy fire to make seven trips to the battlefield to carry the wounded back to the rear.[24]

Very few women joined the regular armies against the French, but the tradition of resourceful, patriotic women was firmly imbedded in the imagination of Vietnamese citizens by the time the Americans entered the war in force in 1964. Noting that the resistance against the French colonial powers brought some women side by side with men in the struggle, a history of women published in Hanoi in 1966 reminds readers that these spontaneous local activities did not yet constitute a nation-wide organized assault. But these women resistance fighters did more than cause trouble for the French; they reminded their countrymen and women that they were reviving an honorable tradition of fighting women: ". . . the memory of those who were the worthy successors of the Trung sisters, Trieu Thi Trinh [Lady Trieu], Bui Thi Xuan and others, is always honoured by the Vietnamese people."[25] The account goes on to suggest that the anti-French resistance served as a training period for women. "Sixteen years ago, our women combatants were armed merely with large knives. At present, facing a much stronger and more ferocious enemy, they are much more numerous, are armed with machine guns and antiaircraft guns, not to mention thousands of rifles. Twenty years of continuous struggle against the French colonialists and now the American imperialists have hardened the arms of our women who are certain of final victory."

THE AMERICAN WAR PRESENTED VIETNAMESE WOMEN with a new challenge, according to Professor Dung. During the French Wars women could decide whether to commit their lives to the resistance. But the American War had to be fought as an all-out war for national salvation. Once the able-bodied men had enlisted, and then the normally exempt only sons, Catholics, and minorities were called up, only the women were left. An appeal to the whole population came on June 21, 1965, when the government issued Directive 71 to establish an "Anti-U.S. National Salvation Assault Youth Unit" to mobilize hundreds of thousands of young men and women to fulfill combat and combat support missions. Most of them would work in the communications and transport units.[26]

Twelve northern provinces and cities were ordered to select 50,000 youths, who would be divided into 41 teams and 337 companies, under the direction of the Ministry of Transportation and the Ministry of Defense. The slogan for the youth indicates their mission: "We will repair any road the enemy destroys. What the enemy continues to destroy, we will repair again."

It was Ho Chi Minh's personal appeal, on July 16, 1966, however, that mobilized large numbers of young people. Ho called for a massive commitment from all the people to counter the large introduction of U.S. troops and the bombing of the North:

Johnson and his 'clique' must understand that even if they send 500,000, 1 million, or even more troops in order to step up their war of aggression in South Vietnam, or even if they use thousands of airplanes, and intensify their attacks against the North, they cannot weaken the heroic Vietnamese people's iron will and determination to oppose the United States for national salvation.[27]

As Ho's message spread through the villages and urban neighborhoods, young people responded more enthusiastically than expected. Professor Dung told me that districts with quotas of two hundred or three hundred recruits received applications from two or three thousand youths, and between 1965 and 1968 a total of about seventy thousand women went out to work on the Ho Chi Minh Trail. Between 1969 and 1971, the cessation of bombing allowed many of the youth to return home and the army engineer units took over most road repairs.[28]

In 1972 the situation changed again. A written history of the volunteer youth describes the Vietnamese assessment and response to the Paris peace talks and Nixon's re-election: "At the Paris meeting the U.S. side was very obstinate. In America, the race for the presidential election was in full swing. . . . Nixon, the aggressive imperialist who replaced Johnson, again won the election." As the air war against the North began again, a call for volunteer youth went out. "It took only a month to recruit more than twenty thousand volunteer youth in eight provinces and cities. Four thousand were sent to Laos, 8,350 worked for the Ministry of Transport and 4,550 others sent to other locations."[29]

After 1973, many of the youths returned home to school or work in the cities and countryside. Those with sufficient education went on to college or training schools. Some young men and women who had displayed particular courage or expertise and maintained good health joined the regular forces. Professor Dung explained the difference between the volunteer units and the regular NVA army units. The volunteers signed on for one year, but could choose to extend their service or return home while regular army personnel were committed to army discipline for life. The volunteers were untrained, while the army units received some training and generally had a higher level of education. Within the volunteer units, some particularly talented or courageous individuals would be singled out for special training—to defuse bombs, for example—by regular army personnel. Firsthand reports show that it was not unusual at some sites to find regular army, volunteer youths, and engineering personnel from the Ministry of Transportation all working together to construct and maintain the roads.

Professor Dung summed up the volunteers' contributions over ten years: "In the two major air campaigns against the North, the United States dropped tens of thousands of torpedoes and shells and over 2 million tons of bombs. On some days 1,200 planes attacked targets—80 percent of which were transportation routes. One hundred percent of bridges were completely destroyed."

"The youth kept open 2,195 kilometers of strategic roads, and guarded over 2,500 key points that were attacked day and night. They built 6 airstrips, neutralized tens of thousands of bombs, shot down 15 planes and transported tens of thousands of kilograms of cargo, weapons, and food by any means, including pack bicycle." Remembering that over 70 percent of this work was carried out by women, one understands why their service made all the difference and why it cannot be overlooked.

HERE IS HOW NORTH VIETNAMESE SAW THE DIVISION between the rear and the front according to Professor Dung: "There was a rear, the North, the Democratic Republic of Vietnam (DRV), the homeland, that was free. Below the 17th parallel, the South, the Republic of Vietnam (RVN), was in the hands of Diem and then other Vietnamese collaborators who worked with the United States. Our people there were not free. The best evidence for this oppression comes from the activities in the South. It was their local protests after 1960 that sparked the war, not the infiltration of soldiers from the North." Their numbers cannot be known in full, but Professor Dung estimates that at least 140,000 women in the South supported the socialist North as spies, propagandists, and crude weapons makers; about 60,000 took part in direct military engagements as Viet Cong soldiers. Almost a million women became involved in protecting villages from the Diem regime's soldiers, members of the Army of the Republic of Vietnam (ARVN).[30]

The American War produced a new crop of heroines. The most visible official heroic models from the late 1960s and early 1970s came out of the South. The official stories produced after 1966 were obviously created to show the world and other Vietnamese women that a total people's war meant that women should fight—and fight well.

Yet these official wartime portraits betray a palpable ambivalence about women's natural maternal roles and their wartime activities. They offer a useful baseline for assessing the personal accounts of ordinary women thirty years later.

One of the most famous published memoirs from the war era records the history of the Deputy Commander of the South Vietnam Liberation Armed Forces (the Viet Cong), charged by Ho Chi Minh with coordinating guerrilla activity in the midst of hostile forces in the South. Madame Nguyen Thi Dinh's life history, published by Hanoi in 1968, depicts a superwoman who manages to make tough decisions, all the while remaining modest and feminine. A peasant girl, the widow of a famous revolutionary who died in prison, she joined the anti-French resistance while still a teen. Her documented exploits read like an Indiana Jones story. She spent time in a French prison

"Women of Thai Binh Province ready to fight while developing production." (*Caption and photo courtesy of the Vietnam Women's Museum*)

camp from 1940 to 1943, led a rebellion in her home province of Ben Tre in 1945, reported on the situation in the South to Ho Chi Minh himself in 1946, and on the way home ran a huge shipment of weapons through a dangerous French blockade to supply her southern comrades.[31]

In 1940, very soon after her husband was taken to a prison camp where he would die, she, too, was sent to prison for organizing against the French. As she turned the care of her seven-month-old son to her mother, she cried as any mother would. But in the very next paragraph, we read that when the French prison guards mistreated her and other women in the camp she organized the women to resist, and when that failed, she persuaded the male prisoners to kill a particularly nasty corporal: "Our women's cell talked over things with the [male] prisoners and suggested that they kill the corporal to set an example for the others." She describes the brutal murder of the corporal and then placidly proceeds to tell her readers how she kept her spirits up by embroidering pillowcases for her family. A poem by a Vietnamese male poet praises both her martial and maternal sides:

> Nguyen Thi Dinh:
> In the assault you command a hundred squads.
> Night returns, you sit mending fighter's clothes.
> Woman general of the South
> You've shaken the brass and steel of the White House.[32]

Less famous but beloved nonetheless by Vietnamese women is Ut Tich, "the fighting mother" in the official publications, who displays even more clearly how difficult it was for a woman to keep the home in order and sow disorder among the enemy's forces.

The public narratives describe Ut Tich as a fighter for justice even when young. In one of many acts of revenge for mistreatment she attacked an abusive landlord with a knife and threw red peppers in his wife's eyes. "Experience had taught her that if you don't want to be attacked, you must strike at your enemy. She was then fourteen." She resisted marriage, but eventually married a Khmer soldier, falling in love with him after he taught her to throw grenades. She produced six children, all the while working with guerrilla forces. "The day after an ambush, she was back home. Giving the breast to her baby, and caressing his hair, she said, 'When my son is old enough to carry a weapon, he will do much better than his parents.'

"Ut's activities took her away all the time. She was never home before midnight and then only to go out again at dawn. Her husband was no less busy, so that their children had to take care of themselves the whole day."[33] Ut Tich, like Madame Dinh, was rewarded with official recognition for her service. She received a medal, a gun, and immortality. Nguyen Thi Dinh became president of the Vietnam Women's Union, a member of the Party Central Committee, and a delegate to the National Assembly.

Their stories are constructed to inspire Vietnamese women to emulate their courage in battle without losing their womanly virtues, for both model women were tough as nails in war and gently maternal at home. Contradictions appear in these portraits, however, hints that in fact these women managed their double duty with difficulty and the help of other women, relatives, and neighbors. Moreover, even the famous Madame Dinh, heroine of the southern revolutionary forces, hints that men did not always accept women as equal partners. In her officially sanctioned memoir she writes about the time she uncovered the identity of a woman guerrilla who had disguised herself as a man during a campaign. When she asks her female comrade why she needed to appear as a man, the answer is telling: "I followed the decision to disguise myself to deceive the enemy but also to put the minds of the men in my unit at ease. They despise us women, you know." These two model women then joked about the contempt they endured from men.[34]

So, too, the official military vision of the war current today, twenty years later, is fraught with ambivalence about women's true contributions to the victory in 1975. As Professor Dung's narrative implies, if the American giant could be done in by diminutive Vietnamese women, how much more effective Vietnamese men must have been! Today's accounts play up women's determination and spirit rather than their military expertise and in so doing remove them from the male realm of technology, relegating them to a domestic supporting role.[35]

CHAPTER TWO

War's People:
Through a Woman's Lens

A hundred years—this life span on earth talent and destiny are apt to feud.
You must go through a play of ebb and flow and watch such things as make
you sick at heart.

> Nguyen Du (1765–1820), *The Tale of Kieu.*

I'm certain that if a majority of women in every country would clearly
express their convictions, they would find that they spoke not for themselves alone, but for those men for whom war has been a laceration—
an "abdication of the spirit."

> Dead soldier's mother to Jane Addams, 1916.

WHEN IT IS A WOMAN WHO DIRECTS THE CAMERA, how does the war
story change? Through Nguyen Thi Duc Hoan's life and art, we can see how
hard-won personal knowledge shapes the way one woman documents the
human side of war. Veteran of the French and American wars, movie actress,
and finally in 1978 director for the Vietnam Feature Film Studio, Duc Hoan
plays a special role in Vietnam, for she is one of the few women positioned to
communicate publicly an alternative to the official heroic stories. She ac-
knowledges that she has led an extraordinary life, but she continues to devote
herself to bringing up painful issues about war's effects on ordinary people,
inserting her messages subtly in a quiet quest to tell the truth as she sees it
despite the Party censors. No alienated dissident, she injects her own hard-
won understanding of human nature into films that nonetheless reflect larger
national and popular issues. Most importantly, her work deals with some of
the most sensitive issues facing women during and after war.

As we sipped tea during our first meeting in Hanoi in 1996, I noticed at
once that she was different from other professional women I had met there,
more flamboyantly dressed, aware of how to make an entrance, every bit the
movie star at first glance. I knew from others that she had divorced a military
man who also worked in the film industry, and had remarried an engineer

Duc Hoan, 1964.
(*Courtesy of Duc Hoan*)

fifteen years her junior. But she has never lived the life of a movie mogul. When I got to know her better, I found that she lived in a humble house, without a telephone or car, moving around Hanoi on the back of her husband's motorcycle. Retired now from the studio, she continues to work on projects that suit her. She remembers fondly the fame she earned as an actress in her first film in 1960, but believes that her work as a director has allowed her to express her own sense of history and social problems.

Duc Hoan views her struggle to remain true to her vision with good humor, laughing as she recalled her trials when she directed her first film, "From a Jungle" (*Tu mot canh rung*), which depicts the lives of Hanoi youth sent to the jungle along the Ho Chi Minh Trail to build new roads in 1966. At the time she made the film in 1978, the official line in Hanoi continued to stress the heroic aspects of war. Duc Hoan was not averse to shaping her story to inspire communal virtues and hard work, qualities needed in the postwar period as the nation attempted to rebuild and reunify. In her film, a young country bumpkin, unruly and cynical at first, learns about discipline and camaraderie from his more experienced peers. The women in the film are competent, at times more than the men. Duc Hoan told me as she recounted the script that she holds a special respect for the young women liaison agents who took responsibility for guiding troops and visitors through their designated terrain. "I wanted to show their contribution. When we calculated the length that the liaison agents walked every day during the war, we figured out that they could have encircled the earth." But Duc Hoan wanted to show too that they were ordinary teenagers, homesick, afraid, and funloving. They miss Hanoi so much that they assign familiar names from the city to these remote villages, forests, and hills. In secluded jungle stations, safe from air attacks, the pretty young girls play games and flirt and tease the boys.

Against the puritanical socialist mores of the time, Duc Hoan allowed her film's teenagers to fall in love. One of her greatest challenges in her directorial debut was to show a couple kissing. "In one scene, I wanted to show two young people in love, kissing by the side of a bomb crater filled with water. I was allowed to show the romantic scene only indirectly, through images of the young lovers reflected in the pond. But I was criticized even for this— because I let the camera play on the reflection too long. I protested that they should either trust me or get rid of me.

"The deputy minister of culture said that the film was 'too much like a poem.' The men in charge of disseminating images wanted films to show bombs and violence, to show off Vietnamese male heroism against the enemy. I had to give up some scenes of daily life that I thought important."

Hanoians appreciate Duc Hoan as someone who stands on her principles and the "kissing scene" has become a defining moment in her cinematographic history. In an article about Duc Hoan in 1988 a reporter from a film magazine quizzed the cameraman for "From a Jungle:" "Our films are very different from foreign films, so it must have been difficult. How did you manage to let a couple kiss on the screen?" The cameraman answered, "It was difficult; but this director is a brilliant, sophisticated woman. She suggested I deceive the audience by letting them think the couple was kissing by imagining their dim shadows. . . . Actually a woman director is always more sophisticated about matters of love."[1]

Duc Hoan has regrets about the film, however, for in portraying a somewhat idyllic world, she feels that she glossed over the deprivations that women suffered. She admits that she was more affected by the heroic mode of the times than she realized then. But she also worked without full information about conditions for youth. "We didn't know how hard life really was for women in the jungles until we saw a documentary in 1990. I was shocked when I saw the thin girls, their lips and eyes darkened by malaria, their shoulders slumped over with fatigue. I regretted casting young, healthy women in the film in 1978." As we talked about problems of interpretation, she told me that she believes that direct experience is the only way to really understand any situation, especially war. And she knows enough about war from first-hand exposure to be able to show its romantic as well as its mundane sides—even if she hadn't gotten it quite right in "From a Jungle."

WHEN WE WENT BACK TO HER OWN LIFE, it became obvious that Duc Hoan is well aware that by telling her story she is recounting the history of her country and that she in turn has shaped the way that history is retold.[2] In the "French" time, she said, the soul of Vietnam was wounded by a century of colonial domination that began in the mid-nineteenth century and ended in her lifetime, in 1954 at the historic battle at Dien Bien Phu. But the very existence of the nation was not at stake then as it was when America unleashed far more deadly weapons in what she termed the "Johnson" and "Nixon" times. She, like so many Vietnamese women of her generation, honed her revolutionary skills during the final decade of the French Wars, and by the time she faced the Americans, had become a veteran guerrilla fighter. And in turn, Duc Hoan's daughter trained in the militia when she was in high school in the late 1960s. "I came back from a trip to the Soviet Union and found my daughter in a straw hat, carrying a gun."

> I left my home to join the anti-French resistance when I was ten. Bigger than other girls of my age, I was able to convince the authorities for a time that I was old enough. Why did I, a sheltered, bourgeois girl, take such a chance with my life? Because I hated the way that my French Catholic school teachers looked down on the Vietnamese students. Because when the French took over Hanoi in 1946, my family had to leave our home to hide in the countryside. Because after my mother died, home had no meaning for me anymore. You see, I was the youngest of six daughters and my father was a traditional Confucian man. In 1948, at age 60, he remarried and had a son, and after that, my sisters and I were pretty much on our own. After all, as the old saying goes, "A hundred girls aren't worth a single testicle." Besides, I knew that my sisters would eventually marry and that if I stayed I would just be a burden to them. And the times were exciting. For all of these reasons, it was easy for me to follow Ho Chi Minh.

After hearing Duc Hoan's story, it came as no surprise to me that her daughter would grow up to be a fighter.

The "tradition" that a young woman like Duc Hoan, coming of age in the 1940s, could draw from was a mixed bag. On the side of the barriers that would prevent a girl from making her own decisions was the still-viable Confucian teaching that placed a good woman in the home and subordinated her to the needs of the patriarchal family. The message she heard from an orthodox version of Confucian teaching—and by her account her father was strict about such matters—was that as a woman she was an inferior member within the family and society, a person of lesser value than a son no matter what she managed to accomplish by virtue of her talents and character. This doesn't mean that daughters were unloved or neglected in all Vietnamese families, but sons were preferred for economic and religious reasons. A boy child meant that the family name would live on, the ancestors properly worshipped, and the communal property guarded. In traditional society only men could serve in public office; they alone could use their power to protect their family interests. A woman's only security rested in her ability to manipulate the affections of her father, her husband, and her son if she had one. If she did not bear a son, she faced a sad old age.

Even progressive men feared the consequences of women's independence. As one male writer put it in 1917 in an essay advocating the education of women: "When men lack virtue, it is harmful to society; but not as harmful as when women become unsound, because unsound women damage the very roots of society."[3] He worried that if their education was not oriented toward moral training women would forget their natural function: to temper crass commercial instincts in men, and to make society a gentler, more beautiful place. Thus, a restless, spirited woman like Duc Hoan had to contend with the deeply held notion that if she didn't keep her place, her actions would harm not just her family, but all of society.

The fact that she was a girl meant that she would never earn her father's love, no matter what she accomplished. When she talked about her family, she admitted how sad she feels after so many years. "I never got over my father's coldness." But she knew her filial duty, and when her father was terminally ill, she left her own children to care for him.

Duc Hoan felt the full force of Confucian traditional notions about women. But her life choices demonstrate that an extraordinary woman could find her own path to personal happiness.

Her first marriage ended in divorce. "My first husband was a career army man, and he didn't know how to take care of a family. I lost my beauty during those years with him. And when I went to the Soviet Union to study, that finally severed the bonds. I was worried when I went to court, but the judge just asked me why I had waited so long to get a divorce. My first husband is also in the film business and we have stayed friends. And when he was alone,

I sent my daughter to stay with him, because a man can't cook for himself, you know!

"When I decided to take a chance and marry my second husband, everyone was worried because he is so much younger than I and this isn't done in Vietnam. His parents made him promise that he would love me all my life. And we are close to each other. It is a good marriage."

When I asked Duc Hoan who her heroes are, who she thought of when she struck out on her own, she mentioned one of Vietnam's most beloved women poets, one of several educated women who through poetry and story have lamented women's sorrows. This late eighteenth century woman poet, Ho Xuan Huong, celebrated single mothers, poked fun at licentious monks and corrupt officials, filled her poetry with sensual allusions, and in general blasted away at male supremacy with sarcasm and mordant humor. In particular, the accepted practice of polygamy for men who could afford more than one wife raised her ire:

> To share a husband with another, what a life! The one sleeps under
>   the covers, well snugged in, the other freezes.
> By chance he comes across you in the dark, once or twice a month,
>   then nothing.
> You hang on hoping to get your share, but the rice is poor and
>   underdone.
> You work like a drudge, save that you get no pay.
> Ah, had I known it would be like this
> Willingly would I have stayed alone, as I was before.[4]

Ho Xuan Huong's critique demonstrates that she wasn't at all fooled by the Confucian view that women's subordination was the only way to keep society in harmony. But she was smart enough to know that her gender would always affect her choices, even if she were a talented writer and critic: "If only I could change my destiny and be a man, I wouldn't content myself with such [small] feats of valour."

Although women in Vietnam inherited a rich body of literature to inspire their resistance against authority, Vietnam's most beloved epic poem, *The Tale of Kieu*, written by a man, dwells on the grim fate of a woman who leaves the protection of her family. Critics argue that the male author, Nguyen Du (1765–1820), uses a woman's story to convey his own ambivalence about loyalty and service to a corrupt court.[5] But women claim its message as well. "You must read about Kieu if you want to understand Vietnamese women," I heard often. And I thought of Duc Hoan as I followed the beautiful, talented Kieu's story of self-sacrifice as she uses her body to redeem her father's debt. It seemed to me that the tale of Kieu provided some small solace for Vietnamese women, because it traces the life history of a woman who is sullied by circumstances beyond her control but in the end allows her to maintain her inner purity. It offered women like Duc Hoan, who would leave home and family and enter the public arena during a time of war and disorder, a model that could resolve some of the social tensions women faced. Duc Hoan, like Kieu and thousands of other Vietnamese women, performed her filial duty best by leaving home.

Of course, Vietnam's female warriors inspired Duc Hoan. "The stories of Vietnam's women heroes, the Trung sisters, Lady Trieu, were sung as lullabies by our mothers. We took the fact that women have always fought for granted. Our heroines were not successful in the long run—but they weren't sad, crazy figures like Joan of Arc." She told me that the French had eliminated the story of the rebellious, mannishly dressed Joan of Arc from the curriculum when Vietnamese women began to take seriously their own oppression under colonial rule. Messages like "liberty, equality, and fraternity" from the French Revolution became too incendiary for Vietnamese ears, she said.

Indeed, Duc Hoan's adult life spanned the history of Vietnam's independence movement. Ho Chi Minh declared Vietnam an independent nation, the Democratic Republic of Vietnam, in September 1945. When French forces returned to fight their final war for control of Vietnam in 1946, Duc Hoan was sent by the resistance to work in the Third Interzone in the North as a teacher. A prodigy, she had been educated in French schools; later, she was trained in literature by a famous professor, Hoang Nhu Mai, and seemed destined for an artistic career. When Ho Chi Minh appealed to nationalists throughout the country to "destroy illiteracy as an enemy," Duc Hoan drew from her elite education to counter French cultural influence, joining teams to teach women, the elderly, and the poor in northern villages how to read and write.

Raised in the city, an urbanite through and through, she remarked that she learned a great deal from living in the countryside, where she observed that rural women gained some freedoms that escaped their sheltered urban sisters. Women were not confined to their homes, but worked in the fields with their men and took the produce to market, because their labor was essential for the family's survival. But village moral codes were strict, and ostracism or worse was a woman's fate if she broke the code. Other forces encouraged passivity. The Buddhist pagoda offered a refuge for both men and women, because Buddhism as practiced in Vietnam rejects the notion of gender and class differentiation.

The revolution provided a rootless woman like Duc Hoan with a community. "In the summers I lived with village families and taught them. During the academic year, we were paid in rice by the month. But in the summers there would be no rice ration and the village families would share what little they had with us—sometimes it was only a sweet potato, but I will never forget how kind they were. The teachers who were in charge of us were good, too, and they would sell their possessions to buy shoes and food for us younger student teachers. I will never forget the love I found with the peasants and my fellow teachers during those years."

Seventeen was the required age for revolutionary teachers, and when the authorities found that she was younger she had to give up her duties. She turned to theater work, where there were no age limits. But she remembers her days as a very young teacher in the countryside fondly. "They were the most beautiful human relationships I have ever had. We were like a big family, and I have kept those friends for my whole life. We still get together whenever we can." She values the experience of living in the villages, and looks back to her time with rural people with fondness, for it allowed her to extend her own feelings of frustration with the old system to help others, and it taught her valuable lessons about hard work and simple affection.

She joined the army in 1953. I had heard from her admirers that Duc Hoan had served as an artillery woman during the siege against Dien Bien Phu, but she did not want her military service to be blown out of proportion: "I joined the E367 Artillery Unit, but I was no different from other women. I learned to shoot a gun, to know when to jump out of the line of fire, and where to shoot." Earlier, in 1953, she was sent to South China to learn to become an interpreter for Vietnamese soldiers in training there. "They could send me because I had no family who would worry about me." But she said the Vietnamese commanders didn't trust her to interpret military matters and made her help the cook instead. She laughed long and hard when she recalled the time she mistranslated a term and told the cook to use a grass seed in a dish that made three thousand men sick. "I cried all day I was so embarrassed."

In the late 1950s Duc Hoan became the student of a Russian theater expert. In the theatrical troup she could use her talents for a time-honored purpose: to teach lessons that needed learning, to bring beauty to the world, to keep the people's spirits up when times were hard. The first film in which she acted, made in 1960, portrays the harsh life of a minority woman who has the misfortune to be the second wife of the brutish son of the village chief. Its didactic purpose is quite clear: to contrast the socialist regime's progressive marriage laws outlawing polygamy with backward customs in a minority village and to legitimize a massive relocation scheme that sent lowland Vietnamese people into minority areas to open up new lands and spread the dominant culture to outlying areas. "The Story of A Phu" (*Vo chong A Phu*), filmed in a village constructed for that purpose in Son Tay Province, was costly, according to Duc Hoan, but the state deemed it worth the cost of filling fields with paper flowers, and training citified actors to get a feel for life outside the realm of the "civilized" world. She suffered through three months in a minority village to learn her part. "I still don't think I can be better than I was in that role," she reminisced. But it was also the most terrible experience of her life, Duc Hoan reported, far more difficult than the bombings during the American War. The burial customs of the minority people offended her, and years later as she talked with me she shivered when she remembered a funeral in which the corpse was fed rice and the relatives ate the kernels that fell out of its mouth. "I spent all of my time worrying that someone would die while I was there." But she was proud, too, that she had learned her role from firsthand experience, "unlike the more shallow actors of today." She looks back with some nostalgia at her triumph as an actress, when her unique beauty and talent—and her capacity to get into the skin of the people she portrayed—were appreciated by the public.

The film was shown throughout the North, in villages and in fields, with simple equipment, and people flocked to see it. It made her famous but it is as a director that Duc Hoan has been able to exert a measure of control over the themes of her films. When I asked her how the transition from actress to director in 1978 changed her life, she answered with typical humor: "I was just more tired because it is much harder work." She went through what she called her "heroic" phase during the American War, when the purpose of art was to inspire the people, to raise their spirits with tales of indomitable heroes. Stationed near the demilitarized zone in Quang Binh, she worked with local entertainment troupes to help people forget their fear as the United States unleashed its weapons in this part of the war zone. "In this heroic commune that had shot down two U.S. planes, people had to have a life when they emerged from the bomb shelters. The government spent money on good props and cosmetics to cheer them. The government knew the value of films then."

She does not view the wartime portraits of women in film, fiction, and newspaper articles as ill-intentioned propaganda. "At no other time in Vietnam's history was the will of the people more necessary for national survival. When even the gentlest Vietnamese woman could be inspired to enter the male world of violence for her country and when she learned to do the job well, the war had become in reality a total people's war."

As a screenwriter and director, she chose to integrate women's problems into the war story. "Love and Distance" (*Tinh yeu va Khoang Cach*), made in the 1980s, deals with a woman's inability to love her disfigured husband. It is a compassionate portrait. Duc Hoan said, "This was a situation many wives encountered: sick, angry husbands, whose war wounds hurt their families. We can't blame wives for their feelings." Nor does she play down the pain that men felt. The theme song in "Love and Distance" sets the scene for a sad ending: "A young soldier who has just left the battlefield, his heart full of love," returns to his sweetheart only to be rejected. In the end, he is constant: "My love is the same. Though you have gone, you are in my heart." A film that forgives a woman for turning her back on a soldier who has suffered on the battlefield flies straight in the face of the official propaganda. But Duc Hoan refuses to place blame or to sell simpleminded morality. Her commitment to take on the messy human emotions that muck up any war is most clear in the 1978 film she considers her best, "Obsession" (*Am Anh*). It is about a North Vietnamese soldier who deserts to the South Vietnamese army in a moment of fear, and the consequences for him and his family. She depicts a deserter as a sympathetic, understandable character. More importantly, the film shows how his wife and son suffer. The mother cannot tell the boy that his father is a traitor when he asks her over and over why they haven't been sent a hero's medal like other families whose men didn't come home. Duc Hoan told me why she made the film: "After the war, Vietnamese people on both sides needed to put the hatred out of their hearts and forgive each other for mistakes. War should never happen, but when it does, sometimes people are forced to use guns. And at the end of the day, even the victorious ones are victims because they lose so much—their families, their sweethearts. The deserters were most hard to forgive. We feared them more than the Americans because they knew so much and could betray so many people. But we have to put ourselves in their position and remember the strong natural human will to survive. At the end of the war we had to find ways to integrate everyone into the community." Others in Hanoi admire "Obsession" because it courageously dealt with touchy issues so soon after the war, when emotions about patriotic service ran high and when cinema was used to push the heroic vision to unify the country and erase memories of suffering and sacrifice.

Duc Hoan's sympathy for people who don't fit again comes from her own life. She pitied her nephew, who was imprisoned for accidentally killing a deaf woman while driving in the 1960s. The black mark on his record marred his entire life. He never married. It was Duc Hoan who had to go to the prison to tell him his mother had died. And finally, when he joined the army in 1965, she thought he might have a chance to make a better life for himself. But he was lost, missing in action. "Because he had no wife or living parents, who might have had power to deal with the bureaucrats, it was almost impossible to get news of how he died or help to locate his body. I wondered if he had been killed by a B-52's bomb, or slaughtered with his whole unit. I wondered if he suffered from wounds before he died." Most troubling for her is that she could not bury him properly, and she reminded me of how important it is for Vietnamese people to bury their dead with the proper rituals to carry them safely to the world beyond. The dead who have not been properly cared for by relatives can become wandering, angry ghosts, harmful to a family. And the family suffers emotionally when closure is not possible.

After the war Duc Hoan's family split up: one brother left Vietnam by boat and a sister emigrated to the United States. She said, "We are a typical Vietnamese family, tied by emotions and memories, split apart by politics and war."

In the 1990s, Duc Hoan has continued to reflect on women's issues. "Love Story by a River" (*Chuyen tinh ben clongsong*), a 1991 film for tele-

Duc Hoan's nephew, Nguyen
Duc Cuong, in 1965. He was lost
in action in 1967. (*Courtesy of
Duc Hoan*)

vision, reveals how she interprets contemporary women's issues. The story features two sisters, orphaned by the war, both disappointed in love. One sister, married to a simple rural man, loves a shallow artist, a Party bureaucrat with neither heart nor talent. She takes up with a fast crowd of young people who are infatuated with Western ideas and clothes, and when her husband finds her dancing to a disco tune, he beats her in anger. Meanwhile, the unlucky sister, who was crippled by a bomb, is so desperate that she allows a traveling medicine man to spend the night with her. Both are war victims. He drinks to chase away memories of the bombs; she calls herself a "lame duck" as she pleads with him to ignore her mangled body and make love to her. When she does not become pregnant from the encounter, she is deeply disappointed, and continues to live vicariously through her married sister and her child. When I asked Duc Hoan about the film's message, she told me that she changed the original story, in which the wounded sister was married, because the problems of single women veterans needed to be brought to light. The

In Duc Hoan's home, Hanoi, 1996. *Left to right,* her husband, Luong Anh; Nguyen Ngoc Tuan; Phan Thanh Hao; and Duc Hoan.

domestic violence in the film, the scene of a husband beating his wife in front of their child, troubled me—especially in light of what I knew about some women's worries about increases in the incidence of domestic violence in Vietnam.[7] Duc Hoan explained, "She needed to understand that her husband became angry because he loved her. She was lucky to have this man. Keeping the family together is a woman's duty." It was the lonely single woman, not the unhappy wife, who was the victim in her view.

Duc Hoan's contribution thus is not a traditionally feminist one. In the end, she is a woman warrior who has drawn from her life history to act as a peacemaker. She ended one of our conversations with her philosophy of life: "Politics change, but human emotions stay the same."

CHAPTER THREE

Broken Promises:
The Lives of a Militiawoman

. . . [h]istory is made up of multiple stories, many of them herstories, which emanate from and then reconstruct events. Each story told by someone who experienced a war, or by someone who saw someone who experienced a war, or by someone who read about someone who saw someone who experienced a war, becomes part of a mosaic the many colors of which make up the totality of that war.

Miriam Cooke, Women and the War Story, 1996.

Some bureaucratic problems were inevitable in wartime, but most people realized that if they were to find solace, the state or the army was not where they would find it. It was from their families, their friends, their neighbours, sometimes their churches, that hope came.

Jay Winter, Sites of Memory, Sites of Mourning, 1995.

THE WARTIME PHOTOGRAPH OF NGO THI TUYEN displayed in the Vietnam Women's Museum shows a young woman standing tall, resolutely gazing into the distance, a gun slung over her shoulder—every inch the model soldier. The official biographies of this now famous militiawoman from Thanh Hoa Province confirm the photo's heroic message, for they describe a strategic bridge, a stubborn young fighter, and a community organized for war. There is another narrative about this woman, however, a postwar story that focuses on a childless, wounded, sick, disappointed, mature woman whose role as a model heroine has complicated her life.

As soon as I began work on this book, Vietnamese diplomats, male veterans, poets, journalists, academicians, and especially women urged me to visit Ngo Thi Tuyen. "You will understand more about North Vietnam during and after the war if you meet her," a middle-aged male foreign service officer told me—while politely declining to help me secure permission to travel outside Hanoi. But it was a conversation with a woman who sputtered with anger when she recalled her own involuntary enlistment in 1966 in the cause

"Heroine Ngo Thi Tuyen." (*Caption and photo courtesy of the Vietnam Women's Museum*)

of the North, who measured revolutionary time by the square meters that the socialist government had confiscated from her family's French-style villa, that convinced me that Ngo Thi Tuyen holds a special place in the hearts of middle-aged North Vietnamese, no matter what their politics.

You want to write a book about North Vietnamese women veterans of the American War? Then you must travel to Thanh Hoa Province to meet the most beloved heroine of our generation, Ngo Thi Tuyen.

She was the one who carried on her back 98 kilograms, over twice the weight of her body, of ammunition to supply the artillery defending the Dragon's Jaw Bridge from the American air attacks in early April 1965.

There was another woman from her hamlet, from the same militia unit. She was more beautiful and knew better how to talk to men and after the war got a high position in Hanoi. But the real heroine is Ngo Thi Tuyen, whose life now is hard mostly because her health is not good. Her neighbors are causing trouble and her house is in bad shape. The local officials won't help her. When you meet her, keep your eyes and ears open. Make your own judgments.

As I unravelled the many threads that make up Ngo Thi Tuyen's public and popular history, trying to sort out why her particular experience touches so responsive a chord in the 1990s, I learned that it wasn't simply her unstinting patriotism that endeared her to the war generation, but the link between her unselfish service and subsequent victimization. I wondered. Was Ngo Thi Tuyen so beloved because she represented the suffering of all Vietnamese women, who felt that they couldn't win no matter how hard they tried? Or because she had literally borne the burden of war on her back, broken her body for the cause, and then received so little for the sacrifice?

Her story points out how memory bends with contemporary worries. It shows as well what one strategic spot on the map of North Vietnam meant to both sides and how constant bombardment affected the all too often forgotten people on the ground, the ones who paid the price for policy and strategic decisions made by distant leaders on both sides of the conflict.

First, there is the bridge, itself a symbol of Vietnamese resilience and ingenuity. All rail and mechanized traffic between North and South on the country's main road, Highway One, had to cross the Dragon's Jaw Bridge during the war. Built originally by the French, it was blown up the first time by the Vietnamese themselves in 1945 to obstruct the French armies. A new bridge, constructed by the North Vietnamese after seven years and dedicated by President Ho Chi Minh in 1964, served as a visible monument to the technical and organizational skills of the new socialist nation. Finally, the Dragon's Jaw Bridge became a major target in the American air war from 1965 until it was finally destroyed by a laser bomb in 1972.

Ngo Thi Tuyen's exploits became a part of the lore of the Dragon's Jaw Bridge soon after she performed her heroic feats in 1965. A publication from Hanoi dated 1966 recounts how she had been trained in shooting down airplanes and had performed brilliantly in provincial shooting competitions. It tells how she organized evacuation teams, guarded the hamlet, fed the gunners, and helped repair telephone lines. A description of her demeanor at the May Day celebration in Thanh Hoa in 1965, as she sat beside other heroes

With Ngo Thi Tuyen at the bank of the Song Ma River with the Dragon's Jaw Bridge in the background, 1997.

and heroines who had distinguished themselves, plays up her youth and innocence: "This nineteen-year-old young woman still looked like a little girl with her round and innocent face and childlike features. She shunned public attention. Her big dark eyes fought shy of admiring gazes and she did not know what to do with her arms, now laying them on the great table before her, now crossing them on her chest."[1]

A more recent version of her story, published in Hanoi in 1994, suggests that the Dragon Jaw Bridge held up as long as it did because of one woman's singular strength and determination.

> Ngo Thi Tuyen, of the Viet nationality, was born in 1946 in Khang hamlet, Nam Ngan-Ham Rong Precinct, Thanh Hoa Province. She is a member of the Communist Party of Vietnam. As a militia woman, she recognized her duty toward the national salvation against the American aggressors. She was always ready to volunteer and possessed remarkable self-determination. During her service at the battlefield she showed great heroic spirit, never shirked danger or hardships, remaining ever ready to accept and fulfill to the utmost her duty and to contribute to the great successes of the armed forces.

On April 3 and 4, 1965, she helped shoot down many U.S. aircraft. On these two days, many planes had been sent to destroy the bridge, and after fulfilling her duty to capture U.S. airmen who parachuted out of their planes, she then helped one of our naval ships anchored in the river, which asked the militia to transport empty cartridges to the bank and in turn to take loaded ammunition to the ship to prepare for the fighting. She volunteered to walk into the river and swim to the ship in the face of the bombs from the U.S. aircraft overhead. She carried ammunition, rice, and water to the ship, and stayed on board to clean cartridges until dusk. That night she returned to shore and helped her comrades dig trenches, fill bomb craters, and cook dinner.

On April 4, at 9 A.M., the United States attacked the area fiercely. She volunteered to carry rice for the armies on the battlefield. When trucks arrived, she volunteered to transport shells from them to the artillery, even though she was exhausted and ordered to rest. Two cases were stuck together, and couldn't be separated out with the implements at hand, and so afraid that a delay would cause problems, she put both cases, weighing 98 kilograms, on her back, walked to the dike at the river bank, and handed them to the armed forces. That night the enemy hammered at the bridge, and under shower of bombs, she gave orders to keep the boats supplied with bullets and rice—as she dug trenches to shelter the artillery.

On May 26, after the enemy attacked the area, another ship asked for volunteers to bandage the wounded. Tuyen ran into the river, began to swim to the ship, but exhausted, was pushed back by the tide. She rested and tried again, bandaged the wounded soldiers, carrying some on her back to the bank. There she stayed, loading cartridges and serving the battlefield's needs until the last minute. As well, she made sure that food production was kept up, encouraging the farmers who were afraid of the bombs. She mobilized the militia and students to till the fields, and the harvest came in on time and the armed forces had vegetables to eat. For this, she was awarded two first class medals and a Ho Chi Minh Badge of Honor and certificate of merit. On January 1, 1967, she was given the title "Hero of the People's Armed Forces" by the National Assembly and the Government.[2]

AMERICAN ACCOUNTS SHOW what Ngo Thi Tuyen and her community were up against and how the U.S. side viewed the bridge and its defenders.

"The March 1965 decision to interdict the North Vietnamese rail system south of the 20th parallel led immediately to the April 3rd strike against the

Thanh Hoa Railroad and Highway Bridge, known to the Vietnamese as Ham Rong (The Dragon's Jaw)."[3] The U.S. Air Force allocated its most experienced pilots and sophisticated equipment to smash it:

> In an effort reminiscent of missions flown in the Second World War and Korea, a huge attack force of seventy-nine planes was assembled for [Lieutenant Colonel Robinson] Risner to lead . . . the plan called for the F-100s to strike first. Then, after the [enemy] anti-aircraft guns had, it was hoped, been knocked out, the F-105s would dive in at the bridge one at a time. Given the symbolic considerations and the initial objective of the American air campaign, the day of the first Thanh Hoa Bridge strike was perhaps the most important of the long Rolling Thunder campaign. If the United States was going to impress Ho and other North Vietnamese with its overwhelming airpower, April 3, 1965, was the day to do it. But the strike was almost a total failure, though not for lack of courage or determination.[4]

What happened? The bridge itself seemed immune to the 750-pound bombs—over 300 of which were dropped on the second day of the strike—and as one American account reported, "firing Bullpups [missiles] at the Dragon was about as effective as shooting BB pellets at a Sherman tank."[5] Technical problems, including the nature of the site, which required the pilots to circle over the bridge while Vietnamese antiaircraft gunners fired from the surrounding hills, confounded the American fliers. They did have an inkling that the battle wasn't just between machines and a bridge, that the people on the ground had much to do with its staying power: "Whenever weather conditions postponed bombing raids, and always at night, North Vietnamese workmen swarmed over the bridge, repairing whatever damage had occurred."[6]

The fight over the Dragon became a contest of wills. In 1967, the American side marveled that the bridge stood after two years of almost constant attacks: "Although the bridge had been damaged many times in the past and the North Vietnamese had paid dearly in men and materiel to keep it open, it had become a paramount symbol of North Vietnamese determination."[7]

WHAT WAS THE SOURCE OF THIS DETERMINATION? When it became clear that roads and bridges would become major targets, Ho Chi Minh called for local people to participate in an all-out fight to keep the roads open: "The war might last for five, ten, or even twenty more years. Hanoi and Haiphong might be destroyed . . . nothing is more important than independence and freedom."[8] His people listened. In 1965, the Hanoi news media reported the reactions of the pilot responsible for leading the Vietnamese counterstrike at the Dragon's Jaw Bridge, a story enhanced by his former trade as a poor fisherman. He had this to say: "A pilot must be calm before he gets on board. But yesterday morning, I was still moved when taking my seat in my cockpit. It seemed that Viet An, my native place, was calling me, that the party and Uncle Ho were looking at me! I was thus flying my plane in an excited state and with great confidence. Confidence in my mates and in myself. Above me, on the ground, in the South, in the North, everywhere I have friends and comrades who protect me and follow me with eyes full of affection and confidence. . . . No wonder that we have had the better of the enemy!"[9]

In the high tide of the patriotic fervor after 1964, this enthusiastic pilot and the militiawoman Ngo Thi Tuyen were simply following orders. After the northern towns of Vinh and Hong Gai were attacked by U.S. planes in August 1964, the Vietnamese Women's Union launched a "Three Responsibility Movement," which aimed to mobilize women for production and other tasks in place of the men who have gone to the front. The official list of women's wartime duties is a daunting one, testimony to the desperate situation and to official regard for women's capacity to work and to sacrifice. "Women must take charge of family affairs in the absence of a husband or son; giving assistance to the fighters at the front and undertaking, if necessary, combat duties. . . . It is not just a question of working harder or longer, but of increasing productivity with the use of better tools and means of production. For example, in the countryside where the labor force is now essentially made up of women, agricultural productivity must be increased through the application of new techniques and the use of better farm tools to lessen the hardship of such tasks as ploughing, transport, harvesting, and threshing. Their new tasks require women to study so as to raise their cultural and professional level. In war time, the technological revolution must be carried out despite the destruction by the enemy. Women play a decisive role in production and greatly contribute to this revolution, which is aimed at raising the economic potential of the country and increasing the people's resistance power."

Added to these burdens, women were also expected to "provide good education for the children, look after the old people so their children at the front will be relieved of caring for them, encourage their husbands and sons to reenlist, volunteer for the army, and always be ready to fight. They must always help the combatants and war wounded, and the families of those who have sacrificed their lives for the country. . . . Women should join in defending the village, and maintaining order and security. They must bring supplies to the combatants, find lodging for them, and look after the wounded. To take direct part in the fighting, they should join the people's militia and undergo combat training."[10]

The three responsibilities movement aimed at keeping production levels up and easing the minds of the men at the front. But histories of women written close to the time revel in the opportunities the campaign opened up for women. The numbers of women in the workforce increased from 170,000 in 1965 to 500,000 in 1969. "No profession—worker, teacher, engineer or physician—was closed to them now."[11] Training programs were established, and no longer could cadres whimsically decide who should be trained and rewarded. Nor could they block women from leadership positions.

A sense of how women in the countryside responded to the war can be detected in interviews conducted by a French journalist who toured the North Vietnamese countryside in 1967.[12] These on-the-spot reports recapture women's anger, determination, and accomplishments.

As one countrywoman told the reporter, "When one speaks of a 'peasant,' it is important to bear in mind that nowadays she is usually a woman of many roles. She is a producer, a housewife, a technician, and a combatant."[13] Militiawomen in the villages bragged to him about their prowess with heavy antiaircraft guns. Here is an example of an unmarried woman of twenty who studied nursing but took the greatest pride in besting the old men in shooting down American planes:

> As soon as I returned to the village [from nurses' training], I was put in charge of a heavy-machine-gun team. We and the rest of the platoon were given training by a regular army officer. The officer spent five days with us, but we trained on our own for a whole month, getting plenty of practice at stripping the gun and reassembling it. We use mobile guns because it is very dangerous to remain in one spot for long. In view of our morale and experience, I'm sure the U.S. Air Force will never succeed in knocking us out.[14]

This young woman's pride that she could shoot a gun shines through her account. She attributed the success of her sixteen-woman platoon, all between the ages of seventeen and twenty, not to guns but to morale and expertise. Her role in defending her village brought her status and recognition and kept her spirits up. She related that after the younger women shot down a plane, the older women in the village would troop out to celebrate with food and sweets. As for the old men, "they don't measure up to us. They can't see well and they aren't agile. So it is the young girls who are charged with the heavy 37 mm antiaircraft guns."

Another young woman spent a year in military training, and it served her well. She gives details to the reporter about the four American aircraft her militia team has shot down, and then predicts that her expertise will surely liberate her from traditional social constraints. "There is certainly complete equality between men and women today. I'm not married, but when I do get married I shall choose my own husband. True, men and women were officially equal even before the attacks started. But the spirit which women have shown under fire has won them far more respect than they enjoyed before. Men's attitudes have changed."[15]

And so, the famous militiawoman Ngo Thi Tuyen was not an anomaly, but one of many young women who learned new skills and proved themselves in battle. But she is the one who is remembered. And, as she was to learn, attitudes toward women didn't change all that much.

HAO RECALLS THAT IN HANOI DURING THE WAR people listened to the radio every day to hear if the Dragon still stood, because they knew that if it fell the supply lines to the South would be rendered much less effective. Even more importantly, the bridge and its defenders came to exemplify the collective staying power of the North as the air war heated up. Hao told me that she had read a lot of articles about Ngo Thi Tuyen and had seen her photos in the newspapers. Everybody admired her and so it was a great opportunity for Hao to be invited to her house in Thanh Hoa in 1991. She recalled that she and Tuyen walked up a hill together, and Hao repeated for me what the heroine told her that day:

> In 1965, just a few hours after our marriage, my husband was sent to B (the southern battlefield). As a militiawoman, I was in charge of transporting ammunition for the regular forces. That very night, the American planes poured bombs into the area and twenty-two of my comrades-in-arms were killed. But we had to defend the Dragon's Jaw Bridge at all costs on that terrible night—and we had to keep the trucks going over it to the south. I don't know why I was able to carry those two big boxes of ammunition at that time. More than once, my strength came from anger and the need to avenge my dead comrades.
>
> Later I was interviewed by many journalists. I had to pose for their photos. I was young then and proud of myself. I was even invited to Hanoi to make a speech. It was so nice to be there. But they made me wear the traditional Vietnamese long dress, the *ao dai,* and it was too complicated for me, and the high-heeled shoes tortured my feet. So I had to hold up my dress to keep it from flopping around and walk barefoot when I finally retreated back to my room in the guest house. And I didn't know how to talk to people in Hanoi—I did not have a high level of education, you know.

And when I went back to Thanh Hoa, I continued to work with the local forces to defend the bridge. We shot down seventy U.S. aircraft, but some fell into the sea and were claimed in the counts of other provinces. We didn't care because we knew what we had done.

Many foreign journalists from the socialist countries wanted to interview me, and one East German television team didn't believe that I had carried ammunition twice my weight. So to prove it I repeated the feat for them, right in front of the provincial guest house. After that my back felt funny.

And then I got the news of my husband's death. I thought day and night of a way to get to the South to find his remains and bury him properly. But when I did finally try, after Liberation in 1975, I couldn't find his body.

Only recently I remarried a wounded veteran who had fought in Cambodia, a colonel. It was not that I had forgotten my first husband, but that everyone felt sorry for me and persuaded me to marry him. And he is not well and needs a companion. He is a very kind man and we desperately want a child—girl or boy, it doesn't matter. But the doctor tells me something is wrong with my spine because I have worked too hard.

So, the upper levels decided to send me to Hanoi and then to Germany for a cure. But I didn't like the way the German doctors treated me and one night someone tried to get into my room. I chased him out, and then went home, too shy to tell anyone why. I knew I could never have a child . . . and didn't want that kind of help. I don't even want to tell you that guy's name.

I am also not happy with the way that things are here, the way the Party leaders deal with the reforestation projects, for example. Too much poverty for too long has made some of them corrupt now that there is a promise of some wealth for a few.

And I still have back pain. Maybe we will adopt a child, but we are poor. A blood child might have more compassion for us as we get older. But an adopted one might resent us for our poverty and need.

Please, when your family takes its summer holidays, come to see me, let me meet your son, let me make him a meal and just look at him.

As Hao and I discussed her encounter with Ngo Thi Tuyen, she told me that she still feels guilty for not keeping her promise to take her son to Thanh Hoa. "I don't know if a visit would cheer or depress her. Or how long it would take me to tell her what I believe: that if there is a creator, he treats every Vietnamese woman the same way—if something good happens to her, something bad will balance it out. I would want her to know that even though I have a nice family myself, I have to suffer other things."

Ngo Thi Tuyen reenacts her heroic deed, 1972. (*Author's photo from Nam Ngan-Ham Rong local commemoration hall, 1996*)

LADEN WITH ALL OF THESE BITS AND PIECES of information and expectations, I finally got out to Thanh Hoa Province in 1997, accompanied by a young scholar from the Center for Vietnamese Studies at Hanoi University. Mr. Nguyen Van Kim, a native of the city of Thanh Hoa, was as eager to meet his famous countrywoman as I, because he, too, admired her. The 108 miles from Hanoi to Thanh Hoa, on one of the North's best roads, took over four hours even though the driver of the old Russian car was an expert—a veteran driver on the Ho Chi Minh Trail during the war, it turned out. The road was in bad shape, the traffic a mix of animals, motorbikes, bicycles, and people walking helter skelter, dodging anything bigger than they. Once we crossed the border into Thanh Hoa, the terrain became noticeably harsher, the vegetation sparse, the soil rocky, and the motorized vehicles few. Mr. Kim told me that Thanh Hoa is one of the country's poorest provinces and that its people have a reputation for stubbornness. As we approached the famous bridge, he pointed out that the Song Ma River runs fast, and pontoons and ferries couldn't be readily used as they have been at other sites where bridges have

Nguyen Van Kim recording impressions at Ban ton tao chua (the pagoda at Ham Rong), 1997.

fallen. On one of the hills overlooking the bridge, where Vietnamese artillerymen and women once shot at American planes, the words *Quyet Thang* [Determined to Win], carved out of limestone, reminds newcomers that the scene has not always been so peaceful.

It was not easy to meet the famous heroine, but I was not really surprised that the local leaders were reluctant to let her talk with me. After all, her fame rested in part on their shoddy treatment of her. They hinted that she was a bit unbalanced of late, spouting off angrily to visitors about official neglect of local veterans, a situation she knows well because as an officer in the North Vietnamese Army she is in charge of veteran's affairs in Thanh Hoa.

Finally, we secured permission and drove to her house. I remember expecting to meet a bent-over, sick, elderly woman. Or maybe a tall, determined, angry woman—like the one I had seen in the photo in the Women's Museum. But when she walked out of her house to greet me, I saw a sturdy, no-nonsense, middle-aged woman dressed in the uniform of an officer of the Vietnamese army. The gifts I had chosen, trinkets to cheer up a sad case, seemed inadequate and I hid them in my briefcase, vowing later to send her something more suitable—a Vietnamese translation of *The Art of War,* or maybe a book about women in the U.S. armed forces. She quickly determined that she was younger than I, and holding my hand she told me she would address me as "older sister."

Not once during the afternoon we spent together, however, did she bring up her own exploits. True to what I had learned already about women veterans, she was far more concerned about someone in worse straits, in this case an eighty-eight-year-old woman who had once been the abbess of the local pagoda. Now sick, poor, and dependent on charity to survive, she, too, had had her time of courage, when she turned the pagoda into a hospital for the wounded. A site for community activities still, people from the hamlet joined us there to talk about how every aspect of life in their home place had been disrupted because a strategic bridge happened to be situated there. They wanted me to know that their precinct had been totally organized for war and as a community still paid the costs of war: the old nun, the widows, the women veterans who became single mothers because no man would have them as permanent partners, the orphans, all of them depended in large part on local donations to survive. And the people were poor, that was obvious. When one of the young nuns asked me to record my impressions, I had to think long and hard for the right words to convey my admiration for them and my guilt for the senseless destruction.

Finally, we found a way for Ngo Thi Tuyen to tell her story, amidst the worn exhibits at the local commemoration house, where a diorama of the bridge and surrounding terrain served as a focus. She talked about how frightened people were when the bombs began to fall, but how they all worked together in spite of their fear. Tuyen did not associate herself with inferior technology, did not present herself or her comrades as well-intentioned but ill-trained irregulars. She bragged a bit, after I asked her how they had learned to shoot so well: "When the Hanoi government knew the Dragon would become a target, the army sent people to teach us how to shoot. In one two-day period alone we shot down forty airplanes." And she said there was competition between local areas about who could claim the largest number of downed planes. When she talked about the American pilots, and how the women tried to protect them from harm after they ejected from their ruined planes, I felt that she was demonstrating pity for a weakened enemy rather than hatred for a powerful one. In fact, one of the pilots who had been captured in Thanh Hoa, Jeremiah Denton, had been back to visit the hamlet just a few weeks ago, she said.

In the end, the historic days of April 3 and 4 did not hold pride of place in her memory as they did in the official accounts. A worse time, May 26 of the same year, haunted her "because so many of our people were killed on that day."

Finally, after we toured the now peaceful riverbank and paid homage to the bridge, she held my hands and said, "We must work for peace. As women we know that." We parted and the nervous local officials sighed with relief

Ngo Thi Tuyen explains the strategy for defending the Dragon's Jaw Bridge, local commemoration hall, 1997.

that she had played her role well by their lights. As we went back to her house, I noticed that it was being repaired. I wondered if she had finally prevailed over her neighbors and secured the long overdue assistance she deserved from local authorities.

THAT NORTH VIETNAM'S MOST FAMED WOMAN FIGHTER came from Thanh Hoa Province made sense to me after I toured the local museums, which display visually a long history of resistance, sacrifice, and courage. The hamlet's dusty one-room commemoration hall is dominated by one wall of photos of the inhabitants who died in the American War. When volunteers were needed on short notice before the official order to create the Volunteer Youth Corps, Thanh Hoa recruited 1,200 "strong boys and girls" to work on the Ho Chi Minh Trail. After Directive 71 was issued in 1965, Thanh Hoa sent a total of 14,500 young people into the Volunteer Youth Corps—almost twice as many as any other province.[16] In addition, some 33,000 people

The wall of the dead soldiers
in the local commemoration
hall.

served in the local militia. Thanh Hoa museum workers carry the list of victims of war in their heads and recite them readily for visitors: In the French and American Wars, 55,000 soldiers died; 136 mothers lost three or more sons; 2,511 mothers lost two or more sons; 94 women lost both sons and husbands.

The larger city museum is in reality a war museum, for the province has a long history of resistance and conflict dating back over a thousand years. Faded photos of five Thanh Hoa women who joined an organized propaganda unit in 1941 attest to the province's long revolutionary history. Hanging there

Memorial statue outside the local commemoration hall.

prominently is a photo of the young Ngo Thi Tuyen, smiling as she shoulders a heavy box of ammunition.

It is a beautiful bronze statue of the woman warrior Lady Trieu, slim, tall, armed, however, that holds pride of place. I recalled her legend—her hatred of housework, her courageous stance against the Chinese—and her enemies' fear of her power. She continues to exercise potent force. On the way out of Thanh Hoa City, we stopped at an elaborate temple complex devoted to Lady Trieu. As Kim and I climbed the stairs to the inner altars devoted to the god-

Statue of Lady Trieu, Thanh Hoa City Museum.

dess, I noticed a crude cartoon-like painting on the wall—the famous lady on her elephant, Chinese soldiers dressed in the olive green uniforms of the modern Red Army—tumbling before her sword. That day a family and a fortune teller were praying to the goddess for help with a family sickness.

And as we drove away from the city, I reflected on the visit. In truth, I had gleaned no new facts about Ngo Thi Tuyen. But I had kept my eyes and ears open. Thanh Hoa has paid a high price in Vietnam's wars for independence, and sadness about the province's local sacrifices is inextricably linked

Temple to Lady Trieu, Thanh Hoa Province.

with its history. No one there advised me to forget about the war, and several times people reminded me that Hanoi had been relatively protected from the bombs because of its status as the capital and its foreign residents.

It didn't surprise me after I pieced together the stories about Ngo Thi Tuyen that she wasn't afraid to speak out about local problems. She was a stubborn, determined fighter during the war—why would she change after it ended? To the war generation, she represents a sacrifice that has never been repaid. In a postwar society that defines a woman by her place in the traditional family system, she has become an object of pity because she has never borne her own children. I knew that beneath Ngo Thi Tuyen's martial dress and bearing was a woman wounded in ways that I, an outsider, could never fully realize. But I also could not help but relish the magical aura of female power that permeates the landscape there. I wondered if the Thanh Hoa local officials treated Ngo Thi Tuyen so gingerly because they harbored a deep-rooted fear that she might one day become a local cult figure—just as the historical Lady Trieu had moved from history to legend to goddess? Certainly, the elements are all there: a superhuman feat, a local notable whose very presence draws outsiders and attention to the community, and a woman with a fierce sense of justice.

Temples to women of the past punctuate the landscape of Vietnam, vivid reminders that women's martial power cannot so easily be invoked in wartime and dismissed when peacetime demands gentler virtues. Will in some distant time visitors to Thanh Hoa be buying incense at a temple dedicated to the heroine of Vietnam's long ago war with America, Ngo Thi Tuyen?

PART TWO

Memories

CHAPTER FOUR

A Bombshell for a Vase: Leaving Home to Save Home

When we went to the district commandant to enlist, we were a class of twenty young men, many of whom proudly shaved for the first time before going to the barracks. We had no definite plans for our future. . . . We were still crammed full of vague ideas which gave to life, and to the war also an ideal and almost romantic character.

Erich Maria Remarque, *All Quiet on the Western Front,* 1929.

We didn't know what we were volunteering for. No one realized what the words "war" or "front" really meant.

Russian woman soldier, 1941, in Shelley Saywell, *Women in War,* 1985.

WHILE NGO THI TUYEN AND HER NEIGHBORS fought to keep the Dragon's Jaw Bridge open to traffic along coastal Route One, tens of thousands of young women labored on the Ho Chi Minh Trail as it wound through the jungles and mountains along the border between Laos and Vietnam. As I had learned from Professor Dung, some were educated urbanites, sent by universities and ministries, but the largest numbers of women entered the war through the volunteer youth corps after 1966. Most were from the countryside and had not progressed beyond the seventh grade. Some volunteers who lied about their age to join up were as young as thirteen, but most of these women were older teenagers, between seventeen and twenty. Armed with shovels, hoes, and AK-47s, they devoted their lives to opening and repairing the "blood roads," the most heavily bombed sections of the Ho Chi Minh Trail. Organized in battalions, platoons, and squads that mirrored the regular army, made up of both men and women dressed in military uniform, the young volunteers were primarily charged with keeping the supply trucks moving steadily to the battlefields of the South. Women also "manned" jungle liaison stations and ammunition depots, made coffins and burial cloth, collected and buried the dead, and tended the wounded. Women with more training and education operated communications networks, staffed and directed jungle clinics, recorded the war as journalists, and organized entertainment. Their work necessarily took them to some of the most dangerous sites. The official history of the volunteer youth admits the sacrificial nature of their service: "Wherever there was danger and death, there were volunteer youth."[1]

Despite their important role, recent reportage from Hanoi suggests that the volunteer youth have been callously treated by the government, initially misled with promises of benefits for their service, untrained and poorly provisioned during the war, and ignored in the postwar reconstruction. An article in *Lao Dong,* a widely circulated official newspaper, dated March 1996, contains a surprisingly frank critique of the government's neglect of these young people: "Each branch [of the government and army] that used volunteer youth was supposed to provide clothing and equipment for them. In reality, however, these branches let units in the local areas care for them, and many carelessly gave volunteer youth goods of bad quality."[2]

The article reminds readers that the youth suffered tremendous hardship: In 1967, on one road alone "every young person dealt with at least one hundred bombs and the road was blocked by the hour, not the day. Every night after filling the craters, the young girls of the Youth Corps took flares and white parasols and ran out on the road to make [living] road marks for the truck drivers. It was these sisters, these volunteer youth, who serve as magnificent models of the life and literature of Vietnam from this period. Moreover, after carrying out their duty, they received no recognition. Many of the volunteer youth now feel as if they have fallen into an abyss."

Women's postwar conditions deserve special attention, as a cadre from the Volunteer Youth Department informs the reporter: "At the moment, there are many cases of women who are ill from diseases or bomb pressure caused by the war and there are no policies to help them. . . . Those are unseen wounds, so they are not taken care of. . . . Society and the state have not fulfilled their duty to these veterans, and this is something we are all really sorry for."

Finally, the article calls for a better accounting of the actual numbers of casualties among the young volunteers. "In the entire country, there are about 170,000 to 180,000 volunteer youth who are still alive and working. But the official data states that for the battlefields of the North and South as well as other sites during the American War, only 130,000 members served."

In light of recent media attention to their collective plight, how do women veterans themselves regard their war experiences and postwar situations? What had propelled young women, mostly from the countryside where a woman's purity is her most prized attribute, to leave home and enter a male realm of violence and death? How do their reasons for entering the war differ from those of the older, more educated urban women? As I talked with women, I discovered that their motives for volunteering were mixed. Some women went to war for patriotic reasons, some resisted socialist propaganda and went unwillingly, some went out of practical considerations, and some because everyone else was going off and it seemed an exciting opportunity. But most women believed that they had no choice. They had to go out to fight once American bombs threatened to obliterate their homes.

"THE WOMEN WHO REALLY SUFFERED, the crazy or sick ones, the ones who never got married, will never be able to talk to you because they are too bitter and angry," a male veteran told me after trying without success to help me arrange a meeting with a single woman who had driven a truck during the war and is now a janitor in his institute. So when I was finally on my way to talk with an unmarried woman veteran, I didn't quite know what to expect. As we careened on a motorbike to a suburb of Hanoi, my young guide, Nguyen Minh Thu, told me that this woman didn't want me to know her name, not for fear of political reprisals, but for shame about her poverty and spinsterhood.

What was it like, I wondered, to be the object of such public pity? She might be unstable, I had been warned, because according to local lore, women who have never given birth often exhibit wilder mood swings than the lucky ones with kids.

When we pulled off the main road to her dirt lane and skidded through the mud to the very end, and I saw her small house, it looked isolated. Or was that simply what I expected from a "lonely household," the term used in Vietnam for a home without a husband?

I noticed right off that she was well dressed and had good, thick hair, and, I was to learn, took pride in it, because she had not suffered the fate of so many veterans who lost their most prized symbol of feminine beauty to malaria and malnutrition. She greeted me warily, but I expected that. Inside, her home seemed far more spacious than many I had visited in Hanoi, where some families live in one room, stacked in layers of lofts, spilling out into the alleys and streets to carry on their social life. Her simple wooden bed, small TV, ancient radio, and rickety table made up the bare-bones furnishings; but there was order and serenity.

As we sat down for the get-acquainted tea, a sinister-looking vase on a shelf caught my attention. It was the shell of a baby bomb, she said, and holding it, watching for my reaction to the grim object, she began to talk about herself.

In July 1966, when our late President Ho Chi Minh called for the whole population to support the armies, I was in middle school. His call, and the bombs from U.S. aircraft, convinced me that I had to go. Actually, I was too young to join the volunteer youth because seventeen was the official cut-off age, but with some of my girl-friends, I pricked my fingers and wrote with my blood to persuade the authorities to let me join. We were all between fifteen and seventeen years old. I had no idea what to expect when we got off the train in Thanh Hoa Province and began to walk to the front, but I can say now that it was the most terrible and interesting time of my life.

I was a roadbuilder until I got malaria so bad that I couldn't talk or hear. So I had to communicate by simple sign language with my comrades—it wasn't so inconvenient, because we knew each other well. And finally, my health was such a problem that I was sent back to the rear. But there was no place for me. My boyfriend had married someone else and I was too sick to find another man and I didn't want to anyway. My family didn't want to give up my plot of land as a dowry. So I went for awhile to live in an all-women's collective farm with other women who had no place to go.

At that first meeting, Nguyen Thuy Mau, the woman I will call Teacher Mau, offered only a sketchy history of her own experiences as a roadbuilder and demolitions expert in the jungles. She was far more concerned with the aftermath, for herself and her troop, C814. The events of the war itself would have to wait until later.

The road to Nguyen Thuy Mau's home outside Hanoi, 1996.

Author with Nguyen Minh Thu and Teacher Mau, 1996.

She brought out her photo album, and turned again and again to two photos of herself: one of a smiling, healthy-looking teen in 1966, the other of a somber, pale adult in 1968. Postwar life had not been easy, and not only because she has remained single and childless. She is sad that like other volunteers, she has never been given veteran's compensation or even recognized as a veteran. Moreover, she has never had medical help for her deafness and worries constantly about the health and well-being of the others in her troop. In contrast to most of the other survivors of her troop, however, she regards herself as well off, because she does have a job as a teacher in a rural school. As one of the few educated members of her group, she feels responsible for the welfare of the others.

Closer to the city than most of her comrades, she is the one who relays news, usually bad news, of deaths in their families, illnesses among the troop, or changes in government policies. In the past two years, Mau has helped organize two reunions, important occasions that brought the survivors of C814 together after they had lost touch with one another for almost three decades. Her photo album is filled with pictures of their most recent July get-together. She pointed to one photo that showed a woman who had tears streaming down her face and a huge, disfiguring goiter on her neck. In another the poorest members of the group line up to receive donations from their peers,

Shell of a baby bomb, Teacher Mau's home, 1996.

who themselves obviously have little to spare. She told me that some members of the troop couldn't come to the reunion because they couldn't afford to buy decent clothes to wear.

What do these veterans talk about when they meet? I asked. "Never about the war. We only want to find out about how people and their children are now, and we talk about the sick and we remember the dead."

These meetings clearly offered solace, but as people traded stories, they also learned about others' misfortunes. For example, a couple from the troop took their dying, handicapped child to the local authorities and asked for medical help. The cadres refused, the baby died, and the parents committed suicide. And then there was the story I heard from others, of the sick older woman from the troop who was offered aid by the higher-ups just recently. A nice gesture, but the cadres decided to make the woman come into town to get the award. It cost more for Mau's troop to hire a car for her than the bonus was worth.

THE THIRD TIME WE MET, on a bright Sunday morning in early 1997, I wasn't surprised to find Teacher Mau acting as the efficient organizer and host. She had gathered together thirty former volunteer youth, members of her

Veterans of Troop C814 in Teacher Mau's home, 1997.

troop, no small feat without telephones or mechanized transportation to ease the logistical problems. Out of respect for her and curiosity, her comrades-in-arms had agreed to meet and talk with Hao and me. We took food for lunch, and our student assistant and friend, Thu, helped us record the conversations.

Tension, curiosity, embarrassment stilled us all at first. They were tired. Only one man had a motorbike. The others had walked or ridden rusty old bicycles for as long as two hours to join us. One of the women quietly reminded me that taking a day off from farm work was no small sacrifice. The men sat close together on one side of the room, talking, smoking; the women clustered cross-legged on the bed, silent, watching. These middle-aged people had known each other since their teen years. Nonetheless, Hao and I, the outsiders, were not complete strangers. Teacher Mau had told them about my project and I had sent a letter and a small contribution to their annual reunion the previous July. But sitting face to face with an American and talking about the war was unnerving, one man told me. "We've never met an American, and we never talk about what happened during the war when we get together for our annual reunions."

The women's worn faces vouched for their hard lives. One woman told me that for twenty years she had wanted to visit Ho Chi Minh's tomb, only a few hours from her home, but it was an impossible dream for her, a woman who survives from day to day as a peddler. Another woman, recovering from

Troop C814, 1997.

a long overdue goiter operation, could not speak at all. Just about the time I thought that it had been a mistake to try to create a bridge between us, one of the men broke the ice with a poem he had composed. He called it "Witnessing," and with apologies to me, nervous, puffing a cigarette, Nguyen Gia Ninh read it out to us:

> It's time to witness the song of the volunteer youth,
> For no longer are they insignificant, silent rocks.
> Or like branches of germinating trees
> Stunted by baby bombs with their dead yellow color.
> Still with us are knapsacks with holes from enemy bombs
> And fragments of poems, forgotten deep in the cupboard.
> Remaining too are tears, darkness
> And light.

And then, moved by the poet's message that it was time to reflect on the past and hope for a better future, ignoring the embarrassed nudges of their companions, the women began to talk:

I joined the volunteer youth because of Uncle Ho's call. I knew that he would never ask us to go if the country didn't need all of us. If the country was at war again, we would sacrifice ourselves, and yes, we would encourage our children to go too. The work we did in the past was worth it, and we are proud. Anyway, it is usual for any people whose country is at war to go out to work for the country. Yes, our lives are hard now. But we don't blame the government. We are like the children of poor parents. Well, sometimes we think they haven't treated us properly, but then we see or read about other people and we know that we have better lives than theirs. So we wish the government would help them first, before it is too late.

There is one thing that we are sorry for. That is that our dead comrade's remains have never been brought back or buried. We carried in our knapsacks the bodies and bones of the ones we could find to put them in cemeteries in the jungles. We are proud of that, because some people from other provinces didn't care. We know where the dead are now, but no one will help us bring them home. Why does your government spend so much money on your men missing in action and why doesn't it care about ours?

Once they started, they talked about how it felt to see people die, to try to live a decent life in the jungle while dodging bombs, what it was like to lose health and sometimes memory to malaria, to come home to shell-shocked, wounded husbands—if they were lucky to have a husband—and then to be afraid of having deformed children. They felt most sorry for the women, like Mau, who had never been able to marry, and they felt guilty and surprised that they had lived at all.

They still revere the memory of Ho Chi Minh and expressed no doubt about their decision to respond to his plea for help. Even men normally exempt from military service went after 1966, Mau's male comrades explained. "I was an only son, and normally I would have been allowed to stay home." Or, "I had many children and a sick wife, and at first I wasn't called, but then I had to go." I know from other evidence that Chinese ancestry or allegiance to Catholicism also removed healthy young men from the regular forces but that even many of these suspect people eventually were called up when the Northern government became desperate enough for support to overlook politically undesirable individuals.[3]

The women, even though imbued with a tradition that called women to war when the nation needed their service, had to justify to themselves and often to their families their decision to leave the safety of home. For some poor women, the volunteer corps beckoned as a way to be fed, relieving their families of one more burden. Some youngsters were caught up in the

Veterans of Troop C814, reunion, Hanoi, 1996.

heady spirit of the times, enticed by romantic visions of life away from family and authority figures, and all the better if leaving home was for a good cause.

The people in Mau's home didn't talk about defending socialism or playing a role in the global political struggle. One woman, sitting on the hard bed, said to me, "The North is our homeland. If it was destroyed, we would have no place to raise future generations. We had no choice." Women talked more openly than men about their anger, their desire to take up arms to avenge dead kin and friends. "After my brothers and father were killed by American bombs, I wanted to get a gun and kill American soldiers" was a refrain I would hear often in these encounters. More than one woman who had not been able to go to the front expressed disappointment and anger at having to play a supporting role. "I wanted to fight for a time when even the children in our country would be safe," was another sentiment repeated during these discussions. Women found themselves in a situation that provoked a complex mix of white hot rage and deeply felt pacifism. And they told me that I had to understand what it was like in the North as the bombs threatened to destroy their homes. One man asked me simply, "Why did the United States come from so far away to bomb our cities and villages?"

AS WE KNOW NOW, there were always doubts among U.S. policymakers about the possible effects of a massive campaign to bomb the cities of North Vietnam. Viet Cong attacks on Americans in Saigon in late December 1964 and a deteriorating political situation in the South in early 1965 prompted hawks among U.S. advisors to urge Lyndon Johnson to authorize raids against the North, not only in retaliation against the Viet Cong, but to break the spirit of the North and to bring its leaders to their knees. General Curtis LeMay in July 1965 argued: "The military task confronting us is to make it so expensive for the North Vietnamese that they will stop their aggression against South Viet Nam and Laos. If we make it too expensive for them, they will stop. They don't want to lose everything they have."[4] What the American side did not factor into the equation was the anger of women, who would sacrifice their lives to save what they had—their homes.

During the air campaign known as "Rolling Thunder," 643,000 tons of bombs were dropped on the North. How did this massive attack affect Vietnamese women on the ground? By late 1965, Hanoians were preparing bomb shelters and evacuation plans as the raids moved ever closer to the city. Many people told me that they never really thought it would happen, that their city was protected as if by magic against destruction, for it had recovered from so many invasions in the past.

Originally called Thang Long, "Rising Dragon," the site that is now Hanoi was chosen as a capital by the Ly king in 1010. For security and protection from floods, a system of dykes was constructed along the banks of the Red River. Never a fortified city, Hanoi's inhabitants simply withdrew into the swamps outside it when the Chinese and Mongols invaded in the thirteenth century and after. In the center of the city, a shrine on Hoan Kiem Lake reminds urbanites of the legend of the hero Le Loi. When the Chinese invaded in 1418, he asked for help, and the lake yielded a sword-bearing tortoise. When he defeated the invader with the magic weapon, it flew out of his hand, back into the lake. When the French took control of Hanoi in late 1946, the Vietnamese revolutionary forces blew up selected strategic sites and evacuated the city rather than allow the enemy to use it and its riches against them. But the American War was different, for the B-52s with their 58,000-ton payloads couldn't be held back with magic swords, nor was there any place to hide. Hanoians learned firsthand the power of modern technology as they watched hospitals, streets, and entire neighborhoods disappear in a flash.

The volunteer youth, mostly rural residents, responded as much to Ho Chi Minh's call as to their fear of losing their homes when they signed on. Urban dwellers were shocked into action by more complex considerations. And there were some who would have preferred to see the city destroyed than support the socialist government. Lest it appear that the entire North was motivated by an unthinking, mass wave of patriotism, one woman's testimony stands as a useful counterpoint to others I heard, for her family background and class had immunized her against the patriotic fever spreading through Hanoi. Politics had taken away everything that she cherished. She hated socialism and the "peasants who run the government." Sent by her university to support the war, she told me how she resented having to go out of the city to work in boring dirty jobs.

> My father was a doctor, and I was educated by the French. We had a beautiful French-style villa in Hanoi, and we had to leave it in 1946 when the French reoccupied the city and the Vietminh made us leave. I wanted to study literature but was forced by the revolutionary government to enter technical school. In 1966, I was sent to work in the mines in the North. It was filthy manual labor, and the miners did not want women underground; it was bad luck. After six months, the director of the mine recognized my class, took pity on me, and offered me an office job. I was back in Hanoi during the Christmas bombing in 1972, and we would stand on the top of our house and watch the rockets and bombs hitting city streets. My father told me that if the house was destroyed, he wanted to die with it. At that time, except for the bombs, Hanoi was so quiet. The men and children were gone, there were no peddlers, no street life.
>
> My sister was away. She had made a different choice from mine. She felt she had to get rid of her middle-class "black mark" and tried to join the Communist Youth Union when she was a teen, but because of her background, they made her go through terrible ordeals to prove her sincerity. The dirtiest work, digging ditches and canals, up to her waist in water for hours on end, she did it all. I don't blame her. Many families in Vietnam have such differences. We are friends. But we all paid for the war. What makes me mad now is that the government is letting the high officials' kids get rich and own property and yet they took everything we had—and we earned our right to it. Now, people are beginning to tell the truth about it.

Family history moved other women to fight for different reasons. Inspired by fathers, uncles, mothers who had resisted the French and who owed their improved lives and education to the socialist government, they served more willingly.

For Le Thi Quy, now a prominent women's studies researcher in Hanoi, there was no question that she would support the war, and she left her studies at Hanoi University to volunteer to work as a journalist in Haiphong in 1972. Her father had worked against the French and her mother had suffered under the old system. Her testimony demonstrates that it was not only fear of death and destruction of homes that hurt her, but separation from family and the disruption of ritual life.

> When Hanoi was bombed, my family went out to a village and I went with my classmates at Hanoi University to another place. My mother was sick with lung cancer, but she didn't tell us, didn't want us to worry about her. She had ten living children, had worked as a fruit peddler, and everything she had she gave to us. One of my classmates happened to visit the village where my mother was staying, saw her, and came back to tell me she seemed better. So when one week later I got a telegram telling me she had died, I couldn't believe it. I wanted more than anything to be at her funeral, and two strong male students helped me push a bicycle down the mountain roads to get to Hanoi as fast as I could—there were no trains or cars to use. It took us a week and when we reached Hanoi, she had been buried already. Her death was one of so many, my family couldn't ask for special privileges and delay the burial. When I got home, I learned that when she was really bad, my father had to put her in a cyclo and take her to the hospital. She died on the way. The night before, she stayed up all night, talking with my brothers and sisters, worrying about their futures. I missed that; I missed the chance to thank her for sacrificing so much for me.

When Hanoi was bombed in late 1972, Quy felt she had to do something when everywhere around her people were dying. As a journalist in Haiphong, she was charged with documenting the damages and could not escape the worst sites. "I will never forget seeing a pregnant woman's fetus blown out of her body by bomb pressure. It was fiercer in Haiphong than Hanoi; the Americans treated Hanoi more carefully, for it was the capital, visible to the world because of the presence of foreign embassies and reporters." In the end, it wasn't the bombs, but the chaos and scrambling the raids caused and her inability to do the right thing for her mother that hurt more permanently than the physical destruction of her home.

Hao, too, described the psychological affect of the air raids. Her motives for volunteering to work outside Hanoi in 1967 and again in 1972 were mixed.[5]

> When President Johnson escalated the war in the North in 1965, any man who could go to the battlefield was accepted, if not in the regular forces, in the volunteer youth corps. And the women who didn't go stayed behind to do all kinds of jobs to replace them. We girls in the school or at the factory set up a volunteer youth group right on the spot. It was our job to rescue people right after the bombing raids inside and out of the city. Life was hard; besides work, we had

Hao reads a letter from Karen Turner, with Teacher Mau, reunion of Troop C814, July 1996. (*Courtesy of Nguyen Minh Thu*)

to learn military training and nurses' training, how to bandage a person hit by a baby bomb when the fragments stuck to them and burned them, what to do when their bones were broken, or they were suffocating from the bomb pressure. We learned only simple methods for dealing with these medical things and there was no equipment for us. No one thought about fear or death as we trained.

We had our first trial when U.S. aircraft missed the March 8 Textile Factory one day and hit a nearby village, in Autumn 1967. After lunch we were sitting in the workshop and suddenly a strong wind, a great force, threw us against the wall. The earth shook fiercely. When you were right near the place where the bombs dropped, you couldn't hear their loud noise. The bombs hit a village on the other side of the dyke, about one hundred meters away on the river bank and the village was on fire. We went there at once and I was in the team that carried water to put the fire out. We got water from the fishponds or anywhere else we could find. But not much could be saved, since the houses were made of bamboo and the fire spread. I will never forget seeing through the smoke a child stuck head down in the debris, his legs making a V shape above the rubble. People rushed to that house. But they couldn't help the boy.

One of my comrades found a shelter underground. We lifted up the roof and stood motionless, because we saw there five burned faces, brown, their hair curled, their noses straight. They looked like ancient Romans. They were so young and handsome. They were killed by the bomb pressure, and the bomb exploded so close that it burned them, preserved them just as they were at that moment. I will never forget those five heads emerging from the soil.

They were four brothers and a cousin, we learned. All had gone home for their father's death anniversary ritual. One took a leave from the battlefield, two came from their military base near Hanoi. The youngest was in university. When their mother and neighbors rushed there, some fainted. Nothing can describe the noise of that day, the cries of wounded people, of survivors who lost family members. And the sight of the mother who fainted, slowly, when she came upon the scene where her four sons and nephew had died. We were ordered to leave so the villagers could bring them up, but then the airplanes came back again. We all jumped into shelters, on top of each other, fearful that the bombing would be worse the second time. But the planes just flew over us. We ran for home to see if our families were safe.

Along the dyke, some corpses were put in coffins, but mostly bodies were laid out on the bamboo trays we use to dry rice. I saw three corpses—mostly broken body parts—on one tray, and the smell of burned flesh, and people crying, and I ran, crying, fast to my home. I had a fever and vomited and couldn't stop and for weeks I couldn't sleep, but just sat staring into nowhere. Even now, whenever I see a V shape, I remember the legs of that little boy and I feel sick.

For Hao, the victory sign would forever be linked with the death of the young and the end of her own youthful innocence. But she told me that she never wanted to take up a gun, only to carry water and care for the wounded. As bombs rained on the city, her family, like so many others, became vagabonds in search of safe places, all the while trying to find work in spite of a "bad" political background. Hao spent the 1960s in glass factories and chalk mines, and earned spare change knitting sweaters at home with her mother.

But life went on, despite the B-52s that came in threes, which couldn't be heard until the bombs hit, and generated so much fear and uncertainty that Hao resigned herself to death. When by accident in 1967 she had the chance to enter a teacher's college, she and her classmates had first to build their classrooms, dormitories, and toilets out of bamboo, and it was at this time that she joined the youth brigades charged with aiding villages after air raids. After a year, she was found out and expelled because the authorities "could not let a prisoner's daughter educate the future generation."

"I was seven months pregnant in April, 1972, when Hanoi was threatened to be wiped away by B-52s. So everybody had to leave the city that night. My son, Binh, was born on 22 June, 1972, and six hours after his birth, a rocket hit close to the maternity house. All of the newborn babies were hastily thrown into the earthen bomb shelters."

Not only bombs but bureaucrats plagued her life, for she had to contend with the baby's delicate health in the face of hospital administrators who often refused him treatment because of her "bad" family background.

> That was when I came to the decision to join a team to reeducate myself. I volunteered to dig canals and dredge the lakes in the youth corps. This shocked and shamed my family and my in-laws. But there, with the volunteers, I could earn the title of state worker, attend the evening university, and graduate with a diploma in French and English. My mother-in-law was so offended she openly looked for another wife for my husband. But I didn't care, because I had proven my proletarian spirit, for my son.

Those who lived through this terrible time do not exult in their good fortune. Hao spoke often of survivor's guilt and the sense of powerlessness in the face of the bombs. "We couldn't hear the B-52s and so the bombs just dropped out of the sky like rain, but even with rain we could see the dark clouds or hear the thunder to know it was coming." She expressed anger when she learned later that sometimes pilots simply dropped the bombs, randomly, to lighten their loads as they flew back to their bases. Hanoians learned the hard way that the fiction that civilian targets would be spared was a cruel lie. "An American bomber shooting for a target is like a stork trying to defecate into a test tube," an observer commented about the B-52s.

Life for those who evacuated not only brought urbanites face to face with the boredom and hardships of rural life, but kept families separated at a time when they most needed support. Children and teachers built schools in the countryside. Duc Hoan remembers teachers and children digging the foundation for their rural school, creating classrooms for study and trenches for safety. "We had no equipment; everything useful went to the armies and so we had to use conical hats to carry dirt—each one holds two kilograms and

Members of Troop C814, Hanoi, 1997.

they worked quite well. We were most afraid of the baby bombs, because their fragments would penetrate the body and cause infections and we had no medicine." Another woman, a teacher in a school northwest of Hanoi during the war, remembers having to interrupt lessons to herd the children into the trenches when the planes came and then calm them down and go back to study when they left. "We constantly told them stories of Vietnamese heroes and heroines to encourage them. The girls were just as stoic about the situation as the boys. But the children's lives were not normal."

And it wasn't just the war that separated loved ones. Massive relocation projects during the 1960s moved people into the mountainous areas to reclaim the land and educate the minority peoples in the highlands. Political struggles wrenched families apart, when solidarity among kin was one of the few respites from chaos and uncertainty. Hao remembers hearing that her father had been sentenced to ten years in prison just as an air raid sent her scurrying to a bomb shelter with her siblings. Instead of saying good-bye to their father, on his way to a prison three hundred kilometers outside Hanoi, the children had to remain hidden. She also remembers that rainy days, when the planes couldn't fly, were times of celebration in Hanoi. And Saturdays, everyone braved the bombs to see family, no matter what the weather—packing the roads with people coming and going. Some never made it to their destinations, and Mondays were days of accounting—who had survived the

Bomb shelter, painting by Nguyen Ngoc Tuan, 1974.

weekend and who had been killed just by venturing out to see family and friends.

She recalled:

> And then we got the news that my father's health was very bad, and my mother had to go to the prison at the end of Tuyen Quang Province to visit him. I remember going to the bus station near the park to see my mother off and these images still come back to me. People lay on pieces of plastic cloth along the bank of the lake, waiting to be in the queue in time to buy a ticket for the next day's bus. My mother, a fragile woman, was carried along with them, with all the food we had saved for months to give to our father. Sometimes she missed the connecting bus and had to walk in the dark, alone, the long distance through the hills and mountains to the prison. She had to be there in the morning, and then had to catch the bus back to the district town and on to Hanoi.

Militiawomen guarding the Red River Dike, Hanoi, 1967.
(*Courtesy of Vu Thi Bich Loc*)

LIFE INDEED WAS NOT NORMAL in the North after 1966. Everything was turned upside down by the war. When Teacher Mau and the members of Volunteer Youth Troop C814 left their homes in the countryside outside of Hanoi in 1966 to work on the Ho Chi Minh Trail, their lives had already been altered forever. And when they told me that they had to leave home to save home, I understood why they believed that they had no choice, and why women could turn to violence in the interest of peace.

When they began to recount their passage from home to the battlefields, they remembered how shocked they were to find that conditions at the remote sites where they were to fight and shovel and dig were far worse than they had ever imagined.

CHAPTER FIVE

Shovels, Hoes, and Guns:
Women on the Ho Chi Minh Trail

With their shovels, hoes and guns, women secured the future of Vietnam.

Colonel Le Trong Tam, 1996.

Turning now to Mu Gia Pass itself—in spite of the many missions, including B-52 missions—the Pass remains open. Primary intelligence sources estimate thousands of coolies maintain this route in a constant state of good repair.

U.S. Air Force briefing notes, 1966.

Armies, like families, are institutions that create a world. Both successfully engender the new member's respect, loyalty, love, affirmation, gratitude, and obedience.

Jonathan Shay, *Achilles in Vietnam,* 1994.

IN 1997, WHEN WE SAT DOWN TO TALK, the veterans of Troop C814 displayed the easy camaraderie of military buddies anywhere. I wondered how in 1966 these inexperienced teens had learned to pull together as a team, how the women remember their lives in an unfamiliar new world where they shared daily hardships and backbreaking work with men. And how did the men regard these thousands of young women working on the Ho Chi Minh Trail? Military accounts and memoirs penned by soldiers, journalists, and artists during the war provide insight into how the presence of women affected the men who depended on their courage and skills to keep the huge human conveyor belt, the Ho Chi Minh Trail, moving smoothly.

When Mau and her comrades-in-arms finally began their stories, they told them in terms of a physical and psychic journey, from home to war, from youthful ignorance to an adult awareness of responsibility and tragedy. Most of them had never ventured outside their villages before. Everything was new, and unlike army regulars and professionals they were given no training. One

Students of literature, Hanoi University, just after volunteering to join the army, Hanoi, 1965. (*Courtesy of Ngo Thao*)

of the women, Mrs. Hoa, quiet until that moment, remembered for us her own passage to the front.

> We left from a place near here—it was farm land then—on July 17, 1966. We were provided with a knapsack, two sets of uniforms, a pot, and a tin can. When they gave me a shovel and a hoe, I knew that we would be road builders. We took the train to Thanh Hoa, and started marching once we got there. We rested by day and walked by night to avoid the bombs. It was so dark that we had to hold onto the shirttail of the one in front of us, just like the game we played as children, "Dragons and snakes make a line to the clouds." We carried our blackened cooking pots on the back of our knapsacks. Sometimes in the dark, someone would trip or stop in a hurry and then the faces of all the people in back would hit the sooty pot in front. When daylight came, we had black faces, and couldn't help but laugh. There wasn't much else to do because it was hard to find water to clean ourselves.
>
> It took twenty-one days to reach our destination in Quang Binh Province. Our feet were torn, infected, and bleeding. We couldn't

Village youth off to war, painting by Nguyen Ngoc Tuan, 1974.

put our feet directly into our rubber sandals; it was too painful. So we had to cover our feet with towels, pieces of cloth from our blouses, anything we could find. And we cried. We were so frightened by the bombs, constantly falling down on us, everywhere.

We came upon a woman about to give birth. We were all young girls, and we knew nothing about it. There was no one else to help her. When the baby came out the cord was wrapped around its neck. We cut it, and the woman stood up, bleeding. The American flares helped us see. We don't know what happened to her or her baby. As we got closer to the battlefields, sometimes we came upon dead women, still holding on to dead babies.

Mau then talked about how she encountered early on the random violence that harmed people who were simply in the wrong place at the wrong time. And then how quickly she got used to a daily life in which air attacks became part of the routine.

One day, on the way to Thanh Hoa, I saw something terrible—some volunteer youth had fallen asleep on the train tracks—it was wet, marshy land and there was no safe place to rest, and the sleeping car of a train rolled down the track and crushed them. I will never forget it. I was young—until that day.

In my troop there were two hundred people, half of us were women and we were in charge of keeping open a segment of the road number 20 that led to the South. We were stationed in Quang

Binh, one of the areas most heavily attacked by U.S. air strikes. We spent one month repairing the road after bombs destroyed it, and one month underground working with communications equipment. We were completely isolated. We worked in teams of fifteen people, and we didn't know anything about what was happening in other areas. We had to protect our fifteen kilometers of the road and that was it. The road came first. We had orders not to run for cover when the bombs came, but to keep on working and to stand up and shoot at the planes. We worked in the daylight, and had to paint our hair ornaments black, because the gleaming metal could attract air fire. We couldn't even dry our white underwear for the same reason. We had to wear damp clothes in that wet jungle. We had no thread to mend our clothes and only two sets of clothing to begin with. When they had worn out, and we got down to one set, the men gave us their clothes to wear when we washed our own clothes in the streams.

At this point, one of the men of the troop broke into the story:

We men felt sorry for the women. It was harder for them. Sometimes they had to work underwater, moving stones. No one can describe it. I was in charge of logistics. I went to find the women one day. I had to be careful to warn them, so they wouldn't be surprised, because they had to take their clothes off to work. These long stretches underwater harmed their health and now they have women's diseases. I know, I am a married man. Some of the women got sick during the war and now they are old and still they have no medicine. Some couldn't marry later, like Mau here.

To divert attention from this intimate talk about women's bodies and her current status, Mau gave her old comrade a scornful look and changed the subject.

When we worked in the tunnels we could go out only at night, and after a month of this we were blinded by the daylight when we emerged like moles from our underground home to work on the road. It would take two days for our eyes to adjust to the light. When we worked on the road, we stayed out from dusk until dawn and we slept in the shelters during the day, except when we had to go out to rescue someone. There was a shelter about every five to ten kilometers and we also used them for classrooms at noon and in the evening. Some people learned to read and write in those shelters.

Most of us carried AK 47s. One time when a bridge had been bombed and there was no time to rebuild it, we used our bodies to

A member of Troop C814 describes how he defused bombs,
Hanoi, 1997.

hold the planks so the trucks could keep moving. Sometimes people
drowned in the mountain rivers and streams. We didn't know the
jungle, and we ate bad things, like a white fruit that gave us hiccups
for days. Some people ate poison mushrooms and died.

Once they reached the battlefield, the untrained and ill-equipped teenagers had no choice but to overcome their fear of bombs and death, for all
too soon both became part of daily life. At this juncture, the men couldn't
help but insert their stories, though they knew I had come to hear the
women. One man had volunteered for a special bomb defusing unit. He explained in detail how by trial and error he had learned to deal with each new
lethal dropping from the U.S. planes. Teacher Mau wanted to be sure that I
knew that women, too, took on this dangerous task:

We had different educational levels and we were young. A few had
finished secondary school, but the majority were still in primary
school—and some were illiterate. We were divided up along the same
lines as the regular army: a company was made up of two hundred
people, a platoon had forty and a squad had twenty. I had more
schooling than others, so I was sent to an on-the-spot training course
for defusing bombs and mines. First we learned to destroy the heavy
bombs, and then found ways to neutralize the magnetic bombs,

leaf-shaped bombs, and so on. But it took us time to find ways to handle them. For every new kind of bomb, people died before they learned the trick of defusing them. The most terrible were the big 250-pound bombs. We would first use baby bombs to explode a crater, and then with shovels carefully prod the big bomb into the hole. We had to be careful of the magnetic bombs. Our hairclips, pens, and shovels could attract them and they would kill us. We would have to use wooden shovels to dig them up out of the soil. We had to get them out of the roads so the trucks and the people who used steel shovels would be safe.

The string bombs frightened us for a while, because they could change color to match their environment—like yellow grass in the dry season, green in the rainy season, or the brown of the soil. After a while, the bombs got more complicated—like the "tropical tree," a sensor that could detect movement. But we learned how to make them harmless, and sometimes turned them into antennas for radios. The leaf bombs didn't kill us, they just blew off our feet or our hands because we couldn't see them. It was so dangerous that we sometimes pretended it was a game. But when this special squad of thirty people who volunteered to do this work started off, we had a service, and we asked our comrades to tell our families we had done our duty if we were killed and couldn't tell them ourselves.

At that point, everyone looked at the bombshell on Mau's curio shelf—and they all laughed and asked me if I wanted to take it home as a souvenir. And to establish even more pointedly that I, the sheltered American, would never know what they had been through, one man said, "Only Vietnamese could do what we did. But I am not sure why I lived. Maybe a spirit looked after me."

In a later talk with the writer Le Minh Khue, I learned more about the brutal conditions the female volunteers in other units endured. She had enlisted at age fifteen on July 8, 1965, in Thanh Hoa Province, and served for ten years, spending four as an engineer and roadbuilder on Road 15 and later on Road 20, and later served as a radio reporter from the front.[1] She shuddered when she described the hard, dirty work.

Men bury the dead in peacetime. During the war, women had to do it. In the morning, they would get up to prepare the white cloth to bury the day's dead, make the coffins, and dig the burial trenches. Getting ready for what was to come. Sometimes, the burial trenches were bombed and they had to take the bodies out and rebury them. Some bodies were in pieces, some had exploded like bombs from the pressure. It was bad luck for everyone. No, they didn't complain. They had to do it.

One night I went to bathe in a stream. It was dark, and something bumped into me. It was a dead body, floating there. What I feared the most was dying naked, while bathing, or having my clothes blown off by the bomb pressure. It happened to a lot of the girls. It was terrible, but we were young and we made jokes. Sometimes we even got in the coffins to play, or to sleep in them. We had no idea when we signed on how life would be. We had to encourage each other. Sometimes we would be so tired we would fall asleep on the march, or not be able to get out of our hammocks. Sometimes as we walked we would come upon a skeleton, someone at the rear of a column who had died alone, of malaria or some other disease.

I wasn't so afraid of the enemy soldiers, but the planes, they were so big, they made me feel that I was only a small woman. I kept going because I had to. It wasn't so much the old heroines of Vietnam who inspired me, but writers like Jack London and John Steinbeck, writers who tell of adventure and courage. And a favorite now of many Vietnamese women is your only war story with a woman hero, *Gone with the Wind*.

When teenagers like Le Minh Khue left home, they had not only to learn new skills to support the army, but also to survive in one of the most rugged landscapes in Asia, the jungles and high peaks in the Truong Son mountain range that runs along Vietnam's border with Laos. There former rice farmers and urbanites entered an alien world of wild animals, poisonous snakes, deadly plants, and dramatic scenery very different from their homelands in the flat plains of the Red River delta. More than one story of young people learning to forage for vegetables, to catch fish with safety pins, and to hunt game with slingshots emerges out of the histories and memoirs of the period. It is no surprise to find that when veterans remember entering the Truong Son Mountains, they describe it as a transition to a new kind of life, marked by isolation from the outside world and the need to adapt to new social arrangements as they moved away from the scrutiny and protection of their families and into the life of an army unit dedicated to only one cause—keeping the road open and the soldiers on the march.

Never did I hear a woman who had lived in the Truong Son range mention its dangerous beauty. For them, the work, the details of survival, human relationships mattered more. Some of the men, however, viewed the natural wilderness as a more benign place. One of the men in Mau's group, still trying to understand why he had survived the war, attributed the miracle in part to "the protection our motherland offered us, with her caves to shelter us, her forests to hide us, her rivers to quench our thirst, and her plants and animals to feed us."

In other men's descriptions of the exotic jungles, beauty and death often intermingle. A communications engineer, for example, retraced his memorable journey through the primeval wilderness in Laos:

> Sometimes we landed in a valley where a multitude of white butterflies fluttered like a huge ribbon in the air. At another spot, we came upon a herd of elephants. To the twitter of birds and the shrieking of monkeys, we followed the tracks of deer along the stream in the immense wilderness that seemed to have no boundary.
>
> But the enemy did not let go of us even in this dark recess of the Truong Son forests. Our lines were shattered by their carpet bombings and we were stunned to see whole hamlets razed by the bombs, only a few charred pillars left standing. At times we were ourselves caught in a bombing, each of us scrambling to find a shelter. When we pushed out of the rubble we embraced each other with tears in our eyes. Our hearts sunk at the sight of several bodies of young women volunteers floating in the stream.[2]

Accounts mention the thousands upon thousands of high rocks and mountains that required that roads be built around steep slopes, where the slightest mistake meant disaster, especially for untrained, ill-shod young people. One writer estimated that in the decade between 1965 and 1975, of the 2,500 days the Truong Son roadbuilders worked, 2,000 were devoted to coping with natural forces.[3]

❖   ❖   ❖

WHEN TEACHER MAU AND HER TROOP BECAME ROADBUILDERS, their personal histories linked up with the saga of one of the war's most hotly contested sites, the Ho Chi Minh Trail.[4]

In the view of U.S. strategists, the Trail served as the main route for channeling soldiers and supplies from the North to Laos and then to the South. A briefing manual, dated July 1966, for use at Air Force Headquarters at Udorn Royal Thai Air Force Base, one staging point for air raids into Laos and Vietnam at that time, outlines the Trail's significance for the United States. It is addressed to visiting U.S. officials and new recruits:

> Barrel Roll is the nickname for our program of close air support and interdiction strikes in Northern Laos. . . . However, we must admit

Women opening the Ho Chi Minh Trail. (*Courtesy of Joiner Archives*)

that the primary interest of the United States in Laos today is to interdict the Ho Chi Minh Trail in the Panhandle. . . . On about April 18, 7AF agreed to launch a modest (32 sorties a day) air offensive aimed primarily at enemy logistics bases. The objective was to destroy the munitions, supplies and food which the enemy would need to mount an offensive. Secondary objectives were to destroy troops and vehicles as the opportunity presented.[5]

One of the most important entry points to the Trail from the north was a site near the Mu Gia Pass, on the border between Vietnam and Laos, named for the goddess who delineates national borders. The "thousands of coolies" who frustrated intense U.S. Air Force efforts to close the pass included young men and women like Teacher Mau and her comrades-in-arms.

❖   ❖   ❖

FOR THE VIETNAMESE SIDE, the Ho Chi Minh Trail, designated a military region under the command of Line 559 on May 19, 1959, held great symbolic as well as strategic importance. By 1965 the Trail had developed from a footpath into a transportation network totaling tens of thousands of kilometers, linking Quang Binh Province in the North to Tay Ninh Province in the South. Some areas could be traversed only by dirt footpaths suitable for pedestrians or pack bicycles. Graveled roads for one-way traffic—and in some areas, multilaned highways—carried truck traffic. Some roads were used only at night and others were camouflaged for travel during the day. Fuel for motor vehicles flowed through pipelines.

The Truong Son Route was divided into three sectors, each with its own command under Line 559, comprising a force equivalent to a division that directed road builders, sappers, drivers, liaison agents, storage workers, guards, antiaircraft gunners, logistical and medical personnel, and telephone operators and linemen.[6] Coordinating personnel so diverse in their backgrounds and training, who were directed by several different ministries and supplied according to decisions made by distant Hanoi bureaucrats, was a challenge indeed. But a special sense of a common mission pervades the memoirs and accounts written by those who commanded work on the Trail during the American War.

In his wartime memoirs, Major General Phan Trong Tue, Commander and Political Commissar of Line 559 in 1965 and a veteran of the anti-French wars, romanticized his personal link with the Trail. "In 1946 and 1947, when I was political commissar of the command of Resistance Zone 9, I was told by high-ranking cadres from Hanoi about this strategic road and it was my dream one day to set foot on it, to travel along it to see Hanoi and Uncle Ho and revisit my mother and my native village. My mother had just been released from prison and extradited from Laos."[7]

He goes on to describe the current situation on the Trail in 1965. "When American aircraft attacked Hong Gai and Vinh and the Marines landed at Danang in March 1965, the destructive war escalated. Bridges became major targets and roads were damaged. At that time the Trail was not a road suited for mechanized vehicles. I was made a commander of Line 559, which was equivalent to a military region, a few days later. My job was to direct the work of transforming the network of paths and dirt roads that wound through the Truong Son Mountains, now used by pedestrians carrying supplies on their backs, to a system of roads passable for big guns and carriages in both the rainy and dry seasons, to step up supplies to the South. I felt extremely enthusiastic when assigned the task of building the historic road along the Truong Son mountain range because by now the enemy had completely blockaded our sea route." He expressed pride that the Americans attached great importance to the road: "On October 30, 1965, the enemy carried this news report: 'For the first time, motorized units of the Vietnam People's

Army are heading south along the Ho Chi Minh Road.'" His commentary is instructive: "They have dropped the word 'Trail' and call it a 'Road'!"

A Vietnamese journalist reveals how engaged both sides became in the symbolism of the Trail: "Ironically, the Western press has spoken of the road much more than we have, yet some journalists have never set foot on it—they call it the 'Indochinese legend,' an ever reviving dragon and a magic road that spreads out continuously as if blessed by the power of the Buddha. For us, too, it is a sacred thing."[8]

No such romantic images temper the stark historical record compiled from seasonal reports written by commanders of Line 559 from the field.[9] These accounts concern themselves with the logistical nightmares involved in keeping the trucks running and the soldiers marching. The road came first, before the health, food, or safety of the people who kept it open, because it was the main artery connecting the supply depots in the North with the battlefields in the South. The reports document constant struggles between field commanders and Party leaders at the rear, showing the Party leaders as reluctant to commit resources and unsympathetic to their problems with natural disasters, sick, demoralized troops, and inexperienced workers and drivers.

The need for an infusion of workers to support Line 559 becomes obvious from the entries for the period April 1965 through October 1966, the period when the United States intensified its attacks and just before the largest influx of volunteer youth would reach the Trail:

> In the program "to bring military pressure" by attacking the North, the Americans concentrated their efforts mainly on the roads, bridges, ferries, depots, and military installations. Even at the beginning, the roads in Zone 4 were out in many sections, especially those linking strategic roads; thus transport became a front hotly disputed between us and the enemy. The war waged by the enemy against the North was precisely an attempt to save him from a setback in the South. So if our victory in the South could be stepped up, it could possibly check the enemy's local war there, and halt the expansion of the war to the North. Thus it was the primary task of the North to supply the South and to help the Lao and Kampuchean revolutions win brilliant successes.[10]

More than one field report comments that diseases and natural disasters took more casualties than the enemy's weapons, at least before the 1968 Tet Offensive. In late 1965, officers were more worried about the fight against food shortages and malaria than enemy raids. In the first months, more than 20 percent of the work force on Road 128 was struck by malaria and in some units the rate was as high as 80 percent. Major General Phan Trong Tue states the grim facts: "At times we had to send a whole unit to the hospital and replace it with a new one. Women made up a high proportion of the volunteers —40 percent in some units. Some squads are all made up of women. To ensure sanitation for them in humid weather conditions wasn't simple. We had made careful preparations, however."[11]

Malaria comes up in every account of the war as the most persistent of enemies. The Malaria Institute sent teams out to the work sites and battlefields to try to figure out a way to counter malaria, but while on a research trip even the Director of the Institute succumbed to the disease.

Weather and untrained personnel also thwarted the best plans of the officers of Line 559 and created tension with Hanoi-based decision makers. Some of the truck drivers had so little training that they barely knew how to put the trucks in reverse, much less handle bad roads: "The lorry drivers had to fight hard against mud sticking to the wheels of vehicles, which stalled and couldn't move. Tired and weakened by malaria, the road workers did their best to help them, but the work was completed only by half."[12] And after two months, Line 559 had to suspend the work. As the seasonal report warns,

> If it continued another month, our men would all collapse. We gave an order to give our men a rest and repair vehicles, hoping that the next dry season would come soon to the Truong Son to make up for the time lost. Meanwhile, the opening of the road became more pressing. . . . The rainy season starts in West Truong Son in May, submerging roads and carrying away bridges . . . the trucks were immobilized and with no food left, our men had to hunt and catch fish to live on. . . . Because of outside lack of support . . . we had to build roads by the 'road jump' formula, that is leaving out difficult sections or obstacles such as blocks of stones standing in the road because we had no mines.
>
> Not only did we maintain the roads, but we took charge of the traveling soldiers marching to the South. We handled twenty-nine thousand men from June to October 1965. The liaison lines set up food and medicine. But when the rainy season came, bad health and air raids undermined them and Line 559 did not meet its plan of transport and road building.[13]

After describing the hardships the workers endured on the Trail and the numbers of soldiers they channeled to the South, the report comments that their failure to meet their quotas was blamed by the higher ups on poor leadership.

In November 1966, the roads were still in bad shape. Sappers lacked equipment and couldn't work; some were unfamiliar with the topography.

Women unloading a truck on the Ho Chi Minh Trail. (*Courtesy of Joiner Archives*)

Transport units were untrained, and when the raids came ran helter-skelter. A respite for the workers on the Trail came when the Americans concentrated their strikes on the cities of the North in February 1966, a grim trade-off that gave Line 559 time to recoup its losses.

By the dry season of 1966, the field accounts mention the presence of "shock youth" teams. Although we know from other sources that thousands of women were in the field by then, they do not yet appear in the military reports. The reports do indicate, however, that work was getting done more efficiently and various labor forces were better coordinated than before. They comment as well that the volunteers were taking their turn with rifles and shovels, building and repairing bridges in broad daylight to keep the road open. Medical and agricultural production improved as well, and the latter benefited everyone, because the units of Line 559 were expected to fend for themselves. Hunger for road workers was a nagging problem; because all supplies first had to be saved to go to the marching troops and then to the South, the young roadbuilders learned to hunt and fish out of necessity.

The Party Central Committee dictated that for 1967–68, Line 559 would have to increase its activities and handle between 90,000 and 100,000 soldiers traveling from the North to the South. In spite of this burden, the reports from this period indicate that conditions improved: "Vehicles crossed rivers mostly on bridges . . . enlarged roads guaranteed bigger formations of soldiers, who now had lighter loads, better rations, including fresh meat and vegetables, better political work to raise their morale, and theatrical performances to entertain them. The Ho Chi Minh Trail now became not just one route but a system of complex roads in a practically indestructible maze of communications lines." The volunteers were making a difference.

Then, during the first ten days of November 1967, the air raids stepped up. "Planes struck 38 percent more often, pounding the line, raining bombs on bridges and fords. The Americans used new methods and weapons—reconnaissance planes, striking the same place with bombs time and again, delayed action bombs, pellet bombs, phosphorus bombs, sensors, and mines to prevent us from remedying the situation easily and causing traffic jams."[14]

IN THE AREA CALLED "ATP," near Road 20, the fighting was fierce. "The enemy struck the trucks and storage places at night combining bombs with flares to intimidate our drivers, and this slowed our movement. They aimed for the roadbuilders themselves; any place where they suspected encampments or streams we might cross, they bombed and strafed. They intended to instill fear in our hearts and intimidate the roadbuilders." And at this dark time, women appear for the first time in the field reports from Line 559.

> The platoon of female sappers of Battalion 33, commanded by Nguyen Thi Nha fought heroically at A-shaped bend and moved to Pakhe, west of a frontier post and Road 20, where she and four mates died heroically on January 5, 1968. Nha was replaced by Mai Lien, her second in command. The platoon has been fighting since the early days of building Road 20. Their determination to fight bolstered the morale of the men of Line 559.

Nha and her comrades were killed at one of the most bombed out intersections on the Trail, a place pocked by at least one huge bomb crater every five kilometers. One Vietnamese writer called it "the hottest point of contention between us and the enemy on the whole of the Indochinese battlefront. It is called 'death gate,' for it bore the brunt of fierce air attacks for seven years. It would not breach any military secret to say that almost all of the provinces in the North of Vietnam have sent antiaircraft gunners there to train in shooting at live targets."[15]

Major General Phan Trong Tue explained in his memoir why Road 20 had to be built, why it was so important to both sides. "I had expressed my opinion in Hanoi that we had to build new roads if we were to cope with American air raids, in line with the policy of 'fighting a bigger force with a smaller force but taking the initiative in all cases.' As I saw it, Road 12 from North Quang Binh across the Mu Gia Pass into Laos was the only passable road, the only route to receive supplies from the great rear. If it was cut off, our whole operation would halt. So we had to find a way to build a lateral road across the Truong Son range, from east to west, at the shortest and most accessible place to link up with Highway 9. While surveying the geography on the map, we found that the mountains in this area are all very high and difficult to cross."[16]

He records how worried he was about carrying out this job in light of the terrain and the need to work fast:

At the Ba Thang slope, according to the calculations of the engineering corps, without the use of a large quantity of dynamite, the work would take two years. Meanwhile the order was to complete the road before the rainy season of 1966 in order to prepare for massive traffic during the dry season that followed. So we were given only four or five months to build the road.

When it rains heavily all of the temporary bridges built by our engineering troops are swept away, all the storehouses flooded, and huge rocks blocked the road. In one terrible season in 1971, all of the roads we had built were impassable, and we had to haul a volume of 150,000 cubic metres of rock before traffic could be resumed—and the engineers and road builders had to work from sixteen to eighteen hours a day to repair the road.

It was built through the most rugged terrain, out of nothing but the determination and spirit of the young volunteers with their primitive tools. It was called by different names: 'Determined to Win,' was one, and because of the volunteers who built it the average age was 20, we baptized it Road 20.

This road, eighty-five kilometers long, with over nine hundred hairpin turns, became one of the most potent symbols of Vietnamese determination to win against all odds. In the dry season of 1966–67, Defense Minister Vo Nguyen Giap commended Line 559 for its achievement, opening up a press and radio media blitz and inviting writers and artists to visit the units and learn about 559.

And so Road 20 became a favorite spot for eager journalists who wanted to see for themselves what life was like at a site already famous because of the sacrifices and achievements of the young people who built it. For the military men who had to juggle supplies and logistics, the writers and artists presented new headaches. But the commanding officers tolerated these outsiders, because they knew that word of the high morale on the road would raise the spirits of the people in the rear who were fighting their own battles to survive.

A reporter native to Quang Binh described what Road 20 meant to him: "Road 20, one of the portions of the Truong Son transportation network, is very dear to us. Its existence in our home province makes us proud. Its construction in the midst of great hardships is an object of wonder and awe. At night from the coast, I had often gazed across at the Western mountains where the road was being laid. The whole area was lit up with flares and it seemed as if there were a big city under that illuminated portion of the night sky. Also I had often heard rumbling sounds from that direction, which seemed to be coming from hundreds of drums deep down in the ground—they were the muffled explosions of bombs from a B-52 strike."

Once on site, however, he came face to face with the realities of life in that distant "illuminated city." A seasoned soldier warned him not to romanticize the situation of the people who lived and worked there:

> I will not tell you how we went about our work, because roads are built the same everywhere, in the same manner, with the same equipment. . . . What I want to tell you is how we lived. The first meal we had gave us a foretaste of what was to come. The rice came from stocks long hidden in caves and it was moldy and tasted like straw. The only thing to go with it was a kind of local shrimp that smelled terrible. The girls who came from the North vomited at the first sniff of it. . . . When the rainy season came in September and flash floods cut off our supplies, rations were reduced and we ate porridge. . . . During the dry season, a different problem faced us and we had to fetch water over long distances and sometimes we had to press banana leaves for a few cupfuls of water to relieve our thirst.
>
> Malaria was another scourge that affected everyone. Privations were absolute. No extra clothes, no shoes, no gloves for protection, no toothpaste. For the girls it was really miserable. For months they did not have a cake of soap to wash their hair. Once we received five kilos of detergent, and I summoned all the company leaders and declared: "This is for the girls alone. Any man who touches it will be disciplined."[17]

An engineering student who worked with the roadbuilders understood full well the extent of the misery and violence that marked daily life. "Road 20 was named without exaggeration a bloody road, and someone had described thirty-seven different ways of dying on this road—of bombs and shells, exhaustion, malaria, labor accidents. No words describe the hardships of the roadbuilders. At times each received only nine kilograms of rice for a month—and at times the sick rate was 100 percent and no one was left to take care of the others."[18]

Another visitor, a writer, marveled at how well the young volunteers had adapted to their environment: "The meals of the road workers on the Ho Chi Minh Trail were as irregular and unpredictable as the rainstorms and even more so than the U.S. air raids. . . . Once we writers and journalists were treated to very special dishes: dough-baked bats, squirrels fried with mushrooms, and fish soup. We dared them half jokingly to procure fresh green vegetables, and they brought in onion and coriander that they had grown. But normally, the soldiers and workers ate only wild vegetables that anyone could find in the jungle, and they would make your head turn just to hear them name all of the edible plants."[19]

The roadbuilders could not depend on nature for sustenance, however. Another writer who traveled with the volunteer youth on Road 20 in the dry season for several years noted how the landscape changed as napalm stripped the area of life: "The primeval forests had vanished and in their place only denuded stumps and branches remained—so much so that a flying bird could no longer find a place to perch. The road builders dared one another to find a living creature on the ground, even an ant, and the loser would have to offer a cigarette. Remember that a cigarette in such a place was not a trifle."[20]

At one of the most dangerous spots, this outsider described in detail how a team of young volunteers handled a direct hit—one crater in the middle of a ford was stopping traffic and had to be filled, and two time bombs had to be reckoned with. A platoon of young women volunteers was assigned—and accepted—this deadly job.

> The larger company of young volunteers wanted to organize a farewell ceremony—for what they felt might be their last meeting with the special platoon. But the commanders didn't want to allow them to do it—because it made the situation look too mournful. Night fell. The battle began and at one spot sappers discussed how to handle the time bomb, deciding to roll it down a ravine to spare a kilo of dynamite. Where the bombs had caused landslides, men and women earnestly shoveled the debris down the road bed. From the broken bridge came the sound of picks, hammers, and pounders—it sounded like a shipyard. Around me the site was like a beehive, each person enthusiastically and dutifully looking after his or her work in spite of the constant threat of even more bombing.
>
> But without doubt, the focus of attention was on the ford where the platoon of young women volunteers had taken up position. There was more than a score of them in all. Their chief concern was not the two time bombs that they decided not to touch, but the big

Women working after an air attack on the Ho Chi Minh Trail.
(*Courtesy of Joiner Archives*)

bomb crater that would hinder the passage of the lorries later in the night. In the light of the kerosene lamps, they seemed drenched from the water, their voices rising above the rumble of the stream. Suddenly, the platoon leader detected one girl too many, one who had been ordered to stay behind because of a fever. When the others took her by force out of the stream, she refused, instead taking up a rifle and offering to stand guard beside the ford.

Judging by the way she held her rifle and the look on her face, I imagined that she thought she could defend the whole platoon, the whole ford, and the whole area with her small rifle.

Soon her hair and clothes had been dried by the wind and she began to sing, one song after another. The other women joined her. A U.S. spy plane came and dropped a flare and another flew past, probably to take a picture, and another came and fired a few rockets. But nothing could change the determination of the women workers who repaired the ford before another day would break. At half past eight in the evening, the woman guard fired her rifle, signaling to the drivers that the ford was now passable.

In this account, it is not just the women's courage and cheer in danger that impressed the writer, but their devotion to each other. He notes as well the tension between the young volunteers who want to mark with a ceremony their comrade's almost certain decision to die, and the intransigent leaders who believed that such a display would harm morale because it would reveal too clearly that the situation was so desperate that only a human sacrifice could resolve it.

These Vietnamese teenagers knew instinctively the healing power of communal mourning. A recent study of post-traumatic stress disorder among American veterans of Vietnam argues that the frequent turnover of personnel on the American side, the constant attacks that allowed no time to mourn the dead, and the indifferent bureaucratic treatment of soldiers' corpses, prevented the survivors from grieving with the only other people who could truly understand their collective experience, their combat units. The author, Jonathan Shay, contrasts the American Vietnam veteran's isolating experiences with the communal nature of the Greek warrior's life. Shay concludes: "If military practice tells soldiers that their emotions of love and grief—which are inseparable from their humanity—*do not matter,* then the civilian society that has sent them to fight on their behalf should not be shocked by their 'inhumanity' when they try to return to civilian life. . . . Greek remains stayed with the combat unit for the duration; American remains flew away from the battle site sometimes in a matter of minutes and from Vietnam within days of death."[21]

I remembered when reading this passage how Teacher Mau's group had held a ceremony for the special team that volunteered to defuse bombs and how it helped ease the burden for those who left and those who stayed behind. Troop C814 decided on their own initiative to carry the remains of their dead comrades in their knapsacks in order to bury them properly and they considered this care for the dead an essential aspect of their humanity.

IT IS CLEAR FROM READING THE MEMOIRS AND HISTORIES that some officers did not heed Ho Chi Minh's order that the commanders of Line 559 must watch over the particular needs of the young people. Ho had said: "In their homes, they were looked after by their parents, elder sisters and brothers. At the construction sites you and the other cadres must take care of them, on behalf of their families, and look after their smallest needs."[22]

Some of the more conservative military men did not approve of the citified youth and even less of making life pleasant for them in the midst of war. Others pushed for more entertainment, and so we find urban artists, composers, and musicians recording their experiences on the Trail. The diary of a composer sent to organize entertainment with local talent and props offers a different slant on life in the jungles than the military men's memoirs. The composer admits his own ambivalence about his assignment and gently mocks the uncultured military men to whom he answers. In 1965, he began his diary with this entry: "I felt bitter about my professional development—a composer becoming an organizer? But I didn't dare to say anything. . . . My wife will have difficulty, because she is in a training course and she's always worried about the children. And she will worry about me. Poor her. But in reality, it is my situation I am concerned about."[23]

Once on the Trail, he met other reluctant recruits—and more importantly, he was willing to depart from the pervading spirit of recording only stories of heroic sacrifice. One man, newly recruited, told him not to use the word "volunteer," but "forced" in his case. The composer noted that this man didn't hate the regime, just the working conditions on the Trail, and though he was angry, he did his job. Another volunteer confided that he didn't trust his wife to remain faithful to him. But when the skeptical urbanite came upon cases of real heroism, he was willing to record them.

The young women impressed him. We find in his diary:

January 1966. Second day climbing the slope. With my exhausted feet. I met the marching soldiers and the volunteer youth transporting goods. It is as joyful as an anti-American festival day. They are so young, but they all have a deep way of thinking. There were young maidens, and I felt a deep pity for them. Anyway, they are women, just out of seventh grade. They have been here only seven months. Their skin is still smooth and not yet tanned. How beautiful and how youthful they are. They hardly laugh or talk since they must carry heavy burdens, and they are worn out. At home they had to work hard, but not as hard as here, where they carry the rice on their shoulders. Some push bicycles laden with supplies, and all with bare feet.

Two days later he met a group of volunteer youth from Ha Tinh Province and heard their stories.

As small town dwellers, they used to be well dressed, to ride bicycles, to carry water as their hardest work. . . . Entering here, each squad was supplied with two big knives and ordered to build makeshift dwellings in two days. It was cold and rainy. But surprisingly they finished thirteen makeshifts, one meeting hall, one storage place, and two toilets in two days. They didn't have enough baskets, so they had to use their trousers and hats to carry things. The road wasn't in good shape and they slipped on the slopes, and crept slowly along the cliffs. After delivering their supplies, many cried, even Party members. They cried because it was too hard.

A few months later, April 26, 1966, he wrote:

Last night I crossed to Phulanich to visit the platoon of Miss Nha. These women volunteers laugh all the time and are very determined. I was so moved when talking to them. In their early twenties, their menstruation has stopped and they look pale and ill. But they don't complain. They work too hard. Most still have parents alive at home, and they talked a lot about their mothers, but not so much about their fathers. They missed their mothers more. They asked one of my artists to draw pictures of them working under the moonlight to send back to their mothers, whom they dream of all the time.

❖   ❖   ❖

HOW ARE THE WOMEN WHO DIED REMEMBERED? What did their sacrifices mean to the men who observed them under fire and paid homage to their graves?

A self-described greenhorn engineering student, intrigued by the lore of Road 20, wrote about what he called his "baptism of fire" on his first day out.

> It was a mournful day. Company 339 included an all woman squad, composed of twelve girls, and led by a young woman named Nguyen Thi Mai. During a fierce bombing attack they lost five members, all in their teens. They buried them right on the side of a road. During their meals afterward, the remaining members of the squad continued to set out twelve tin plates, as though the five girls were still alive. And they decided to take on the workload of their dead comrades.[24]

There was one woman who so moved the men who knew her that her name pops up again and again in the memoirs and diaries: Nguyen Thi Lieu. From the different renderings of her story that appear randomly in passages from the memoirs, the modern reader can piece together just what it was about her that made her special. She was well known as one of the first women to deactivate time bombs on the Trail. Her parents were in the South, working with the Viet Cong, and she had stayed in the North with her grandmother. At age seventeen, she joined the volunteers.

The soldiers who worked with Lieu interpret her behavior to the outsiders who come their way. When a visiting artist hears her sing and asks if she is a professional singer, he provokes an indignant response from a male comrade: "You're wrong buddy; she's no professional at all. Haven't you ever heard of Lieu, head of the volunteer platoon at Ta Le? Six times she and her friends were buried under bomb-triggered landslides and each time they managed to get out and go on with their work."[25]

But the visitor is shocked when he sees Lieu's performance in a play one night:

> Lieu had been given a male part to play. It was a serious drama, but the audience broke into laughter when she made her entry, grotesquely

Preparing for a jungle play on the Ho Chi Minh Trail. (*Courtesy of Joiner Archives*)

dressed up as a man. Lieu, however, did not flinch, but went through her part with admirable poise. Then before making her exit, she turned to face her audience. "I'm ashamed of your bad manners," she declared.

The visitor is embarrassed, and after Lieu's display refuses to use her in his own productions because she "would wreck everything." But the men who know Lieu have a different response to her high spirits, as he records: "The men loved the sermon. The political commissar roared, laughing, 'That's the first time in my life I have been told to watch my manners. What a girl.'"

The Deputy Director of the Political Department, however, seems disturbed: "I suppose it's her frequent encounters with death that have made her so fearless."

Eventually Lieu's luck gives out and she is killed. One of her male comrades wants to let a visiting reporter know what she and the other dead girls meant to them:

I suppose you noticed the cemetery on your way in. The hundreds of people there all died very young. The oldest, as I remember, was twenty-four. Just the other day, we lost Ly, a girl just nineteen, nicknamed "Ly canary" because she was so small. . . . And there was

Lieu, whose death filled us not only with sorrow, but self-reproach. She was the first girl in our group to be trained in dynamite. She deactivated more bombs than the rest of her team. In addition, she sang very well . . . she could breathe life into any folk song. Not only in our regiment, but throughout the road, everyone loved her. Even so, she was not completely trusted because of certain points in her personal record, and she died without ever getting complete clearance. We, or more exactly, some of us, did not believe in her as she believed in us. When she was still in Nam Ha, she was almost rejected by the recruitment board for the Young Volunteers because of something in her family background.[26]

What had these seasoned military men learned from knowing Lieu as a soldier? One remembered: "If the Truong Son is a university, as you people often call it, for me it is first of all a school to teach me to love and believe in mankind. In my judgement this love and this belief is actually the source of revolutionary heroism."[27]

AS I RECONSTRUCTED LIEU'S STORY FROM THE SOURCES, it struck me that elements of her life history resonate with the most beloved literary heroine in the Vietnamese tradition, Kieu. Just as reading *The Tale of Kieu* helped me understand Duc Hoan's life decisions, so too the old poem explained to me in part the romance that had grown up around the young volunteer, Lieu. Both women were wrenched from their families while young, endured trials, captivated men as much for their singing and intellect as for their beauty, were capable of tough revenge against their enemies, and in the end remained pure of heart despite their unconventional lives. The story of Kieu, believed by many Vietnamese to speak for their collective experiences as a nation, allows for redemption and tolerance when human beings are placed in situations where they cannot operate according to normal rules and when bad luck tests their strength of character.

Lieu's history had a dark spot in it, however, for clearly her political record contained information that rendered her suspect. Other women, too, were caught in politics between North and South—one young woman volunteer met her soldier-father after nineteen years apart. Her mother, his wife, had been forced to marry a Saigonese military man, to forsake her own family in order to spy for the North.

Lieu's tale, however, is significant because it offers an example of a curious reversal of normal reactions to war. Most women performed men's work with competence and assumed an air of quiet authority. In the case of Lieu,

who went so far as to don male clothing, the men who fought with her tolerated and understood the source of her reckless courage in a way an outsider
simply could not.

But the frown on the political commissar's face after Lieu chided her superiors may well have revealed not only his pique that a subordinate had challenged the military hierarchy, but a certain foreboding about the ultimate
consequences of allowing women to gain equality on the battlefield.

CHAPTER SIX

Only Soldiers: Women and Men in War

War is man's work. Biological convergence on the battlefield would not only be dissatisfying in terms of what women could do, but it would be an enormous psychological distraction for the male who wants to think that he's fighting for that woman somewhere behind, not up there in the same fox hole with him. It tramples the male ego. When you come right down to it, you've got to protect the manliness of war.

Commandant of U.S. Marines, General Barrow, 1980.

In fact there was no distinction between men and women's work. They used the same equipment and they both used weapons when they had to. The job of the volunteer youth was to make sure the trucks and marching soldiers moved along the Trail. Our success depended on them.

North Vietnamese Colonel Le Trong Tam, 1996.

ANECDOTAL AND WRITTEN EVIDENCE from Vietnam suggests that North Vietnam nearly became a gender-neutral field during the war. Le Thi Quy, the women's studies researcher, told me that she once rode her bicycle alone from Haiphong to Hanoi and feared nothing but the bombs. A woman who had spent ten years in a jungle hospital told me that she had never thought about harassment from her colleagues or the soldiers who passed through. Some women hinted that problems did occur, behind the lines, where women in offices with superiors became vulnerable. Others declared firmly that the leaders couldn't allow women to be victimized, because that would have adversely affected the fighting men's morale.

The question that had been hanging in the air but never addressed directly in any of my discussions with women was addressed by Professor Dung, the military historian: "I know, because Japanese and American friends always ask me, that you foreigners want to find out about sexual relations between our men and women during the war. We had no comfort women like the

Japanese. People were sick, tired, trying to survive. You must understand that."

Comfort women were certainly not in my mind after what I had learned thus far about Vietnamese women. But I couldn't help but wonder how men reacted when women took leadership positions, and whether professional and sexual tensions prevented young people from working together efficiently, in isolation and in circumstances that inevitably heightened emotions. The silences in women's accounts about such problems seemed odd. Maybe, I thought, I was simply reacting to the recent, almost obsessive, media interest in the American military's confusion about women's roles.

A recent article in *The New Republic,* "Sex and the Soldier," for example, asks, "Can a man of say, 35, be trained not to stay his hand when he needs to send a 20-year-old girl into a mortar-strafed field? Can the impulse which, still, impels men to try to protect women be overridden? Do we want it to be? Won't sex always gum up the works? Would we really prefer if it didn't?"[1]

I was able to learn how a Vietnamese commanding officer articulates his thinking about these issues during two days of conversation in 1996. Colonel Le Trong Tam, a founding member of the command team for Line 559 and a section secretary throughout the American War, is now retired. He travels to Hanoi to meet foreign youth groups and reporters, and to try to help former enemies understand one another. At home in Ha Tinh Province, he spends his days tending his garden. He is poor, Hao tells me, for his army pension amounts only to about the equivalent of 800 U.S. dollars a year. A patriot to the core, he told me how proud he is that his native area had nurtured famous martial women. The highest ranking woman in the Indochinese Communist Party at its founding in 1930, Nguyen Thi Minh Khai, began her career as an organizer there and the survivor of the now-famous ten young girls who died at Dong Loc cave is a native of his province. War had also touched the women he loved. Like so many of the veterans I met, he expressed guilt, sorrow, and pride when he talked about them—his sister, Le Thi Phuong, was killed in 1967, and his first girlfriend died during an air attack just as she was returning to the battlefield after a trip home. His wife saw hard fighting and contracted malaria while in the volunteer youth corps.

He arrived to brief me, armed not with statistics or tales of heroism, but with poetry, letters, and photographs of the women he had loved and lost to the war. Not that he wasn't interested in standard military histories; he was one of the compilers of the official histories of the Ho Chi Minh Trail. At this point in the old veteran's life, however, it is the costs for the young people who worked on the roads, his own personal losses, that preoccupy him. His perspective on the war reveals too that there is no single official line, and that the boundaries between official and vernacular culture in Vietnam are not rigid. Moreover, he reminded me that poetry, fiction, diaries, and memoirs are just as much a part of the history of war as official accounts.

Colonel Le Trong Tam and Lieutenant Phan Ngoc Anh, Hanoi, 1996.

We began the interview with a poem he had penned to his first love:

You joined the army at age seventeen to fight the Americans.
How cheerful you were when you visited home.
The day when you left and I saw you off at the train
You were smiling, in love with life.
I have your diary, with its wishes and hopes
For your country and family.
Each page tells of a young girl in her teens
Hoping for a rosy future.
Your godmother made a sweater for you
But you will never wear it or feel its warmth.

What his young girlfriend might have felt as she left home that day we can only guess from other women who lived to talk about their leavetakings. But I could ask Colonel Tam what it had been like for him, one of the decision makers, and a man so aware from personal experiences of the costs of war for women, to send teenagers into danger.

We had never planned to use women on the Trail, and we knew very well the risks and hardships for women. In fact, our late President, Ho Chi Minh, cautioned us to watch out for women's welfare and

special health needs. But we couldn't spare our able-bodied men after the United States expanded the land and air war against the
North in 1965.

The Trail was just a dirt road and we needed to make it a real
road. We have a saying, "With shovels, hoes and guns, our women
secured a future for Vietnam."

Yes, people fell in love. These young people were very romantic,
especially the educated ones. They had had ten years since 1954,
when the French Wars ended and before the American War began to
be felt in the North, to study literature, to develop a sense of beauty
and history. I think that this love of beauty sustained them during
the hardest times. They wrote, they sang, they loved life and their
own national history. If women got married or pregnant, we had to
send them back home. If they were pregnant and not married, sometimes we forged birth certificates that made the babies legitimate,
because we didn't want the children to suffer and we knew how
much disapproval the mothers would face, especially in the countryside.

WHEN I ASKED WOMEN IN 1996 what it had been like to work with men during the war, to a woman they replied: "Men were better then," with empha-
sis on "then." They remembered wartime hardships, of course, but at the
same time, they longed for an imagined past when a collective struggle had
muted gender differences and selfish professionalism.

There were problems, women admitted, but a constant struggle for food
and shelter created a tight working group that could not afford to break the
bonds, as I learned from Le Thi Linh when we talked in March 1996:

1968 was a terrible year. My mother didn't want me to go to the
front. But my sister had been killed and my two brothers wounded
by an American bomb. I wanted to fight to avenge my family. When
my workplace, the Ministry of Communications, called for volunteers, I was ready to go. I was eighteen years old. We walked in a
group of 500 young people south, to an area at the battlefield near
Hue. There, we worked in groups of five, in our case, three men and
two women.

Because we handled top-secret information by radio, we could
have no contact with anyone outside. We had to build tunnels to live
in and to grow our own food, and because our equipment could give
us away, we had to move at least three times a month to escape air

Le Thi Linh rereads her
letter, Hanoi, 1996.

raids. We couldn't cook because the smoke would betray us to the
American planes and helicopters, and so sometimes we ate grass, we
were so hungry. In order to keep the lines open, we would go for
days without food when the fighting was fierce. We shared the work
equally, according to our best abilities. We had to. Very little news
from home ever reached us. I had one letter from my boyfriend, and
we all read it over and over again. We lived this way for six years.

Young people like Mrs. Linh, who volunteered for specific tasks or technological work, were given some training as were regular army personnel, and
so were better prepared for what was to come than the volunteers. I was told
that these training courses took place in the Hoa Binh Mountains outside
Hanoi and in Tan Diep District in Ninh Binh Province. Urban teens were
hardened to physical work by carrying ten, twenty, then thirty kilograms of
bricks in their knapsacks, up mountain slopes from dusk to dawn. When
everybody in a team could manage thirty kilos and walk for twenty kilometers
without rest, the group would be sent south. Political work was part of the
course and secrecy was all-important. For example, some units were ordered
to march south at dusk with all their belongings. In reality, however, they had

made a circle right back to the training camps by morning—to ensure that no one could betray the location.

Mrs. Linh remembers that no training course could replicate conditions at the front, but concludes that women were better suited to endure the deprivations and isolation than the men.

> I tried to keep myself clean, to maintain some feeling of order and routine in these conditions, which were terrible, especially for women. There were no sanitary supplies, but women's menstrual periods often stopped anyway because of bad diet and stress.
>
> I lived this way from the age of eighteen to twenty-four. The men did the harder physical work and they got sick more easily than women. We made our own clothes and helped them with their sewing. Some people couldn't live in this way, and some went mad. Women seemed better able to endure. We gave the men our best rations, because we felt sorry for them. The most terrible time came when two of my male comrades-in-arms starved to death. We couldn't take time out to cook rice because the smoke would attract the planes. Their diet of freshly picked grass wasn't enough to keep them alive.

It was one thing to pull together as equals in a small unit, but what happened when a woman took a leadership role? "Of course, men wanted to show how strong they were, and sure they didn't like it at first when I was made a platoon leader. But they soon learned that I knew how to talk to both the men and the women and they accepted me," a woman commander of a mixed platoon of volunteers from Thanh Hoa Province remembered, as her women friends joked about how many men it took to make trouble in any group.

Another woman, now in Hanoi, who has made a career of the military recalled her disappointment when she trained for combat and then found herself working as a cook. Eventually, however, her leadership qualities were recognized. Lieutenant Phan Ngoc Anh was reluctant to meet me at first because as she admitted later, "I don't deserve to be in a book about women heroes of the American War because I served after the Paris Agreement of 1973, which ended active U.S. involvement." She entered the military with a career in mind, as well as for patriotic impulses. She told me that women like her who went into battle in the early 1970s admired the pioneering women who went out in 1966 through 1968, into the fiercest fighting. But her story, like those of the volunteers from the late 1960s, bespoke her decision to put her personal future on hold out of necessity:

> I was the youngest daughter of a rural family. My father is a Party district head and my mother a farmer. In my childhood, I saw how

the airstrikes devastated the North. I wanted to join and thought, if men can fight, so can I. Yes, I had read about the past heroines and I knew about the women of the late 1960s and that did make it easier. In 1973, I had just finished high school and I wanted to go to university. I passed the exams. And I had a real conflict. I loved books, and as the youngest daughter, I was sheltered. But the desire to go was stronger than the desire to stay and I joined. I felt that if I had chosen the army life I had better stick with it. First, I trained in a company in the jungle, learning how to survive.

In all of the companies there were women like me, between seventeen and eighteen years old. I thought I would fight. That was why I joined the army. But I was assigned to be a cook. I was angry and disappointed. But after a month, I became a sapper, working with dynamite, filling craters, and rebuilding bridges along Highways 9 and 14. I was the head of a company. There were twelve people under me, all in charge of explosives. We worked in three teams, and we did everything by hand, including moving rocks. Most of the time, I did not have trouble with the men.

She said that eventually she didn't have to give orders. People worked together as a well-oiled team, not only out of habit, but with respect for others—"each of us understood that our lives depended on the actions of each and every one of us."

When we lit the sticks of dynamite, we had to run fast. Sometimes women would get killed or hurt by fragments. We were skilled, but we saw terrible things, trucks running off the mountains into deep ravines, people buried alive.

A typical day? We got up at 5 A.M. but it all depended on the bombs, whether we would work by day or by night. I assigned our tasks when we knew the situation. We ate out of tins with branches because we had no chopsticks and we cleaned our tins with leaves. We hated leeches but had to live with them, and we dreaded snakes when we had to go underground. We drank out of streams and ate on the job, right on the road. I don't know now how I could stand it.

We tried to preserve a normal life. We carried books and we read. At night we would try to forget, and write home or read. Sometimes we would put flowers in our hair, to try to look nice for a while. We sang a lot, because we believed that "songs are louder than the bombs."

Hard as her life was, she contended that her husband had done much more dangerous work.

My husband was an officer, a political commissar, in communications. He worked with short-wave radios. Men did this, because it was so dangerous. They could be targeted; one person would have to set up the antenna as a decoy and sometimes be killed. Only army regulars had maps and knew the communications networks—this was not entrusted to volunteers or women.

As this anecdotal evidence affirms, the army regulars constituted a mostly male elite: they were entrusted with the big picture, they provided the special training for the volunteers, and they were better supplied. The army field commanders exercised the ultimate authority over the volunteers. But beneath them, men and women volunteers pulled together to get the job done. In the jungles, roadbuilders, engineers, liaison agents, and sappers could be men or women. In effect, they all played a supporting role for they were caretakers who dedicated themselves to the road and the troops on their way to the battlefields and the visiting officers from the rear. Gender was not the criterion for distributing tasks, and the sources show that women were involved in every aspect of work. For example, the liaison agents made up a critical element of the military team. They were the guides who took responsibility for ferrying soldiers and guests through their 15 kilometers of territory between stations. Mostly they were women, but men too took on this role. One male observer painted the image of the liaison agent in feminine terms, even while witnessing men doing the job. "The liaison agent resembles a sweet mother, mild, kind, ready to stand any hardship for her children, who are the passengers, some of them quite coarse, hard to please, and authoritarian. The image of the comrade liaison agent comforting her guests is worthy of respect, like a big sister caring for her little brother and sisters."

These Vietnamese memories of a better time when men and women could forget their differences and work together square with accounts from other armies. Lily Adams, a nurse of Chinese-Italian background who worked in the U.S. Army's hospital in Cu Chi from 1969 to 1970, reported: "I was lucky enough to witness the special friendships between men that you rarely see in so-called real life. I learned that men can be gentle, tender, and loving with each other. I learned that men and women can work together with mutual respect and admiration. But no matter what positive experiences we had over there, I know war is not the answer to anything. That's why I'll continue to work on peace issues for the rest of my life."[2]

In a similar vein, Soviet women soldiers, when queried about sex at the front during World War II, told an interviewer in the late 1980s: "Men and women were shy with each other then. . . . Today, it seems impossible to think of a million women with the front-line troops without a great deal of sex going on. But then we weren't like that. The conditions were hardly conducive to sex anyway. We were filthy, exhausted, and hungry. We were just trying to survive."[3] This Soviet woman admits that some married men at the front fell in love with female comrades they met there. But rape or harassment among equals at the front was not an issue of great importance. Vietnamese women hinted that women became vulnerable only when they stepped outside this circle in which individuals depended on one another for survival.

WRITINGS FROM WARTIME ITSELF, HOWEVER, portray a somewhat darker picture of Vietnamese women's struggles to be accepted as equals than oral histories collected twenty years later. Written evidence suggests, moreover, that men's and women's memories of a better time in the past might be in part influenced by postwar nostalgia for community and cohesion.

Indeed, documents and memoirs from the late 1960s reveal that a gap between ideals and realities still troubled women who were then being asked to serve the Party and the military because their labor was needed. An article in the official Party newspaper, *Nhan Dan,* dated March 6, 1966, shows what women were up against.[4] The author, Vu Dung, argues in "The Number of Women Party Members Must Be Increased" that men must help women overcome their limitations so that they too can operate as leaders. The article betrays how reluctant most men were to accept women—not only as soldiers but as partners in making decisions.

> In the struggle against U.S. imperialist aggression, women play a very important role and their capabilities are very great. Millions of women are volunteering to take charge of the heaviest tasks in the rear areas in order to support the front. . . . There are Party committees which have encouraged the admission of women members . . . but there are Party branches which have not for years admitted any women members. . . . Many Party members do not want to admit women because although they think that they are courageous and diligent, they also believe 'women cannot lead but must be led.' . . . Today in the patriotic war of resistance against U.S. imperialist aggression, more and more of our women are appearing as advanced workers, labor heroines, army heroines, guerrilla heroines. They are the best daughters of our motherland, and models in production and fighting.

The author, echoing the Party line, exhorted men to allow women into their ranks, to give up their "feudal" ways of thinking and to learn to understand women's difficulties.

In life and work, women have still many problems: childbirth, raising children, tackling most of the family duties. Due to the influence of the old society, many women learn less than men and are still bound by backward customs and habits. Therefore they often have an inferiority complex because of their sex and must make great personal strides to become Party members.

That women were not readily accepted even when they had proven themselves as soldiers is obvious when we remember that even so prominent a female warrior as Madame Dinh, deputy commander-in-chief of the Viet Cong forces, admitted in her memoir that she and her fighting sisters had to find ways to cope with the contempt of their male comrades.

Another document from the period, a woman's official *curriculum vitae,* the record of life and service that everyone carried, offers an unvarnished glimpse of the past. Taken from a thirty-five-year-old woman captured by a U.S. unit in January 1967 and preserved in the Combined Document Exploitation Center in Saigon, her life history poignantly demonstrates the effect of discrimination against women.[5] She is from a poor farmer's family, she is married to a poor farmer who is also in the army but she doesn't know where, and she left two children in the village. She records her official life history: "In 1946, I was young and did housework and herded buffalo and in 1948 I was wounded and entered the 303 military hospital for six months. After I was released, I entered the hospital troop unit for one year." She then described the many ways she had worked against the French—building fences, running missions, and transporting goods. By 1965 she was a veteran soldier; in that year alone, she mobilized seven battles commanding between fifteen and twenty people, and single-handedly directed seven combat missions. Back in her village, she taught school between battles: "In June 1964, the village began a school and we have one hundred pupils." Was this superwoman ever afraid? In her self-criticism, included in the report, she admitted that her fear of the enemy was a weakness, but that she always managed to overcome it and go on. How did the Party evaluate this valuable soldier? Their comments stated that she is brave and diligent, but "hot-tempered and quarrelsome." More damning—they wrote on her *vitae* that although she has performed several missions, she still "doesn't understand her part very well."

Not all women accepted second-class status. A commanding officer's memoir from 1968 yields intriguing clues about some men's prejudice against women in the field and women's resistance. New to the area, an officer describes his encounter with women who had been fighting with a volunteer unit:

> I decided to keep only the fittest and to transfer the girls back to the second line. Girls could be good at bookkeeping, handling freight, or even manning antiaircraft guns. But they would be no match for

Saigon infantry. Some time earlier, in fact, areas south of Highway 9 had been declared off limits to women. And several all-women units had gone on strike against the decision. These girls at Ha Lap also refused to go back North.[6]

Indignant, the young women presented him with a petition: "As human beings, we are not inferior to other people. We're members of the Youth Union. We want to know if you really have a bias against us."

The commander, fearing an "interminable diatribe," firmly told them to pack their bags and go back. They had no choice but to leave. The only girls allowed to stay—three nurses—were ordered to sing and care for the mortally wounded soldiers.

Few instances survive in print that detail such struggles between male officers and women soldiers. These women at Ha Lap who voiced anger at being sent back to a safer area after having proved their mettle, however, should not be considered unusual cases. In more quiet ways, most of the women veterans I met believed that their war service entitled them to full rights as citizen patriots.

FICTIONAL ACCOUNTS BY VIETNAMESE WAR VETERANS take up problems of doubt, sexual tensions, and daily negotiations between men and women. Initially most of this writing was by men, but women are beginning to write about their experiences. These ficitionalized portraits display a far more charged atmosphere between men and women than the oral histories, memoirs, or official narratives.

The most interesting short novel about wartime male–female relations, *The Maiden Stars,* came out in Vietnam in 1986.[7] The author, a male veteran, tells the story of a twenty-eight-year-old soldier, who by accident is charged with leading to the battlefield four young girls who have been left behind by their units. He is a taciturn peasant; they are "real Hanoi maidens." The women know nothing about how to survive in the jungle and the veteran, Trong, knows nothing about women. The story focuses on a journey toward understanding between individuals of different class and gender, and different views of the war and its consequences.

Right from the start, the teenage girls have the upper hand. After the girls take what he considers silly risks, the frustrated soldier reflects that it is difficult to manage the girls according to the army regulations he had learned by heart since he was in officer school. When he declares, "From now on when you go to bathe it will be when you have my orders," the girls burst out laughing, and one, pretending to be embarrassed, responds, "What if we get ringworm or scabies, who will scratch us?"

Once Trong finally lets go of his military regimen, his sexual and emotional feelings begin to trouble him.

Trong found it difficult to live with these girls. It wasn't their work, but relations with them that mattered. He always spoke carefully, afraid of their sharp tongues. At meals he kept his head bowed over his bowl of rice, but he could not get used to their jokes. He calmed down somewhat when they called him "father-in-law," and although not really pleased, deep in his heart he thought it best to be stricken out of any possible love affairs.

In spite of his determination to avoid romantic entanglements, the soldier cannot avoid embarrassing moments,

which always made him hawk like a tubercular patient when he came into his team's camp—like a man walking in a minefield. Once he made a mistake, and it made him sweat to think about that dreadful night . . . when as if by mistake his legs carried him to the tent of Hong, the youngest girl in his team. He switched on his flashlight and nearly fainted. In her hammock, the girl was sleeping soundly, a mass of hair over her angelic face. The buttons of her blouse burst out showing her soft and white throbbing chest. Trong put the light out, and turned as fast as he could, bumping into a tree trunk.

In time, the need to survive replaces all other emotions and the girls earn his respect. At first, when they falter on the high slopes, he has to carry their rucksacks. He comforts them when leeches attack. But he notes that they bring beauty and life to the jungle, decorating their camp with flowers, foraging for food. They toughen up and learn what poor working women have always known, how to balance a shoulder pole, to carry heavy loads through rough terrain. The author reflects, "This was the first time in her life that this Hanoi girl knew the heavy burden of a shoulder pole pressing on her shoulders and felt so clearly the taste of sweat."

Their high spirits in the face of danger temporarily bolster Trong's flagging enthusiasm for the warrior's lot. After a particularly hard day, "Trong sat silently, smoking a cigarette, as the girls giggled and joked. He said nothing, but he was happy too, for their small joys were contagious. It softened hardships and bitterness; it was the fellow traveler of energy and strength." Now, Trong realizes that he cannot stand the march without their laughter. But the girls' lightheartedness does not please everyone. One day an elderly comrade hears them, and complains—"Going to Truong Son is not a stroll in the fresh air."

Trucks along the Ho Chi Minh Trail. (*Courtesy of Joiner Archives*)

Trong, who would have once agreed, reminded his superior: "They are still young. Youth is always like this, they can go without food, but not without laughter." The older man is furious: "This is a war and there are no boys and girls in a war, only soldiers." One of the girls jumps into the argument: "I think there is no contradiction. A soldier is not a fighting machine."

Men and women share anger and a need for vengeance in this war story. After trying to reassure the girls that losing their hair, their greatest fear, doesn't really matter, as they try to laugh themselves out of melancholy, Trong muses: "These are only fledglings. Is there any pain greater than this one? Those warmongers must be killed. If the war could be ended at once, he was ready." And similarly, one of the young women reflects, after hearing of the death of yet another loved one, "The war had once more touched my fate with its hairy hands. It lay on me its burden of suffering, but added duty. In my debt register between myself and the aggressors, I added another name."

This war story, written by a man, does not present emotional distress as a female problem. Trong begins to break down after one by one the girls become sick and wounded and one, a young widow, is killed. "He could not repress his feelings. It seemed that the creator had given the women the superhuman capacity to suffer things that the men could not." As he raves, reporting in his hallucinations to the famous military woman, Madame Nguyen Thi Dinh, the doctor wants to know what is wrong. Hong, the gentlest of the Hanoi women at the outset, now takes over and tells the doctor that Trong has a disease of the heart: "It is different for the men at the front, their pain can be poured out. In front of them is the enemy. Here there are no simple boundaries between good and evil." And in the end, it is she who goes on, marching cheerfully to "the destination" with a new troop that calls her "little sister," and a male comrade who carries her rucksack. She cries in front of them, now a competent, seasoned, but still feminine warrior.

The only slacker in the story is a man, a cameraman, a spoiled only son, who is in the jungle to make a name for himself. He steals precious food and plots for ways to better himself while the women become more and more unselfish—sharing food and sandals. He is the one unfit for war, not the women, for he "liked to sing solo, not in chorus. War needs not blazing heroes, but sacrifice, fortitude, mute and enduring." And who, the male veteran-author implies, is more willing to sacrifice, to endure, to give to the common good than a woman?

AS I TALKED IN HANOI with two male veterans who are very openly sympathetic to their female comrades-in-arms, the writer and poet Nguyen Duy and the literary critic and writer Ngo Thao, both men declared that women's courage inspired them. Duy's novel about the war, which he titled *The Gap* to reflect how misunderstandings even among the best of comrades can affect the course of their lives, aims to commemorate the courage and survival skills of communications linemen on the Trail.[8] It is a tale not of macho heroes, but of complicated human relationships between boys who get involved with the same girl, tease each other, and hurt each other. The author's admiration for the women shines through his tale. In one bad spot, giant leeches attack the group, and the men hate them as much as the women. Duy writes, "They were no less dreadful than the bombs. After a day of walking our clothes were full of blood. Most dreaded were the 'needle leeches' because they are as small as a needle and penetrate the deepest recesses of the body, to feed on blood without the victim knowing it. Of course the leeches caused more trouble for the girls than the boys. [The girl] Thanh Ha did not complain openly. Only when they were alone did she confide her fears and exhaustion. But before the others, she was the most exemplary girl in courage."

Duy includes boyish pranks in his account—in one scene the boys rig up a way to watch girls take a bath. I asked him if he had sanitized relations between men and women. He said, "We were actually that innocent in those days. War is not a normal situation. Our actions cannot be judged by what others consider normal." He reminded me that not all men were in contact with women regularly. "I went for two years without hearing a woman's voice and one day, listening in as I repaired a telephone line, I heard the voice of a girl. It was one of my happiest moments."

In the literature of the 1990s, images of gender relations take on a darker cast than in the novels that came out right after the war. A short novel, *The Tale of the Inn of the Three Angels,* by the veteran and writer Xuan Thieu, tells about a major in the regular forces who cooks up a plan to start up an "inn" in a cave in the Truong Son Mountains, a place where truck drivers can stop for a brief respite as they journey into dangerous territory.[9] He needs a respectable woman to run it and chooses Mai, the leader of a platoon of volunteer youths working on the road. Despite her previous status as a heroic fighter, he places her in a servile domestic role. Isolated in the jungles, the nineteen-year-old widow struggles with her own sexual frustrations and fears. When she requests that a man be assigned to protect her and her female companions, he impregnates one of the girls in her charge, who then has an abortion. Desperate and afraid, Mai pleads with the commander to replace her and her crew with a team of men. He refuses and she knows that the only way out is to oppose the major and endure his inevitable punishment, a stint in a shock troop with a high casualty rate.

"She could not tell him about her loneliness and her revolt within herself . . . she knew that Major Lam, without any constraints, could send her to a most vicious spot." He does. She is killed, a victim of war and the scapegoat of a rigid military man who abused his power and refused to reckon with normal human emotions.

The deeply antiheroic tone of other male-authored literature is most obvious in Bao Ninh's *The Sorrow of War,* one of the great anti-war novels, compared with good reason to the post–World War I novel of disillusionment, *All Quiet on the Western Front.*[10] There is a difference, however. The German novel is exclusively about men. The only hero in the Vietnamese novel is a woman.

When the protagonist, Kien, meets a young female liaison agent who cannot find the right path and endangers his unit in retreat after the Tet offensive in 1968, he curses and threatens to shoot her for her mistake. But eventually she succeeds in her task and Kien softens toward her. As they smoke a Salem cigarette dropped by the Americans, they trade war stories. He learns her age and realizes that he was about to shoot a teenage girl, and they share a moment of intimacy. And then, an American commando unit with a tracking dog comes close to them. The young woman, Hoa, slips away, and Kien hears a shot and sees the dog charging toward Hoa.

"Kien, now behind the patrol, was astonished to see little Hoa step from behind a clay anthill. She was a magnificent portrait of courage; she stood against the setting sun, her lovely slim body erect, arm outstretched firing at the dog and the dog only."

She hurls her pistol at the Americans, and runs away from Kien's unit to deflect the fire of the enemy. She is caught and raped as Kien watches:

"Kien with a single hand grenade to fight with was almost totally powerless. Hoa had saved fifteen sick and wounded men from certain death by first shooting the dog and then diverting them from the trail. . . . She saved me, too. With that thought, he eased the grenade lever back to its safe position."

The most brutal aspect of Hoa's sacrifice is that none of the men she saved ask about her and then Kien, too, finds himself forgetting her. "Was it that such sacrifices were now an everyday occurrence? Or that they were expected, even of such young people? Or worse that they were too worried about their own safety to bother with others?"

For Bao Ninh, war has no redeeming moments and even the meaning of a young girl's heroism is muted by the men's need to survive. In war, human beings become mere tools, he warns, and by definition everyone who is touched by violence becomes less than human.

Pollution is the theme of one of the few novels written by a female veteran. Duong Thu Huong, at the age of twenty, led a volunteer group of North Vietnamese youth to fight the Americans. She was one of three survivors of her group of forty, living for seven years in tunnels with North Vietnamese troops. Her *Novel Without a Name,* published in 1995, refuses to romanticize war in any fashion.[11] This is not a woman's war tale, because the story is told through the eyes of a man, a disillusioned soldier with an obsessive fear and hatred of blood, particularly women's blood. Through his eyes, women in war lose not only their femininity, but their humanity. The male protagonist is repulsed by naked, rotten, maggot-ridden female corpses, and by the women soldiers he encounters in the course of his travels. He meets a woman in a forest supply depot. Initially excited at finding a woman alone, once he takes a good look, he is repulsed by her hideous, animal-like face, her hulking body, and her sickening odor, which she tells him comes from handling and burying corpses. She complains that she has no soap to wash off the smell of blood, but tells the man he'll get used to it. He doesn't, and deprived as he is of sex finds himself impotent when she begs him to make love to him. He knows that she is a brave soldier, but he can't help but see her as an animal, and chides himself for lacking the courage and generosity of a legendary king who slept with a monkey on a deserted island—not only out of lust but to boost the ego of the poor ugly creature. Why is he so repulsed?

> She had dragged three corpses in the sunset. She had closed the eyes of three dead men. Alone, she had buried them on the other side of the hill. She lived here, guarding their belongings, keeping watch over their shadows, these mementos of life.
>
> This woman was born of the war. She belonged to it, had been forged by it. It wasn't just because she was ugly that I had rejected

her. I had been afraid to face myself, scared of the truth. I was a coward. Ten years of war had gone by. I had known glory and humiliation, lived through all its sordid games. I had needed to meet her to finally see myself clearly. I had been defeated from the beginning. The eighteen-year-old boy who had thrown himself into army life was still just a boy, wandering lost out there, somewhere just beyond the horizon. I had never really committed myself to war.[12]

Here is a woman veteran creating a fictional male antihero and a degraded woman soldier. Does Duong Thu Huong's bitter story speak the unspeakable, that war renders women so polluted by blood that they are no longer fully human? That it drives them so crazy that they turn the tables on men and become sexual aggressors? Does it betray the author's doubts about her own femininity? Or is it simply an exposition about the costs of war for all humans who must cope with blood and death routinely?

CHAPTER SEVEN

Only Women: Maternal Soldiers

The armed forces may get nervous when nurses start telling their stories because they reveal so much about the nature of war itself.

Cynthia Enloe, *Does Khaki Become You?* 1983.

When we Chinese girls listened to the adults talk-story, we learned that we failed if we grew up to be but wives or slaves. We could be heroines, swordswomen. Even if she had to rage across all China, a swordswoman got even with anybody who hurt her family. Perhaps women were once so dangerous that they had to have their feet bound.

Maxine Hong Kingston, *The Woman Warrior: Memoirs of a Childhood among Ghosts*, 1975.

THE WAR TURNED CONVENTIONAL HUMAN RELATIONSHIPS INSIDE OUT. Women soldiers called on domestic imagery to describe their wartime duties, and longed without any pretense to marry and have children when it was all over. At the same time, women expressed vengeful threats and handled lethal weapons with competence. Vietnamese male soldiers knew full well that the very same women who comforted the wounded and dying were also capable of handling an AK-47. Moreover, women who survived the tests that war imposes on human beings gained a certain unshakable confidence. "Nothing will ever frighten me again," remarked a woman who headed a medical clinic at the front for ten years.

In the jungles, the tunnels, the clinics, when Vietnamese women turned their gaze toward their men, they saw not powerful patriarchal figures but comrades trying to survive with dignity and sometimes losing the struggle. For example, the writer Le Minh Khue, who served as an engineer and journalist on the Trail, remembers that caring for wounded and dying men was part of daily life: "After I held in my arms officers who had once been stern and authoritarian, hearing them cry for their mothers as they died, I no longer feared them."

Vietnamese society did not erase conventional notions of male–female relations during the war, but buried them temporarily. It is not surprising, as

135

traditional boundaries between men and women's work dissolved at the front, that some men would express ambivalence about women in war, by trivializing them as aesthetic objects in an otherwise bleak landscape, by downplaying their competence, or by reminding them that they would not in the end be judged as warriors but as wives and mothers. In general, the men and women who worked closely together in the lower ranks expressed mutual respect. It was the outsiders, the higher ups from the rear, the reporters and writers living the war vicariously, who didn't understand the bonds that developed among comrades-in-arms. But not always.

"BE CAREFUL OR YOU'LL DESTROY YOUR SEX," male soldiers yelled at female volunteers pushing pack bicycles up a steep trail, according to one observer.[1] Other men expressed their worries more circumspectly. An engineer on the Trail in 1969 took account of the effect of poor conditions on women's health:

> Humidity was such that everyone's clothing was damp all year round. Drinkable water had to be taken from deep ravines. At our lunar New Year's festival, there wasn't a single fresh vegetable, no meat or fish. It was a breeding ground for malaria.
>
> Uniforms wore out quickly and our soldiers had to dry their clothes at night over bonfires in order not to go round only in knickers the next day. It was much harder for the women . . . the higher command decided to move the sick and weak to another place where the climate and conditions were less rigorous, but most of the women protested. Only after much persuasion could I talk them into obeying the order.
>
> To a girl who had passed her thirtieth year of age, I said: "We are in wartime. The Party knows your high devotion but also cares about your future. You must return to the rear, get married and have a family of your own."[2]

Other men overlooked the hardships for women and rhapsodized instead about the ways that women enhanced the aesthetic quality of the exotic jungles. A high-ranking officer on an inspection tour of the Trail described a sight that seems incongruous in light of what other men and women themselves reported about actual conditions in the jungles:

"As we reached the peak of the mountain, a very poetic sight appeared beneath us. White clouds drifted past in the middle of the mountain slope. On the branches of trees, the girls in the Young Volunteer forces had hung their colorful garments to dry. These would move when a strong wind blew, making them appear like the blossoms of flowers on the mountain slopes. The girls were singing as they cut trees, quarried rocks, and repaired the road."

He lamented his lack of poetic ability, but nonetheless composed a poem to be included in his memoir, as "a small tribute to the services of those innumerable silent heroes and heroines:"

> Pink brassieres hanging on the trees
> Frail heels trod everywhere in the Truong Son Forest,
> Their songs resonate across the mountains,
> Determined to get the trucks to the blood-filled south.

Ironically, however, the poetic officer is brought down to earth by a veteran volunteer who reminds him that there are real problems, with latrines, for example, that must be attended to at once.[3]

ONE WAY TO GET AT THE HEART of some of the ambivalence about women in combat that surfaces in the Vietnamese writings from the war is to examine how women medical practitioners talk about war and how others viewed them. It is the female nurse or doctor who operates within an ambiguous space, between the domestic and military arenas, who is expected to render the kind of unselfish care mothers give naturally, yet perform efficiently amidst a world of carnage and violence believed to be men's unique province. Women in their role as caretakers witness up close the blood, gore, and indignity—and the costs—of war.

On both sides during the American War, nurses and doctors faced the hard fact that the war was fought by the young. Lynda Van Devanter, an American nurse who worked in an evacuation hospital in Pleiku from June 1969 to June 1970, rails against a war machine that allows boys to be mangled beyond repair: "We were just tired and lonely and sick to death of trying to fix the mutilated bodies of young boys."[4] Vietnamese women, too, expressed their deepest sadness for the young boys and girls who died without knowing love or who went home to languish in government recuperation centers because their families couldn't care for them.

Not all female medical personnel remained in safe base hospitals at the rear, where a strict boundary between the nurturer and the fighter could be preserved. Some American nurses traveled with evacuation teams into the field. In base hospitals they worked their medical miracles amidst danger from incoming fire and guerrilla attacks, all too often hampered by inadequate equipment. Vietnamese medical workers made do with far worse conditions, for

A jungle hospital. (*Courtesy of Joiner Archives*)

they moved with the front, transporting their wounded to temporary safe havens, operating only with the equipment they could carry as they ran from the bombs.

A Vietnamese doctor who worked near the battlefields in the South for ten years, from 1965 through 1975, remembers those days. Now, like many prominent patriots, Kim Cuc holds a high position, Director of the International Office and member of the Presidium in the Vietnam Women's Union. When I first met her in 1996, I noticed at once her devotion to her mission to raise living and working standards for all Vietnamese women. At the end of a long interview conducted in English, which she is learning "on the side," I had an inkling of how well her moral courage and sheer determination, evident even in peacetime, must have served her during the war. By her account, family history and a deeply ingrained patriotism contributed to her will to survive and carry out her work. Madame Cuc's matter-of-fact account of giving birth in the jungle and then having to run from a shower of bombs demonstrates yet again that women themselves often perceived no hard and fast distinction between regeneration and death in this war.

> I was born into a family of patriots. My father and uncles were active in the French wars. It wasn't Vietnamese heroes like Lady Trieu or the Trung sisters who inspired me so much as the Russian heroines,

Author with Madame Kim Cuc, Hanoi Women's Union, 1996.

like Alexandra Kollontai. And I liked to read about Soviet women pilots and soldiers who fought during World War II because they were modern heroines.

When I finished secondary school, I wanted to be a photographer, but my father told me to become a doctor and so I entered Hanoi Medical College to become a pediatrician—because I loved him. I graduated in 1965, and when Ho Chi Minh's appeal came, I decided to volunteer my services. I went to Quang Nam Da Nang, the most terrible area of the fighting. We traveled for three months on foot, carrying our supplies. For the first five days, I felt I couldn't go on. I was so tired and I couldn't eat anything. But I had to march at the end of the group, because I was a doctor and could help anyone who got sick and fell behind. I was ashamed to go back because my parents were so proud of me. After the seventh day my spirits came back.

After 1968, the war became more fierce because there were more helicopters that could travel anywhere and spot people. We had to disguise the hospital. Living in the jungle for ten years, I ran the hospital almost alone because my nurses had to go out to forage for supplies. Some of them left and never returned and I had no way of knowing what had happened to them. I had to take on any duty that came up. I was the chief of the hospital and there were fifty women and seven men who worked for me.

She said over and over again how lucky she was to have survived, as she ran from explosions so close that she had to touch herself from time to time to make sure she was intact. The war was so near that she lived with violence day and night; often she could hear American soldiers shouting at each other.

Kim Cuc was twenty-three and married when she went to the front. In 1969 she thought the war would end, and she and her husband decided to have a child, although her husband, a soldier, had to leave for another front.

In the jungle, the delivery was hard. The day after I gave birth, the hospital was bombed and we all had to leave. I put my son on my back and we ran from the helicopters. If my son cried, I knew we would all be killed. I breastfed him to keep him quiet. If he whimpered, my heart would stop. But he was a miraculously happy baby. When I established another hospital, the amputees looked after him, and befriended him. He played with sticks, empty bottles, anything he could find.

Did she have conflicts with the men in her hospital? Did tension between the men and the women on her staff complicate her work?

I didn't have time to worry about that. The men on the staff supported me in my work. I felt sorry for the male patients and they helped me whenever they could. We had to work as a team. We had no choice.

We moved to keep up with the front and whenever the clinic was bombed. In some ways we felt safest in the jungle, because the Americans were afraid of it. But there were wild animals there that harmed people. When I heard about a man who had been mangled by a bear away from our camp, I had to go out alone where I knew the bear lived to carry him back to the clinic so I could operate on him. I was frightened. Snakes were a problem, especially the green leaf snakes that hide themselves so well.

I had an anatomy book that I used for new situations. Sometimes there was no anesthesia and the men screamed. It was terrible to hear them.

On a typical day, I would get up at 3 A.M. to clean cassava. I would have to soften it in a stream for two or three days, and then boil it. Sometimes I ground it into a powder to mix with water as a cake for patients. We didn't have enough food, and if there was rice, the staff saved it for the sick and ate leaves from the forest. At 4:30, I would finish with the food preparations and if I had nurses, ask them to take water from the stream to wash the patients. I would then examine the patients, treat wounds, wash bandages in the stream, and prepare dinner at 6 P.M. Sometimes when I was too tired I would accidentally burn the food. After dinner I washed the patients, washed our clothes, and wrote the medical records. Every now and then we would have a special dinner, and we would eat the husks of termites that had hatched in the rice. Even today, I hate more than anything to see rice wasted.

Then I got virulent malaria near the end of the war and had to mix quinine with water and inject it into my own body. It was so harsh that I lost my memory and my speech. I couldn't recognize friends or family. I had to do exercises to remember how to talk—it was as if I had frozen up. Then I went to China for special treatment and a rest and I began to get my memory back.

What kept her going? She said she could resist U.S. propaganda to surrender to the other side because of her family heritage, because she dreamed of reunification and curing people in peacetime. And she had lost so many friends that she wanted to be worthy of their sacrifice. What happened when she returned home?

I will never fear anything again after living through this time. In the jungle, I slept in hammocks for ten years and sometimes the bombs would break the strings of the hammock; they were that close. When I got home, all the beds were too hard for me. I worked in Hanoi as a pediatrician and then the Women's Union asked me to join the staff. My son now talks with a Quang Nam Da Nang accent! He is a good young man, not spoiled. He still remembers the years in the jungle, when he would stand by me late at night when I did surgery, encouraging me.

To my final question, she responded: "What did I long for most? To dry my clothes in the sun. It was so hard, in the jungles, wearing wet clothes all the time."

When I told Hao what I had heard from Madame Cuc, she showed me a poem written by one of her closest friends, the late Xuan Quynh. It is called "My Son's Childhood," and some of its lines translate into verse what so many women like Kim Cuc must have felt as they raised their children and fought for their lives.

What do you have for a childhood
That you still smile in the bomb shelter?
There is the morning wind which comes to visit you
There is the full moon which follows you.
The long river, the immense sea, a round pond
The enemy's bomb smoke, the evening star.
At three months you turn your head, at seven you crawl.
You toy with the earth, you play in a bomb shelter.
I long for peace, every day, every month for a year.
For a year, you toddle around the shelter
The sky is blue, but way over there,
The grass is green far away on the ancient tombs
My heart is a pendulum
Pounding in my chest, keeping time for the march.
The small cricket knows how to dig a shelter
The crab doesn't sleep; it, too, fears the bombs.
In the moonlight, even the hare hides
The black clouds hinder the enemy's sight
Flowers and trees join the march
Concealing troops crossing streams, valleys, villages.
My son, trenches crisscross everywhere.
They're as long as the roads you'll someday take.
Our deep shelter is more precious than a house
The gun is close by, the bullets ready
If I must shoot
When you grow up, you'll hold life in your own hands
Whatever I think at present
I note down to remind you of your childhood days.
In the future, when our dreams come true
You will love our history all the more.[5]

This intermingling of maternal sentiment and fighting spirit in women, who could be at once softened by maternal love and toughened by war, was noticed by male observers. In October 1968, a reporter from *Nhan Dan*, the official Party newspaper, wrote about these qualities in a nurse, a member of the volunteer youth corps, whom he chanced upon as he walked down the Trail.

A girl was sitting on a ledge by the stream, her chin and hands resting on her knees. That was Hong, the nurse. She must be watching for fish coming upstream. I asked her what she was doing. She blushed, "Oh, nothing, just girding for a bout of malaria."

I thought she was joking but she looked serious. "It's true, most of the girls have it already, and now it is my turn." "But you're a nurse. I suppose you can scare off the germs." "No, no one is immune to malaria. A doctor died of it the other day—he had just come from Hanoi."

I could see that Hong was really ill: her cheeks were no longer scarlet, but pale, and her lips too. I asked her to take a rest, but she refused, preferring to stay on her feet. She told me, "I don't want to be forced to stay behind, I want to be out on the road tonight. It will be reopened for traffic. I don't want to miss it."

She was a brave girl. One night, as the last convoy had been through, she was on the way to camp with friends and heard three rifle shots, the usual distress signal. Retracing their steps, the girls found a lorry on fire, and the driver and his aide wounded. One man was able to walk and Hong's friend helped him to his feet. The other was wounded in the chest and abdomen and unconscious. Hong dressed his wounds and dragged him to an emergency shelter a short distance away. She didn't want to put him on the ground, which was wet from a recent rain, and so she sat down on a log and cradled the man in her arms.

Then light from the burning lorry attracted a group of jet fighters, and they lit up the area with flares, dropping a pattern of delayed action fragmentation bombs around the vehicle before firing rockets on it. The wounded driver recovered consciousness just for a minute and then died peacefully in her arms. When the rescue team came, they had difficulty taking Hong's arms off the dead body. Like her legs, they had become stiff from staying in the same position for hours.

Curious, I asked her about herself, and whether or not her mother had cried when she left home. "No. Mother only said, 'You've always been a good-for-nothing. It's time you did a grown-up's job.'"[6]

Medical work in wartime brought a chance for advancement for women like Hong, who had no place at home. A written Party résumé carried by a woman who commanded a medical company and was captured by an American infantry unit on February 19, 1970, preserves an ordinary woman's chronicle. Her history traces her family's economic status and her own political and medical education. A native of Binh Dinh Province, she was from a landless farm family: "Her parents and four siblings had enough to eat when they were all healthy enough to work, but half-starved when they could not and sometimes had to hire out their labor to make ends meet." She started giving food to the Viet Cong in her village in 1964, and joined the army in 1965 after having been imprisoned by the ARVN soldiers as a suspected Viet Cong propagandist. She studied nursing in 1966–1967 and then went to a medical school in the Fifth Interzone in 1968. She became an army doctor

A Vietnamese doctor, Dr. Le
Thi Phuong, Laos, 1967.
(*Courtesy of Colonel Le Trong
Tam*)

and platoon leader with only a first-grade education and two years of medical
training.[7]

Other women doctors and nurses with inadequate training performed
their duties as healers at the most dangerous sites, because they were charged
with the first line of medical treatment for the wounded. A diarist, who was
often chided by veteran soldiers when he clouded his admiration for the
women he met on the Trail with condescending concern, wrote about a nurse
he encountered sometime in 1968, just off of Route 9, at a spot that had just
been bombed. The fires still smoldered. He and his group came upon a girl
running in front of a van, asking them to let it pass because it carried casualties. The diarist's female assistant pulled out her first-aid kit to help the nurse,
and the two women worked on the wounded men, hoping that the surgical
team was not too far down the road. The diarist took a close look at the
nurse:

> She had a pleasant voice. Her face was haggard and her helmet
> clearly too big and heavy for her delicate head. When she looked up
> at me, I saw a whitish patch beneath the helmet and laid a hand on
> her frail shoulder.
>
> "Are you wounded, too?" I asked. She winced and complained that
> I was hurting her.
>
> "I have a cut near the left temple. If it had been the carotid, I'd
> have died."
>
> A male comrade who watched the scene interjected brusquely,
> "Don't you worry none for her. She's very tough and very brave.

Dr. Phuong (second from right) with her staff. (*Courtesy of Colonel Le Trong Tam*)

Didn't you see how she carried a wounded man a long way, getting covered with blood?"[8]

AS THE WAR WOUND DOWN, as the mythmaking began, some male writers began to tune out women's tough competence and play up their feminine qualities. For example, in 1975, a journalist in search of the romance of the Trail at a now famous army hospital traveled to the heart of the Three Border Region, the "malaria pocket" of Indochina, a place he calls "Honey Bee Mountain." There he describes for his readers the "quiet, the sunshine dancing through the primeval forests, the murmur of birds, the wind caressing the silky hair of the girl soldier who also exuded a lovely scent." He muses, "Was it the perfume from the girl with the moonshaped face? She told me that she had been a student in the ninth form before joining the army. She came from a coastal village in Thanh Hoa Province and had been on the Truong Son route for three years. Even supposing she had carried a bottle of scent in her knapsack, how could it have lasted until now?"

The journalist is greeted by a rather cynical hospital director, a man, who wants to know if there is a hidden agenda behind his visit. "No, far from that.

People say your place is isolated, but you have managed to make it warm and hospitable." With the current staff, including a nurse "shy as a bride," he re-traces their history as a mobile medical unit team for the Army Medical De-partment. The staff tells him that their team, DT13, was set up in 1965 and after 1966 traveled with the army to the hottest spots. In the heat of battle, surgical shock troops went in to give first aid and many were killed. Con-stantly on the move to find safe places for the wounded armymen, the hospi-tal staff of necessity became construction workers, cutting bamboo and tim-ber for operating rooms, digging earth for air-raid shelters and mess halls—a whole village of one hundred and fifty houses each time they moved. He hears about women's service back then: "The nurses carried the wounded soldiers on their backs to the shelters and all those who could handle a rifle concentrated their fire on the choppers. The doctors and nurses gradually got used to this roving life, but it was never a makeshift life. They not only had to handle dexterously the scalpel and the injection needle, but the spade. But that was not all, for the doctor on this Truong Son range must also know what kind of vegetable to grow and how to catch fish. And he must be ready at any time to donate his blood to critically wounded soldiers."

Gendered conceptions of work did not seem to vex the medical team during the war. But now, in 1975, back at Honey Bee Mountain, as the staff concentrates solely on its medical duties, the sexes seemed quite separate ac-cording to the observer, who notes that the women soldier's quarters could be easily identified by their cheerful curtains. Of the caring nurses, he writes that one is "easily given to emotion," because she weeps over a wounded pa-tient. But he couldn't help but see that this sentimental young woman also hunted for food and learned to catch fish—with a needle from her sewing kit—to feed her patient. Her ministrations work, and the wounded soldier walks away, leaving the journalist to think about the moving story of the "sis-ter nurse and the young sick soldier." In this nostalgic piece, women are writ-ten out of the story except as nurturers with a possible romantic interest in the sick; the men have taken charge in the hospital and the reportage as well.[9]

Another journalist on the Trail in 1975 interviews a group of former fe-male volunteers, now sappers in the regular army. Dressed in their Sunday best, they revisit their old haunts with him. He marvels at the discrepancy be-tween their current appearance and their past exploits. Of one woman who had joined the volunteers while teaching in Thanh Hoa Province, he writes:

> She is now a platoon leader in an engineering unit. I could not imag-ine how such a frail girl had stood firm during those long days of the dry season of 1971 to 1972, when on the peak of this mountain American aircraft of all types dropped more than ninety-one thou-sand demolition bombs, magnetic bombs, incendiary and antiper-

Women at a stream along the Ho Chi Minh Trail. (*Courtesy of Joiner Archives*)

sonnel bombs. She took me to a tree which once held the signal light for the drivers. Still there, I could read clearly the words: "Battlefront of Section 3 of the Ho Chi Minh Communist Youth Union."

She pointed to where they had lived—a small upper cave during the rainy season and a lower cave in dry times. A mixture of items that showed a youthful urge for fun, and constant threat of danger, were still there. I asked them about the table tennis table in the cave. "Yes we played," she remembered, "but of course we had to have the dynamite and fuses always at the ready to rush to the bombed places at any moment. At the first bomb explosion, we would send a scout to reconnoiter and we communicated by rifle shots."

"When a bomb hit the road, someone would fire two successive shots and then as many after that as there were bomb craters, so we could send the necessary forces to repair them. Two of us would fill a big bomb crater with a single dynamite charge and run to avoid the

Guns and needles, Ho Chi Minh Trail. (*Courtesy of Joiner Archives*)

next attack. We were scared in the first days, but got used to it. So much so that one of us compared the mending of the road to the mending of a shirt."[10]

It is not unusual to find women describing routinely dangerous work in the vocabulary of the housewife. Cynthia Enloe notes that during World War II in the United States women defense workers likened their jobs welding fighter planes to sewing.[11] A poem from a Vietnamese cache of documents captured in 1966 preserves the voice of a worker in the thick of war, one that celebrates soldiers at the frontline killing the enemy resolutely, while she sews clothing for them:

Sewing machines move quickly.
The forest echoes with the bird's songs.
Our resentment will be changed into silk.
The distant sounds of guns harmonize
With the rhythm of the sewing machines.
We are determined to kill the enemy.[12]

This use of domestic images narrows the gap between the abnormal work that falls to women in war and normal domestic tasks allotted to women in peace.

Men's writings suggest that it wasn't always easy for the men to figure out how to deal with women who could be both tough-minded and feminine. A recent short story from Vietnam yields interesting insights about a Truong Son truck driver's attempts to get the right fix on a female trail guide who guides his truck one dark night as he is pushing on to his destination. The driver is irritable because he knows that the girl's laughter is artificial, aimed at downplaying the true conditions of the road ahead. The female trail guide does her job well, however, "floating" ahead of the truck through the dark path in her white blouse, leading the driver down a secret path, away from the bombed-out road. Yet he tries to diminish her critical role in his own success and survival when he tells her: "Your limbs are as slender as raw silk threads. It seems as if you just left your schoolwork at home only a few days ago. You'll have a tough job building roads and cutting through the mountains. I'll bet at night you're still weeping inside your blankets and calling out to mama, right?"

"You get used to it, brother," she replied, laughing.[13]

THE WAR PRODUCED WOMEN who got used to the constant danger and tension, discovered they could do men's work, talked back to superiors, and lost their fear of male authority. How would these women reintegrate into civilian life?

Even the Women's Union worried about that question. *Glorious Daughters of the Revolution,* published by the Vietnamese Women's Union right after the war's end, reassures readers that warrior women ultimately can preserve their feminine virtues. The story of Brigade 609, all young women volunteers, for example, features fearless, hardworking, disciplined women, whose exploits earn them the nickname "Lady Trieu Brigade," after the heroine of old. They willingly accept the hardest tasks, become skilled carpenters and metal forgers—they made their own shovels and hoes—and built a 1,600 kilometer road by moving 40,000 cubic meters of earth and rock. This is how their service is described: "The reputation of the Lady Trieu Brigade was due not only to the courage and resolve of its members, but to other qualities: industry, thrift, integrity, uprightness. These qualities are indispensable if one wants to fight the Americans and build socialism at the same time." Reading between the lines, we learn that the brigade had not always been so well oiled; at first the women balked at wearing rubber-tired sandals and straw hats that interfered with their good looks."

The tract ends with a reassurance that in the end, feminine concerns win out. "Classes are regularly held for the brigade members, at which they acquire a general education and learn sewing and embroidery etc. Brigade 609's idea of a good woman is one who works diligently, fights courageously, shows good morals and is likely to become a good wife and mother."[14]

Leaders, Thanh Hoa Women's Union, 1997.

Here we have the Women's Union, founded on revolutionary principles and devoted to women's emancipation, asserting in a postwar publication that women's ultimate value in society rested in their domestic function. But for many women, life didn't work out as it was supposed to. And so, many women veterans would be caught in a bind at war's end: their unselfish, patriotic, wartime work, undertaken just at the time in their lives when they would have married and settled into family life, in many cases rendered them ineligible to compete for mates, incapable of carrying out their duty to the postwar nation as bearers of future generations of patriotic citizens.

CHAPTER EIGHT

Picking Up the Pieces:
Going Home

After every war, someone has to tidy up. Things won't pick themselves up,
after all.

> Wislawa Szymborska, *The End and the
> Beginning,* 1993.

Wars have their endings inside families.

> Cynthia Enloe, *Women After Wars:
> Puzzles and Warnings,* 1996.

To marry and have a child, how banal! But to become pregnant without
the help of a husband, what an achievement.

> Ho Xuan Huong, late eighteenth-century
> Vietnamese woman poet.

BY THE WAR'S END, nearly every family in Vietnam was in mourning. Three
and a half million people died during the decade between 1965 and 1975.
Over 300,000 children were orphaned and four million people disabled from
the consequences of war. Seven hundred thousand wounded soldiers were
brought to the rear via the Ho Chi Minh Trail alone. And the American War
was not just a struggle with a foreign aggressor, but a civil war that generated
irreparable conflicts within families and the nation itself.

Most women stayed in the field as long as their health held up, for as
long as ten years in some cases. News from home could not be counted on
and some families knew nothing of the fate of their soldier sons and daughters for years. Vietnam's Missing in Action statistics are staggering: as many as
200,000 men and women were still not accounted for in 1996.[1]

Women left home as teenagers, in their most vulnerable, formative years.
They grew up quickly, out of touch with the flow of life at the rear. How did
they fare when they returned home? And how did they cope with the inevitable tensions of settling back into civilian society?

"We were drunk with victory in 1975," Hao recalled. "But then we began to realize how poor and isolated we were after the United States placed an embargo against us. We had fantasized about the riches in the South, but then reporters went there and found that people in Saigon had suffered too. Then there were families that had been divided by politics since 1954. And relatives of deserters. Most of us just turned back to our own families. What was left of them."

The writer Le Minh Khue observed that all Vietnamese women, not only veterans, had a rough time.

> They had to pick up the pieces, to act as peacemakers, to put their needs behind others yet again. Those who had husbands or parents to go back to were fortunate. How could married women fight with their husbands? Everyone had been hurt. Some of us who had watched men die and suffer so much just didn't want to struggle with them when it was over. Still, many people got divorced—they couldn't pull together again after so many years apart. Some men had been away for twenty years or more, if you count the French Wars.

I remembered what Teacher Mau had told me about her bitter homecoming, when, sick with malaria, she found her former boyfriend married to someone else and no place in her natal family for a single daughter. Like many women, she did not simply accept her fate, but tried to change it. "After living in a collective farm with other homeless veterans, I went back to the city to continue my education in a teacher's college. I tried to raise the child of a friend. But when my friend had a new baby, she wanted the girl back, to help out. And I don't see much of the girl I spent so much time with any more."

VIETNAMESE WOMEN LEFT THEIR HOMES after 1965 to protect the homeland, to secure a peaceful place to raise future generations. In the field, they were sustained by the universal soldier's dream of the day when they would return to home and family. After they were demobilized, they hoped to reap the benefits of their sacrifice, to take their place in society once again as whole human beings.

As I assess women's postwar situations, I want to keep in mind what these women themselves deemed worth fighting for, how they define the good life, as well as the power of the Vietnamese cultural assumption that motherhood is a woman's sacred right.[2]

In the 1990s, men and women, official and popular culture, national narratives and personal accounts, all position the woman who is both a wife and a mother at the top of the heap, in the category of the lucky ones—and bearing a son is the ultimate achievement. Hao constantly talked about the only good fortune to come her way: "I have a nice family and I have a son. I feel guilty about those other women who do not enjoy what I have." Women, from farmers to academic urbanites, confided that they spoiled their sons, dreaded losing them to a daughter-in-law, and hoped that they would never have to see them off to war. But in fact, any healthy child is prized, they assured me, and a daughter is welcome, too—for in fact, it is the daughters who help their mothers manage the household chores, who stay close in times of family trouble.

Women veterans, even if married and fertile, had to weigh the possibility that they might not be able to produce a healthy child. "We had both served in the South, where Agent Orange was used, and we decided not to take a chance, not to have children," a woman whose husband was also in the army told me. Such couples believed that the risk of a deformed child was too great to be taken, even if it meant an old age of loneliness. One of the most poignant postwar short stories from the past decade tells of a middle-aged couple, both in the military, who after finding each other after twenty-one years apart, try to have a child. It is called "The Sound of Harness Bells" for the bells a new father would ring to celebrate the birth of his son. It begins with their reunion:

> She had remained fertile, but her sixteen years in the jungle had left her stricken with chronic malaria. Her skin was unnaturally pale; her hair had thinned and faded to a sickly yellow. Night after night, he held her in his arms. She listened to his beating heart and wondered if it was still strong. He had aged as well; he was already fifty-seven. Every night she noticed the sweat dripping from his tired, liver-spotted face. In his embrace she felt the dryness of his skin and noticed the layers of deadened cells accumulating daily on his back.
>
> If there's no baby by next year, then it's over, she thought to herself. Few women give birth after fifty.

Her body becomes a public symbol, watched over by the division commander and army doctors; the military community rejoices when she finally gets pregnant. But she is haunted. She knows her body isn't fit to carry a healthy child because she had served in an area contaminated by Agent Orange. Her husband, meanwhile, blissfully dreams of a future when he will have a son. The story continues to the inevitable, tragic end:

> In the maternity room, Dr. Giau informed her it was a boy and she smiled faintly. The baby was brought to the postnatal recovery room. . . . His worst fear, a fear he had tried for months to suppress, had finally come to pass. The child was horribly deformed—its left leg

stiffly twisted to its buttocks, its face distorted, with the left eyelid so big it covered one cheek and the lower lip dropping grotesquely below the chin. He knew that God was not so cruel as to create something like this. Only a high concentration of Agent Orange within that poor woman's body could have caused such disfigurement.[3]

Families and communities often bear responsibility for the infirm who remain in their midst. The plight of the family of a sick woman, a former volunteer youth married to a demobilized soldier, attracted the attention of a reporter who wrote that the woman got medical attention and recognition of her problems from exposure to Agent Orange only after his first article appeared and public donations to help her poured in. But she did not live long enough to enjoy the aid, for she died two months after she finally gained entry into a hospital. She left behind a sick husband and three disabled children who, according to the reporter, are still waiting for the official agency in charge of these matters—the Ministry of Labour, War Invalids and Social Affairs—to help them.[4]

Veterans of the volunteer youth corps are not eligible for military pensions unless they suffered wounds that the state covers under disability payments. I was told that a veteran with "light" wounds receives 150,000 dong (the equivalent of about 12 U.S. dollars in 1997) per month and those classed as totally disabled get 400,000. This is not adequate to sustain life for anyone without family or other means of support. Most Vietnamese people I met do not fault the government for the low level of financial recompense for veterans in the past, when everyone was poor. But now concerns are being raised about veterans' benefits in better times, and the pension system is being re-evaluated.

Certainly, Vietnam is not alone in skimping when it comes time to repay its former soldiers. Other far wealthier nations' veterans have voiced complaints about poor treatment once their military duties end. But because in Vietnam so many civilians as well as military personnel were harmed, the problems facing the government are immense. Moreover, as one woman told me, many of the war wounds are hidden, invisible scars that prevent people from living a full, productive life.

Their declining health worries Teacher Mau's comrades, the former volunteers of Troop C814. One woman, whose ill-health has aged her prematurely, commented without bitterness:

Now and then, we think that the government has not cared for us properly. Sometimes we see films or programs on television that show other people's problems and they seem worse than ours. We wish the government would help them before us. We will not live much longer, because of our health problems. Those of us who worked when we returned from the battlefields couldn't stay at our jobs long enough to get a pension because we got sick and had to quit. Some of us were able to marry, by taking much older men who couldn't find any other wives. We want our children to be the same as others whose parents were not volunteers like us. Sometimes we don't know how to bring up our children, how to provide for them and develop their spirit. We were willing to sacrifice ourselves for our nation and succeeding generations, but we don't want our children to pay a price in peace time.

FEMALE VETERANS WHO HAVE ACHIEVED the ideal of a complete family will go to great lengths to keep the family together. Aware of the high divorce rate in the United States, Vietnamese women often asked me who in her right mind would break up a family to seek her own happiness. Statistics do indicate that divorce has been on the rise since 1975, but the figures also show that most divorces occur among the population that is under forty years old.[5]

Indeed, for many women even domestic violence is not considered a sufficient cause for divorce. Feminists in Vietnam, such as Le Thi Quy, have written passionately about the pervasive problem. Professor Quy is troubled by "invisible violence," which she attributes to a postwar resurgence of the backward custom of "honouring men and despising women."[6] According to Quy, this patriarchal system "transforms women into obedient slaves for drudgery and menial jobs, although no one flogs, scolds, or curses them." But physical beating as well occurs all too frequently: her figures for 1994 show that of 22,634 divorce cases, over 70 percent were attributed to violence in the home. She advocates laws and policies to correct the conditions that lead to violence. But like many other Vietnamese feminists, she does not believe that separating husbands from their families is a good solution. One day as Quy and I talked about the problems of families in postwar societies, I recalled Duc Hoan's recent film, "Love Story by a River," in which the single mutilated woman is portrayed as the victim and the married woman beaten by her husband as the lucky one. Some Vietnamese women themselves, then, are admitting that a woman should place her family's happiness above her own, even if it means tolerating an abusive spouse. Such widespread violence and women's tolerance of it can be viewed as another insidious consequence of Vietnam's long periods of war.

MARRIED WOMEN'S ALMOST DESPERATE URGE to maintain the integrity of the family must be viewed in light of the many women who have been left to live alone because of war. Widows and single women are lumped together in the statistics: according to the Women's Union, in both North and South Vietnam, 1.4 million women are classed as widows or unmarried as a result of the war. Despite their large numbers, war widows garner relatively little attention. This neglect is not peculiar to Vietnam. Cynthia Enloe observes that war widows everywhere are useful to the nation as symbols of women's capacity to offer up personal happiness for the welfare of the state and its people. But these women become a financial embarrassment, too, because military widows are expensive for the nation to support. Enloe notes that even in wealthy industrialized countries widows of men who died in the service of their country have had to fight for compensation.[7]

Family tensions, especially with in-laws, trouble Vietnamese widows as much as poverty. Lieutenant Anh, the widow of a soldier and herself a veteran of the American War, enjoyed a brief period of normal family life when her husband was demobilized. She recalls:

> My husband was wounded in the shoulder, and after the war ended, he died, just two months after our daughter was born in 1981. When our child was ten years old, I went to university and then I became a military librarian. The men I work with respect me because of my former war service. But there are some prejudices against me in my job now, just as there are for women everywhere. I don't want to retire at fifty, the mandatory age for women. I am still capable and I can't take care of my daughter's education on a military pension.
>
> I do tell our daughter about our life. I want her to know her history, what it took to keep our country free, why her father had a bullet in his back. It is hard to have a daughter and no husband. I have no support when the families criticize me. I want her to be educated. Women today must be smarter than our generation—we did not have the chance to get a good education because of the war. Today we must integrate science and technology in our lives, but not let our young people be too influenced by the West.

Unease about the widow's place in postwar society can be detected in literature as well as oral histories. The contradictions that arise when a woman who by custom should remain chaste out of loyalty to her dead husband but feels emotional and sexual needs of her own is the subject of a short story by Ma Van Khang, a widely read author. A hardworking lonely widow, gently encouraged by friends to find another man, finally meets someone she can care for. But there are obstacles—and the story brings to light how serious they are:

Long were the days when Duyen had to wrestle with her personal problem. The major wrote to her every week, telling her of his love. He spoke with reason. No, he would not impose his sightless mother and ailing child on her. They would be taken care of by him and his brothers and sisters. But he insisted that he needed her as much as she needed him, not only now but in their old age as well.

In her letters, which she never sent, Duyen always began by refusing his love. Then she would speak of her wish for marital bliss, only to end up in a tangle. . . . How she wanted to enjoy life to the full, with so many years ahead of her. Yet there was the realization that hers was not an isolated case considering all the sacrifices exacted by the thirty years of war. Moreover, there was the love of her children for her and her duties toward them. She loved them with all her heart and they did not want to share her with anyone. Love cannot be shared and happiness once lost can never be regained. How sad that made her. "You cannot acquire peace of mind without losing something," Duyen consoled herself and tried not to think about the major anymore.

Only when her daughter and mother-in-law tacitly give their permission does this woman dare to follow her heart.[8]

This fictional widow has a decent job in the city, while thousands of women in the countryside, sometimes veterans themselves, eke out a living only with help from neighbors and family. For them personal fulfillment is secondary to sheer survival.

IN THE ONGOING DIALOGUES ABOUT THE WAR and its aftermath in Vietnam today, more attention is paid to the single women veterans who want to have children but cannot find husbands than to widows. Sympathy is directed to the women who ended up stuck permanently in isolated state farms or Buddhist pagodas with other bitter female veterans. The terrible irony of their situation is this: Women had gone out to fight to preserve a place where they could look forward to raising their children in peace. When the war went on too long, many women "passed their time" for marriage, or returned sick and tired and traumatized and thus found themselves disadvantaged in the competition for suitable mates. These women lost out in the hard bargain they made when they linked their personal futures with the fate of the nation.

Fear that their poisoned bodies rendered them unfit for marriage informed some women's decision not to marry. A veteran who has become a nun explained to a reporter why she refused the offer of marriage from a coworker in her village who had divorced his wife because she had not produced a son. This man wanted to marry her so that she could give him sons, but she had been in the South, in Quang Tri, and knew that she was infected by toxic chemicals. A comrade's babies had been born deformed and she could not take a chance with a pregnancy. She renounced family life altogether and now devotes her life to praying for other women like her, she told the reporter.[9]

Postwar reportage from Vietnam shows that the Buddhist pagodas in the countryside often take the place of medical institutions for women who have suffered psychic as well as physical damage. In an interview with a nun, Le Thi Than, who had been an assistant doctor with the rank of first-lieutenant during the war, the same Vietnamese reporter uncovered a story all too familiar to students of post-traumatic stress disorder. The nun recounted how she almost lost her ability to function when her fiance was killed on the battlefield while she worked with a medical team in the jungle. Just as she recovered from her personal loss, she found herself in a convoy of trucks that was hit by a Saigonese bomb that pushed the burning trucks and their occupants into a ravine. She was wounded and lost consciousness. Two soldiers in the unit carried her to the ambulance team in a nearby village and volunteered to donate blood to her. But after they went back to their unit, they too were both killed.

In the village she was placed in the care of a Buddhist family after the army medical team moved out. She couldn't stop crying. Her landlady's prayers eventually reached her and one night, she had a dream in which she saw hundreds of people, most of them soldiers and volunteer youth, headless, mutilated, or motionless like statues. In her dream they were leaning toward her, pleading, as if they wanted someone to pray for them to be whole again. She thought maybe they were her dead comrades-in-arms, and the soldiers who had given her their blood.

Though only a dream, she became obsessed with these images as she remembered the broken bodies she had bandaged on the battlefield, the death of the young, the burning trucks, the soldiers thrown into the abyss. Buddhism became her salvation, she tells the reporter, for religion has helped her cope with the memories that haunt her. Her story echoes the accounts of American nurses who struggled with "bloody pictures" as they tried to reintegrate into civilian life. Many of these Vietnamese women, however, cannot, or choose not to, find solace from the psychiatrist or the pharmacist. For them, the pagoda becomes a refuge and religion a healing force.

Yet, not all single women have accepted a childless life. Today, some women's need to bear children is so strong that they are willing to risk ostracism and become pregnant outside of marriage, to "ask for a child."

It is important to note at the outset that neither the plight of the single mother nor the institution of the pagoda and the collective farm as a holding area for unwanted women is purely a result of war. Women workers were sent or voluntarily moved from the Red River Delta to the mountainous areas to work in forestry communes and to teach Vietnamese culture and socialist ideals to the children of the minority peoples in the remote areas throughout the 1960s. Moreover, it is not only war widows and unmarried veterans who are choosing to have children without husbands, nor are these unconventional women all located far away from urban society. Young city women are also having children without marriage—and not simply because of a shortage of men in their age group. As senior women's studies researcher Le Thi points out, 20 percent of all Vietnamese families are "incomplete," headed by veterans, unmarried women in their thirties, war widows, and divorced and abandoned women. Not only war, but internal migration, migration abroad, official duties, and sheer lack of interest in household affairs take some men out of the family for long periods of time.[10]

The focus of academic studies and public sympathies, however, remains centered on single women veterans. Today, 70 percent of the state's 52,000 workers in forestry collectives are women.[11] In these remote, mostly all-female farms they have few opportunities to meet men who would make suitable husbands.

A recent article about a commune in Thai Binh Province defines what is meant when a woman "asks for a child" and reveals how researchers view this unconventional approach to motherhood.[12]

> The mother here is not asking for a child she would bring up as an adoptive one, but the child is born of herself. Many researchers on this social phenomenon pity those mothers as "the mothers who alone give birth to children" or "isolated mothers" or "unfortunate mothers." Indeed they are mostly war victims and victims of "over-agedness" and inability to found a family (as no man would marry them) and they are looking for sexual intercourse with one man (even two men in case of necessity) with the sole purpose of having a child born from him (or them).

This commune reports twenty-one cases of women "asking for a child" out of a total of eighty-five women residents who are over thirty years old. Some women have used intermediaries or economic incentives to help them locate a prospective donor. One woman who is described as "getting on in years" made this offer: "Whoever gives me a child I will give him one quintal of paddy if the child is a girl and two if it is a boy."

Not all communities have been understanding of a woman's decision to bear a child out of wedlock. In another study, a woman working in a silviculture commune in Vinh Phu Province told a researcher from Hanoi's Center for Family and Women's Studies: "When I decided to have a child [in 1984]

I and he [the father of the child] had to write our self-criticism. The management organized a meeting lasting for several nights in order to oblige me to receive [acknowledge] all the mistakes. Afterwards my salary was demoted, my bonus and all other subsidies were cut."[13] Another woman, twenty-eight years old, had a second child out of wedlock, because her first was a girl and she wanted a son. She was penalized and made to work as a babysitter for other women. The article condemns society for sneering at these women, especially those who are placed in the position of loneliness because of the war. The author calls for an end to feudal morality and for policies to help the children. She presents the single women as objects of pity and victims of men, as well as active agents in finding personal solutions to their childlessness:

> Because the number of men at the farms is small, many girls have resigned themselves to their fate, handing their bodies to married men or unfaithful lovers. . . . After sneaking love affairs at the working site, a number of those men have returned to their native land and to their wives. They have left behind the women workers with children of a tender age. But what can these women do further when the law only protects monogamy?

In 1986, the numbers of women bearing children without husbands became too great to ignore, and for the sake of the children, and under pressure from the All-Vietnam Women's Union, a law was passed declaring children without fathers to have the same rights as those born to married parents.

Sociological studies do not always differentiate the veteran who decides to have a child outside marriage from younger women who cannot marry for other reasons. But anecdotal and survey data do indicate that the lonely single woman veteran who has a child out of wedlock stands as a powerful cultural symbol of the human cost of war. Denying them a stake in society is cruel, by everyone's account, and so these women's needs are taken seriously, even when they threaten to disrupt other women's families.

One case from the commune in Thai Binh Province involved a forty-year-old woman who was an executive member of the local Women's Union, and presumably a veteran because most women with high positions in the organization are veterans.[14] She asked to resign her post because she intended to seek a child and felt it would reflect badly on the organization. Her colleagues tried to assure her that it wasn't necessary to resign—indicating their sympathy for her plight—but she did anyway and began having relations with a married man from the same subhamlet, who had four daughters. He wanted her to become his second wife, but she refused: "Either you give me a child or I shall ask for a child from another man. I don't agree to be your concubine." She bore him a son, and reported to the researchers that she didn't mind the taunts about her sexual relations out of wedlock. She decided to sever relations with the child's father out of respect for his wife and fear of her jealousy. But in fact the wife helped her after the delivery and has cared for her like a close friend. The baby has been given a birth certificate and a ration of the rice land from the village cooperative, indicating that he is recognized as a full member of the hamlet.

In postwar Vietnam, it is married women who pay the price of the single mother's fulfillment. Caught between guilt about women veterans who cannot have children, concerns about the effect of illicit affairs on the community, and worries about temptations for their own husbands, some of these women are anxious. When I met with four leaders of the Women's Union of Thanh Hoa Province, the talk turned to the female veterans in their communities who were reaching their mid-forties and becoming desperate for a child. Married, veterans themselves, these women cadre talked about solutions, about the need to find some way to help single women have what is rightfully theirs, without endangering the married women's family happiness. They said that these vulnerable single women yearning for a child often become easy prey for lustful, unscrupulous men. But short of a massive, costly program of artificial insemination—which these women felt might alleviate the tensions in their community—they see no easy solution for this problem.

SO MUCH MYTHOLOGY CIRCULATES about single mothers in Hanoi today that it is hard to get behind the statistics and sociological studies to discover what is really at the heart of the practice. Marriage resistance is not unknown in Asia. In China, for example, studies of women silk workers in the late nineteenth century describe communal vegetarian halls, where women who decided to preserve their chastity lived collectively with like-minded women and adopted daughters to care for them in old age and maintain the rites when they died.[15] Moreover, the Vietnamese poet Ho Xuan Huong's late eighteenth century ironic paean to women who achieve motherhood without husbands indicates that the deliberate act of becoming pregnant outside of marriage is not a recent phenomenon.

Today, most Vietnamese women do not view adoption as a viable option. They yearn for the full experience of carrying and giving birth—indeed, as I remembered when my friends warned me that the childless Teacher Mau might be a bit unstable—they would never be considered fully functional adults without experiencing a woman's most important rite of passage.

A woman's decision to place the need for a child above the need for a husband and a family can be read as an act of resistance against the dominant ideal of the traditional Confucian patrilocal, patrilineal family. The "lonely household" headed by a woman renders men and the family structure itself of secondary importance to the raising of children. Moreover, researchers indicate that villagers and single mothers alike report that while most women have trouble supporting and caring for a child alone, their children are singularly healthy and robust. "It is commonly agreed that compared with other children, the physical and intellectual standard of the child 'asked for' is more healthy, intelligent, and handsome. This is in full agreement with another opinion shared by many people who notice that the woman who asks for a child on her own initiative knows how to select a 'seed sower.' "[16] Here we find a female researcher declaring that some of the women who "ask for a child," or seek artificial insemination, have made a clear decision to view the male partner as little more than a suitable sperm donor. Men become irrelevant for these women except for their value as agents in the reproductive process.

What little is known about these postwar single mothers indicates that single-parent families are counted among the disadvantaged in terms of income and quality of life in their areas.[17] Indeed when she visited one of the women's collectives and met some of the children, Hao remembers that "the children were so poor that some did not know what candy was when we offered it to them."

For some women, however, hope for any sort of family is out of reach. An interview with a seventy-eight-year-old woman who has worked for twenty-four years in a munitions factory in Gia Lam, across the Red River from Hanoi, brought to light for me the sad lives of the truly forgotten women, the workers who volunteered to produce the war material and never left the factory. Today, these women live in groups of fifty, in shacks provided by the factory, completely isolated from even the villagers around them, so poor that they do not have the proper clothes or the basic social skills to venture outside.

WHEN THE IDEAL FAMILY IS THE COMPLETE FAMILY, and building an intact, "cultured" family with a husband, wife, children, and, if necessary, aged parents, is still seen as the path to a stable society, even by women themselves, single women will be viewed as objects of pity, less than fully participating citizens in their communities and nation. Yet the belief that a woman has a right to children may explain why, despite state directives aimed at limiting families to two children, the birth rate continues to rise.[18] I remembered how the women of Mau's troop laughed in the face of the two-child policy, proudly noting that they had more than two children because they deserved some rewards after all they had gone through.

A memoir by a man who once worked on the Trail as an engineering student and has now become a cadre shows that even a bureaucrat can put government policies aside when confronted with a woman veteran. He writes:

How could I recognize her from the thousands of girls of those days who had in common the same pallid complexions caused by prolonged malarial fever—falling hair and dark rimmed eyes? Suddenly it reappeared very clearly before my eyes, their shining youth and smiling mouths even during an attack of malaria when they could hardly sit up to eat a bowl of rice. We in the command staff thought that it was only normal for the young men like us to suffer during wartime. But for them, the girls, what would happen if the war dragged on and they "passed their time"? So we had decided to transfer gradually all the girls to the rear. But to my surprise and consternation and admiration, very few applied to go home. Some candidly said that they were too old to consider marriage and even if they wanted to find husbands, who would consent to marry such sickly spinsters as they had become? Others went further by saying that even if they got married they did not believe they could bear children after so much sickness.

This woman now standing before me was one of those girls of the Truong Son days. She was once reputed as a most skillful time-bomb and leaf-bomb defuser and she could even deal with "tropical trees." . . . She smiled at me, shyly, "I already have three children, yet in those days, I thought. . . ."

I felt a deep grip at my heart and tried to make a joke: "You thought you would not be able to marry didn't you? Now, you take care or you'll bear more children than you are allowed." . . . We both smiled joyfully."[19]

THUS, WHILE MANY ACADEMIC WOMEN IN VIETNAM rail against the moral straitjacket imposed by patriarchal society, and women and men praise family stability as the foundation of the nation, society in general takes a relatively tolerant stance toward women veterans who break out of the mold to try to find solutions to the personal problems directly linked to the war: The widow who is tacitly encouraged to remarry, when the ideal of the chaste widow is still upheld; the single woman veteran who can raise a child without marriage, even when sex outside of marriage for women is decried; the veterans who have many children even when the official policy mandates a limit of two—they are all given special dispensation by their communities, who at present have no other means to repay them.

PART THREE

Meanings

CHAPTER NINE

A Rice Meal Without Rice:
The Costs of War

The struggle of man against power is the struggle of memory against forgetting.

> Milan Kundera, *The Book of Laughter and Forgetting*, 1981.

The language and literature of disillusionment would be on the whole a postwar phenomenon—everywhere.

> Modris Eksteins, *The Rites of Spring*, 1989.

A REFLECTIVE MOOD ABOUT VIETNAM'S PAST characterizes public and private discourse in Hanoi since the open-door policy and renovation have altered the direction of economic life and foreign relations in the late 1980s. Despite the omnipresent Party censors, surprisingly strong critiques of the state and its policies have appeared in documentaries, literature, and reportage produced in Hanoi in the past decade. Writers and film and television producers are echoing a widespread call for an accounting: Who paid the price that bought the state its chance to move into an international political arena as a unified nation?

At the same time, the possibility of a more vibrant economic system raises questions about how the new wealth will be distributed. Now that the state need no longer be forgiven as a "poor parent" but must decide how to disperse resources, the time has come to raise the touchy issue of paying back debts. In public venues and in private talks, middle-aged Hanoians in particular worry about the decline in moral values, especially among the postwar generations, who may all too quickly forget the sacrifices of their parents and turn toward individualism and greed.

Despite the flurry of media attention I observed and many conversations about these concerns with friends in Hanoi, it wasn't until I was able to stand at a famous war memorial, that I understood the sadness of ordinary people when they look back at the history of the past fifty years.

❖   ❖   ❖

AFTER WE HAD JOLTED FOR SIXTEEN HOURS over rocky mountain roads in a Toyota van, the town of Dien Bien Phu was a letdown when we reached it in late May 1996. Its isolation—for it is situated in a valley ten miles from the Laotian border, ringed by mountains and jungles—was no surprise. That was part of its legend. The small town's symbolic value has always outweighed its commercial or cultural significance. There in May 1954, Ho Chi Minh's revolutionary Viet Minh armies literally tunneled their way into the heart of the well defended French fortress to end a fifty-six-day siege, a decade of war, and nearly a century of French colonial rule.[1]

But a recent building boom that would transform the town into a provincial capital seemed designed to erase all traces of its unique history. Chinese-style cement block buildings emerged out of the dust, in stark contrast to the lovely wooden stilt houses of the minority peoples in the surrounding hills.

It wasn't until we found the cemetery of the Vietnamese dead, one of the only spots of quiet and beauty in the town, that we felt the power of the place. Standing at the gravesites with Vietnamese pilgrims, listening to them quietly speculate about the past, watching their reverence as they offered Buddhist prayers and incense at each grave, it became clear that reckoning the human costs of Vietnam's most recent wars is not only the province of disenchanted urban intellectuals, but a matter of deep concern for ordinary people as well.

The cemetery's five hundred graves represent only a small fraction of the nearly eight thousand members of the Vietnamese People's Army who died in the final battles against the French. The Vietnamese architects of the memorial site did not forget the others: a wall, eerily similar to the Vietnam War Memorial in Washington, lists by province of origin the names of all the dead combatants. But left unnamed are the more than two hundred thousand or so porters—including minority peoples and women—who made the victory possible. Their contribution is commemorated in a carved stone mural that shows them doubled over with the burden of hauling ammunition and food on their backs and dragging heavy artillery by ropes to the front. Standing proudly over the cemetery are two large statues of women, one Vietnamese, the other an ethnic minority. The women shield a kneeling, boyish Vietnamese soldier.

The message for a Vietnamese citizen burdened with the memory of all that happened later is inescapable: the victory at Dien Bien Phu on May 7, 1954, was a costly one, and even more suffering was yet to come.

No one there questioned Ho Chi Minh's determination to call on his people to drive the French colonial government out of Vietnam once and for

Cemetery of the Vietnamese dead, Dien Bien Phu, 1996.

Commemoration stone at the cemetery at Dien Bien Phu, 1996.

Statue at the cemetery at Dien Bien Phu, 1996.

all. At stake was a voice for the Viet Minh at the Geneva conference that would decide the disposition of territory and power in Indochina. But was it necessary to sacrifice so many people, and was the military's "human wave" approach the only way to secure a timely victory? At Dien Bien Phu that spring day in 1996, people were coming uncomfortably close to questioning the costs of war in general, not just the assault against the French fortress forty some years ago. They talked about the debt the survivors owe the millions of victims of the wars, the need to keep history alive so that younger generations will guard their traditions rather than discard them as old-fashioned and irrelevant. They asked what kind of society must be created to ensure that the costs have been worth it in the end. And, who, after all, are the true heroes?

IN BAO NINH'S ANTI-WAR NOVEL *The Sorrow of War,* published in 1991, the protagonist, like the author a soldier-writer and one of ten survivors of a volunteer youth brigade originally five hundred strong, rails against the "damned idiots up there in the north enjoying the profits of war." He speaks on behalf of the peasants, "whose special characteristics had created an almost invincible fighting force because of their peasant qualities, by volunteering to sacrifice their lives. They had simple, gentle, ethical outlooks on life. It was clearly those same friendly, simple peasant fighters who were the ones ready to bear the catastrophic consequences of this war, yet they never had a say in deciding the course of the war."[2]

A less direct but still pointed critique of indifferent Party bureaucrats emerges even in some officially sanctioned revisitations of the war. A documentary produced by the Military Film Studio in 1994 to be shown a year later for the anniversary of reunification—or the fall of Saigon, depending on one's standpoint—features a modern, well-attired navy team traveling down the coast with cameras to retrace the history of the "No Name Ships," the fleet that ran supplies from North to South from 1959 to 1972. The metaphor of the sea, which erases all traces of the dead, provides the narrator a convenient vehicle for recounting the stories of forgotten, no-name people who died. "History is not abstract. . . . It is made by humans," the narrator intones, and it is the human story that the program brings to life.

In one poignant episode, an old woman peddler in a fishing village remembers how she gave up her gold to buy a boat and a Japanese engine for the navy, and sent the army her son as well for the cause. "Has the government ever repaid you?" Predictably, she replies that not only was she never reimbursed, but has never even been thanked. And her son, imprisoned by the Saigon regime, has never been recognized as a veteran. Similar stories come forth throughout this surprisingly frank journey to the past, as the film team interviews a man who had plastic surgery to change his identity for the cause, and records the memories of a simple fisherman who helped out with what little he had to offer.

A recent article in the national newspaper, *Lao Dong,* muses about the Vietnamese people's willingness to sacrifice, to forgive past hurts, to carry on with seeming good cheer no matter what the circumstances.[3] The author, a respected scholar and linguist, declares that the very nature of the Vietnamese people renders them vulnerable to official exploitation. He conjures up a powerful cultural symbol—the mothers of war martyrs—to make his point:

> Ask Vietnamese mothers if they know anything about [Marxist] notions of class struggle or surplus value. . . . Then ask them if they know how to sacrifice, how to bear hardships to preserve the honor

of the family and the nation. . . . Ask them if they respect their own interests more than the common interests of their village and their country . . . ask the widows whether they care for themselves more than for their children's lives and honor.

His message seems to be this: These women are the most unselfish citizens in our country. They have given all that they had to give, and they didn't do it for selfish or ideological reasons. If we cannot let them live as dignified human beings, we have all failed. He uses the image of the neglected martyrs' mothers to make a larger point: "The Party and the government need to have concrete and effective policies to improve the lives of the people. . . . If there are food shortages . . . if people are ignorant . . . or unhealthy, the mistake rests with the Party and the government."[4]

This identification of the patriotic, self-sacrificing mother with pure unselfishness appears in other forms in the reportage and literature of the 1990s, most of it by male authors. And in turn, these pieces argue in one form or another that to neglect the war martyrs' mothers is to neglect the best element of Vietnamese culture.

The government's belated attempts to honor the mothers of martyrs are met with derision by many Hanoians. "Look at them, sitting so stiffly, their faces grim, as the officials try to honor them now, after all these years," a middle-aged woman commented with anger as we looked at a newspaper photo of the hero mothers celebration in Hanoi in 1996. This public ritual—that offered the saddest members of postwar society, the mothers who had lost their sons, and with them their economic and ritual security, too little too late—seemed to epitomize how out of touch with real people the Party bureaucrats have become.

For example, a widow's only surviving son, who accompanied his mother to an official ceremony because she was too weak to go alone, terms the absurd spectacle "A Rice Meal Without Rice" in an article in *Thanh Nien,* on January 18, 1996.[5] He describes ironically the fancy dining room with its foreign beer, Coca Cola, and expensive meat dishes. When he urged his aged mother to partake of the grand feast—for it is a rare occasion that the provincial officials treat the people so well—she answered, "How can I eat? I have no teeth left for chicken. . . . I was told that we were invited to a rice meal but there is no rice or porridge here."

Finally, the officials figure out the problem and have rice brought in, but these old women are not used to eating such rich food and ask for the humble boiled spinach or sweet potato leaves to which they are accustomed. And in the end, the author makes his point by reporting what his frail, politically naive mother had to say: "The cadres don't understand the people."

The patriotic mother who offers her sons to safeguard the nation is a universal figure of unselfish sacrifice for the common good. And in turn, every nation that needs warriors must honor the mothers who produce them, must

"Mother reunited with son, Le Van Thich, who had been sentenced to death and imprisoned by the French for ten years in Can Dao." (*Caption and photo courtesy of the Vietnam Women's Museum*)

find some means to legitimize and compensate their losses. The martyrs' mothers are especially tragic figures in Vietnam because their only hope for ritual and economic support died with their sons. There are small government allotments for these women. But poverty isn't the only issue. A woman's son, far more than her husband, is the source of her identity, her worth as a person. For all of these reasons, the plight of the neglected martyrs' mothers has roused tremendous anger against the cold-hearted bureaucrats who waited twenty years to honor them and then bungled the banquet. But the duty to help these women is not simply passed off to distant bureaucrats, for just as the son traditionally expressed his filial duty to his parents by "tiling mum's roof," so too must society find a way to provide for mothers whose surviving sons have died.[6]

❖ ❖ ❖

SECOND ONLY TO THE WAR MARTYRS' MOTHERS as symbols of sacrifice are the young women who died before they had the chance to bear children or who survived the war and now live in poverty. As Colonel Tam told me, remembering the deaths of his own sister and young girlfriend, "The hardest part for us was to send young girls into battle, knowing what would happen. We had no choice, but we were sorry, especially for the ones who had never known love." The mother-patriot and the teenage female fighter share a common quality: They are victims of war because they have been deprived of the family life they had every reason to expect.

Reporters and filmmakers are rediscovering young women heroes, comparing their past exploits with their current situations. The current condition of one group of survivors is the topic of an article about the Ngu Thuy female artillery company. Composed of thirty-seven village women, it became legendary when it set a U.S. destroyer on fire in February 1968 off the coast of Quang Binh. The women had been invited to Hanoi to meet Ho Chi Minh and were given badges, and some even traveled abroad. How are they living now? An article in the newspaper *Lao Dong* on December 22, 1994, describes their situation: "Now we are sitting here in Ms. Xu's house. It is called a house, but it is really a tent made from old masts and broken planks from boats. The floor is just sand. We sat on broken planks. In front of and beside me were all those women with their wrinkled faces, and their children in tattered clothes."[7]

Narratives of forgotten heroines sometimes seem prompted by local pride, because they often end with pleas to officials to help a community that sacrificed their young women to the nation. A report of a visit to Truong Bon, where twelve young girls died in 1968, recounts their heroic decision to guide the trucks along the roads through the night by the light from their white bras and then records the reactions of the Party officials and others who had gathered to hear the survivors remember their story. A reporter from the Party newspaper, *Nhan Dan,* visited the survivors with a local delegation in July 1993.[8] He tells his readers that everyone who heard the story cried and expressed hope that the Party and the people would create a special policy to help these women and their home villages. One woman, a local official, speaks for her native place: "As for we My Son people, we never had a single hesitation about sacrificing for the national salvation. Now we are the poorest people in the district and the province and we hope that we do not let the 'young millionaires' forget the youth of previous generations who sacrificed their lives so they could live well today."

This story of the young girls of Truong Bon is rich in symbolism, for these young women are described today as so pure that they forgot all modesty and stripped to their underwear to guide the trucks through the night. Their young bodies could not protect the trucks from the bombs, but the bombs could not destroy the power of their selflessness. Young men were involved in the fight, and many died. But it is the women, who should not have been there in the first place, who call up more powerful feelings of victimization and anger.

The reporter admits that poverty in this area of Vietnam is still a problem and that it will take a long time to eliminate it. But he appeals to the central and provincial leaders to commemorate the dead and help the living by directing resources to the area. He warns the government that it is on the backs of these simple local people that the current institutional stability has been constructed: "Remember the source when you drink the water."

Current media productions aim to remind audiences that behind the heroic images are real people, with families, feelings, and economic needs that must be recognized. In a poignant article, a photographer recalls the history of a picture he snapped during an air raid in a suburb of Haiphong in October 1967. "Through the smoke curtain, I recognized the artillerywomen whose laughter drowned out the sound of the explosions and I saw how brave and active they were. . . . I didn't want to miss the chance, so I pointed my camera toward those faces as they appeared through the smoke, and pressed the shutter."[9]

The photographer carried the photo to Hanoi, and it was printed on the front page of the *People's Army Newspaper* the next day. The woman in the photo was identified as Nguyen Thi Gai from Vinh Niem Hamlet, near Haiphong. As time went on and the war became more fierce, the photographer forgot about the photo and its subject until he received a letter from her parents asking for a copy to help them remember their dead daughter.

The photographer relates his ambivalent feelings about the photo: It had brought him success because it won a prize in Germany. But he wants his young readers to remember the person behind it: "Listen to me . . . that photo was not only a work of art, but a life. The young artillerywoman has passed away, but her portrait will exist forever, as a reminder of what has been given to provide a new, beautiful life for the younger generations in our country today."[10]

NOT ALL LITERATURE AND MEDIA PRESENTATIONS put forth a sympathetic view of women or honor their patriotic contributions. The well-known male writer Nguyen Huy Thiep has angered many Vietnamese women with his short story about a greedy woman who collects aborted fetuses from the maternity clinic where she works to feed the dogs she raises for profit at home. His creation, "The General Retires," is important because it is one of the first fictional pieces to bring to the fore thorny questions about Vietnam's heroic history and current culture.[11] But Thiep paints a dark picture of Vietnamese women, contrasting the simple, upright general who is the protagonist in the story with his manipulative, amoral daughter-in-law. When at his talk at Harvard University in the fall of 1996 Thiep was asked by some of us in the audience whether his fiction reflected his real feelings about women, the author admitted honestly that he is ambivalent about women, and hasn't thought through the issues of women's place in society.

In another instance, some Hanoi women reacted strongly against a television show about women in the jungles during the war for quite a different reason. The series was based on a written text and created an outcry when it deviated from the original story. The written version is an important piece because it is written by a woman who raises sensitive issues. "The Last Survivor of the Jungle of Laughter" shows the worst aspects of the lives of five teenage girls who try to survive in a remote jungle post for three rainy seasons during the war.[12] It discusses madness, senseless death, and sexuality. One girl, Thao, is considered the lucky one, because she has a fiance back in Hanoi, a very eligible man, a student of literature. Her romance becomes the focus of the attention of her four lonely comrades, for she has a chance for happiness after the war. But like the others, she loses her hair and her beauty as the jungle saps them of their vitality. One day as the fighting moves closer to their remote post, three male Vietnamese soldiers hear crazy laughter and what looks like a white orangutan jumps down from the trees and grabs the neck of one of the men. The animal-like creature is one of the girls, naked and laughing crazily. The soldiers snap her out of her fit and leave. But then the enemy fire draws closer and four of the girls are killed.

The writer reminds her readers of the female soldier's particular dilemma: "The events that become legends didn't happen in this place. They couldn't counterattack the enemy because they had reserved the last bullets for themselves, to avoid rape."

Thao survived, hidden behind a tree during the attack, and as she buries her comrades, remembers what one of them had said once: "Remember, don't let men feel pity for us."

Thao returns home to her urban boyfriend, thin and sick, traumatized, and though he tries to love her out of respect for her service in the war, he eventually succumbs to the charms of a rosy-cheeked healthy girl who stayed home.

As the written story goes, one of the soldiers who witnessed the women's crazy behavior does pity them. He recorded his impressions in his diary: "I can never forget what I saw in the Jungle of Laughter. The fact that women have been drawn into war is horrible. I'd die twice to avoid putting women in this situation. I shiver to think of my sister or my sweetheart laughing crazy like that, somewhere in that immense jungle." He lost his chance for a medal when one of his superiors read this passage.

The television show, according to some critics in Hanoi, violated the original story on several counts: the women were made too glamorous, their suffering was downplayed, and a hint of lesbianism surfaced. Moreover, women were angry that the film neglected to remind people of the sad fact that many forgotten women, like the survivor, Thao, ended up in remote state farms when they could not fit into civilian society. But something else troubled women like Phan Thanh Hao. She disliked the way the movie played up the emotional instability of the girls in the jungle, ignored their survival skills, and overlooked their patriotism.

> The written story was distorted in the film. Not all women became hysterical and certainly not so early in the war as the film implied. It made the girls look as if all they thought about was sex and ignored their real friendship with each other and their loneliness. The costumes weren't right, either. One of the characters wore a traditional *ao dai*, a white party dress. She looked as if she belonged in the French film, *Indochine*, instead of a real film about the war. The girls wore baggy white t-shirts and swam naked underwater—no one would have worn such clothes or acted so carefree back then. The audience was mad at the filmmakers because they didn't show the women's sacrifices and their devotion to the country. They were casual about depicting the women and they put in too much personal nonsense.

MEN STILL DOMINATE THE IMAGES OF WOMEN projected into the wider culture, but women are beginning to speak out, and as they do, their portraits challenge the idealized image of the courageous, pure woman warrior. "The Last Survivor of the Jungle of Laughter" takes up some of the same hard questions about female sexuality and war that Duong Thu Huong addresses in *Novel Without a Name*. After talking with Hao about these women's writings and reading very critical reportage about the state's neglect of women veterans in male writers' stories, I wondered: What does it mean, this interplay among male writers and media producers and women's issues? I asked a senior editor of a weekly magazine in Hanoi, a woman of about forty, to describe to me who controls the media. This seasoned journalist lamented the problems her magazine faced in finding suitable women journalists, who have the necessary education, training—and courage—to pursue the reporter's competitive, fast-paced life. Those women who do investigative reportage are vulnerable to criticism, she said—even a small technical error in an article can discredit a woman's otherwise accurate report if it gets too close to politically problematic themes. So women have not taken their rightful place as interpreters of women's problems.

When I asked how the pointedly critical documentaries like "No Name Ships," novels like Bao Ninh's *The Sorrow of War*, and the written version of "The Last Survivor of the Jungle of Laughter" have made it past the censors, I was told that many of the men who are gatekeepers are in fact very sympathetic to women's problems and believe they should be aired.

In the public arena, one safe—and face-saving—means to express complicated and politically sensitive concerns is to couch them in terms of women's issues. As historian Hue-Tam Ho Tai has noted, similar techniques were used by male writers during the 1920s and 1930s: "Gender acted as a coded language for debating a whole range of issues without overstepping the limits imposed on public discourse by colonial censorship. The French rhetoric of empire which presented France as the mother country, the Governor-General as a father figure, and the colonial people as children at various stages of immaturity met its match in the Vietnamese literary practice of commenting on the human condition through the device of female characters."[14]

How effectively a contemporary Vietnamese male author can use a woman's voice to express anger not simply toward the war's costs but toward the powerholders who neglect all veterans surfaces in a recent article, "The Woman with Her Face Covered," published in the journal *Literature and Art*, March 18, 1996.

The narrator is a male army veteran, Ha, who meets a woman on a train. He notices that she is dressed like the young volunteers he had met in the jungle in '72 and '73, but her face is covered with a kerchief. She called to mind a young woman he had known in wartime, who also had covered her face. Her name was Bo, and she was the head of a squad of young girls in charge of an ammunition and supply depot at Cam Ly cave. He was stationed "one jungle away" from them, and knew that the area the girls guarded was bombed twenty-four hours a day. Ms. Bo was a legend, even then:

> Miss Bo who could explode a timing bomb in three minutes, but screamed and fainted when a snail crawled on her chest. Miss Bo who was buried alive by a bomb and after two days, when she was dug out, revived. Miss Bo who always had her face covered, with just a space for her eyes.

The memory of this woman, with her feminine squeamishness and stalwart courage, stayed with Ha, and he couldn't resist asking the woman on the train if she is the Miss Bo who tied up a downed pilot in his parachute and filled it with stones to keep him there. She admits that she is indeed Miss Bo, and tells him what happened at the end of the war when the regiment moved on:

> Peace returned and everybody who lived in the jungle poured out to the delta, to the cities. . . . You guys, the commanders of the regiment, left at dawn and forgot us. . . . I told the other three girls,

"You find your way home. As for me, I will stay here. I can't leave the ammunition depot with no one to care for it. Certainly someone will come to replace me." . . . But no one came. Alone in the jungle and the mountains, haunted by bodies buried in the regiment cemetery, I did not starve, because there were food supplies. But I was afraid all the time until I became so busy chasing away moths and mending clothes that I killed the fear, became numb. After one year and nine months (I counted time by using branches from a tree) . . . a group of geologists came to the cave in the rain. I left everything and ran out, out of the jungle, without papers or luggage.

She went back to her village, to the place and the lifestyle she had volunteered to preserve when the bombs exploded over the rice fields in 1965. Her father, whose son in the United States had sent money to fix up the family home, died before she returned. So when Bo reached her village, she had to deal with a greedy Party chairman, who told her that she didn't need so big a house because she didn't have a family. He offered to build for her a smaller place.

Something exploded in Bo, and she stood up and threw her knapsack on the floor . . . pulled the kerchief off her face and screamed: "No husband and no child, is that what you say? Look at me, look at me carefully. First I was scarred by a fish hook and then by American bombs. Look at these scars and remember. And shut up because we have nothing more to say. I gave you all, all."[15]

VIETNAM WON THE WAR against a far more powerful enemy. And yet the heroic mode has not had a long life in the postwar period, despite official efforts to sustain it. In today's Vietnam, the image of the disappointed, disillusioned, ill-treated female veteran provides men as well as women with an acceptable vehicle for railing at the state not only in the name of women's rights but also in the cause of all those who gave their youth for a unified, independent nation. In the 1990s, the young women who died bravely and the survivors who live poorly have become potent symbols of the costs of war.

EPILOGUE

Women's Worries

In the field, the men respected us—our brains, our strength. . . . They now respect make-up, nice hair, being a proper housewife.

> Amair Adhana, former guerilla fighter,
> Eritrean People's Liberation Front, 1994.

If there were another war, I would gladly go out to fight for my country. But I don't want my sons to go, and I don't want my children to suffer.

> Vietnamese woman veteran, 1997.

Why do we Vietnamese smile when we hurt the most?

> Phan Thanh Hao, Hanoi, 1997.

AFTER I FINISHED MY INTERVIEWS and prepared to leave Hanoi in 1997, still troubled by nagging questions about women and postwar society, I went back to the Women's Museum, for its artifacts so clearly display competing conceptions of women's place in the nation-state and its official narratives. I had learned that just as the giant mother statue at the entrance overshadows the photographs of serious fighting women in the historical section, so too, in the long run, a woman's reproductive function is more important to Vietnam, as to any nation-state, than her fighting ability. As studies about women, war, and national identity show, "emerging . . . nation-states and nationalisms seek to exert their control over their community's women and girls in their effort to protect, revive, and create nations."[1] When the North Vietnamese government sent thousands of its young, fertile, healthy women to war after 1965, it placed at risk its future mother-citizens and potentially weakened the strength of the nation. Clearly, the American War challenged the idea that women could at once fight and nurture.

The traditional national story casts the mother-warrior as the emblem of the best elements of Vietnam's national character: its commitment to stable families, to cultural purity, and to national independence. But the old narratives of maternal warriors did not take account of the situation with which thousands of women contended during the American War. Historical martial

Woman in Hanoi, 1996.

women, like the Trung sisters and Lady Trieu, resisted foreign aggressors from a firm position within their communities, united by local pride and loyalty against an outside enemy. During the wars of resistance against the French, women displayed great courage, but they mainly operated in local forces, rooted in a network of peers, neighbors, and kin. During the American War, in both North and South Vietnam, the militiawomen and guerrilla fighters who stayed close to home seem to engender less postwar anxiety than the women who lived with men in the wilderness for long periods of time. Women who moved outside the boundaries of family and neighborhood faced a double bind. They would be judged during wartime on the basis of their ability to perform manly tasks. But their post-war positions within their communities hinged on how well they could preserve their womanly qualities.

The damaged Miss Bo's angry exchange with a greedy, indifferent representative of the state can be construed as the universal cry of the demobilized soldier who is marginalized in postwar society. All over Vietnam, in full view of more fortunate citizens, men in ragged army uniforms work in menial jobs, as bicycle repairmen or cyclo drivers, for example. But although they are poor, these veterans are not regarded as less than men. Former soldiers who are women, on the other hand, are judged not by their work lives but by their capacity to bear children. The concrete contributions of women who served in the armies and volunteer brigades during the war are diminished in the postwar era by a collective outpouring of pity for those who have lost the essence of their womanhood.

As I tried to disentangle women's own estimations of the quality of their postwar lives from the cacophony of well-meaning, pitying, guilty voices speaking on behalf of the childless female veteran, a line from the fictionalized story of women in the jungle, "The Last Survivor in the Jungle of Laughter," kept haunting me: "Don't let men pity us." I remembered too how women in their oral remembrances and in fiction agonized about losing their hair and their health, hoping that in the end men would still find them attractive.

They were so right to worry. A short story by a male author, published in Hanoi in 1992, hits hard at women's deepest fears. It speaks directly to the plight of the woman veteran. The story, "The Blanket of Scraps," dwells on the fate of Minh Xuyen, who in 1966 joined a volunteer youth brigade at the age of fifteen, leaving behind a sad, widowed mother. First stationed, like Teacher Mau and Troop C814, in Quang Binh, she moves south, closer to the front, and signs on for three tours of duty. After some years, her health deteriorates, she stops menstruating, and she ends up in a convalescent camp with amputees and mental cases. She considers herself normal, but is told otherwise by a woman doctor: "My conscience demands that I have to re-store to you your right to be a woman." After the peace treaty, the camp is disbanded and she returns to her village ninety kilometers from Hanoi.

Eventually she owns her own hut and secures a contract to farm, but after a disastrous flood she goes out begging with her fellow villagers. In Hanoi, she meets a friend from the old days, Thu, who volunteered at the same time. Thu's life has been lonely—she has never married and lives with sixteen other women in a dormitory. But she has a child. What makes this story interesting is that it is not poverty alone that marks these women. Thu's desire to find a mate is constantly thwarted. Xuyen meets widower Bien through the medium of a quilt she long ago created out of scraps, and she begs him to make love to her, because she wants a child. He tries, manfully, but then tells the forty-one-year-old virgin that she is no longer a woman, for her breasts have withered and her reproductive parts are good only for "excretory purposes."

This woman's long service in the army matters less than her current state. She has been reduced to a tragic, pleading figure, dependent on the goodwill of any male partner she can seduce for a moment of human warmth and the most prized of all possessions, a woman's only insurance against loneliness and poverty, a child.[2] In the end, she and Bien decide to live together in a platonic relationship. "The war had robbed her of the right to be a woman," the author reminds his readers.

WHAT IS THE LINK BETWEEN the postwar literature of disenchantment and women's memories of war as a better time in human relations? It is important to remember, as studies of European culture after World War I have shown, that postwar versions of war do not necessarily reflect the real situation back then. Erich Maria Remarque's novel, *All Quiet on the Western Front,* which like Bao Ninh's *The Sorrow of War* carries an antiheroic message, was written over a decade after the end of World War I. Remarque himself contended that the novel was not about actual events during the war but a diatribe against the old men who send young men into war, turning them into feral creatures as they try to survive in unbearable conditions. But the bitter veteran of the German army in World War I also wanted his readers to know that soldiers were not mere robots even then, but capable of deep friendships and firm attachments to common values.[3]

In Vietnam, contemporary narratives that cast women as pure heroines, tragic victims, or mad sexual aggressors need not be read as straightforward portraits of their behavior during the war, but as expressions of nationalistic pride, critiques of postwar policies, or revelations of anxiety about gender relations. When women tell their own stories, they draw from culturally and historically approved ideals, even as they inject their individual perceptions and experiences. As so many Vietnamese women told me, sacrifice is associated with womanhood, in war and in peace. It is no wonder, then, that women's deeply ingrained belief that they must put the welfare of others first stayed with them in the worst of times. Their memories of stoic courage, and male observations of their selfless determination to endure hardship during the war, ring true. Moreover, in a culture that equates sacrifice with the good woman, linking women's unselfish patriotism with their victimization might well serve as an effective "weapon of the weak" for women and their advocates, a path to having their situation improved that makes sense within a contemporary Vietnamese context.

When women become symbols, however, their individual voices are muted. Oral histories offer women a means to shape their own position in war and civil society. Listening carefully, one hears threading through their tales of patriotism and victimization a countertheme. Pride in their accomplishments, against obstacles and amid conditions that everyone recognizes as extraordinarily difficult, rings through their narratives. Yes, they dealt with male prejudice, they said often. But, they overcame it. Yes, they yearned for domestic life during their long years away from home. But they also wanted others to know that they developed expertise with weapons and machinery. They do not want to be relegated to the realm of simple luddites, or protected as symbols of Vietnam's pure, traditional culture—especially as status becomes linked with a global culture that values technological expertise.

Sewing class, Hanoi Women's Union Vocational School, 1996.

VIETNAM'S CELEBRATION OF MOTHERHOOD as the only route to full female personhood has many ramifications. When motherhood is considered the natural right of women, one given her by the Creator, as a female sociologist asserts, then a woman's right to children takes precedence over her obligations to social harmony and family stability.[4] When some women see no alternative but to use a man's services for the sole purpose of insemination, and when society views the children of these unions as particularly sturdy specimens, we can see how the maternal ideal serves as a vehicle for resistance to the equation of motherhood with marriage and family.

But as we have seen so vividly, this identification of motherhood with women's essential human nature also marginalizes women who cannot, or choose not to, marry or bear children. Lesbianism is almost never allowed to be discussed in a public forum in Vietnam, and as the audience reactions from "The Last Survivor of the Jungle of Laughter" reveal, some people abhorred the film's suggestion that women in the jungle could turn to one another for physical love. The maternal ideal also places pressure on the daughters of peace, the women who have come of age in the postwar era. The women students I met in Hanoi, in their early twenties, are studying hard to earn the credentials they need to secure an independent income. But they know full well from observing their mothers that maintaining a family and a work life is a constant juggling act.

"We are the first generation of women raised in peace since 1945," they would marvel, and then begin to worry aloud about finding and keeping a husband, and then bearing and raising sons for him. One young woman from a famous military family told me that her family tradition—a grandmother in the anti-French resistance, a grandfather who was one of the planners who opened the Ho Chi Minh Sea Route, and father and mother both officers in the military—has taught her by example to be independent. She took leadership positions in school, and she wants to follow in the footsteps of her country's famous heroines. But when we talked over her professional aspirations, she set modest goals: "I can't aspire to a director or manager position. It would interfere with my duties to my family too much."

And another young woman, educated at one of America's elite universities, told me in despair that she doesn't want to become exposed to too much feminist theory in America. It would make her life back home harder, she said, and she can't do anything to change the structure anyway.

Other women voice similar feelings of powerlessness. One very intelligent and independent-minded economics student informed her English instructor that her ideal world was one where there were no men, only women. And one of my friends, an ambitious professional, confessed to me that her kids were spoiled rotten and a trial to her. Her husband is away most of the time and her male colleagues exploit her, she said. For this woman, the only recourse is to seek a scholarship to work on an advanced degree abroad. She harbors little hope of working within the system at home.

NATIONS THAT ARE RECOVERING FROM WAR all too often put women's issues on the back burner—despite promises to link women's emancipation with national liberation in socialist countries like Vietnam.[5] Many forces contribute to this neglect of women's economic and political rights during postwar reconstructions: the nation's need to keep women in the home and out of the workforce as male veterans seek jobs, economic priorities that stress modernization over social welfare, political systems that view women's active participation in national affairs as a temporary expedient, and families and communities that turn to the past for a comforting, nostalgic view of life.

Women veterans, who have so obviously won the right to full citizenship, should be the strongest advocates for better policies for all women. I began this book by asking how women in Vietnam would parlay their war service into a strong postwar political force. I end by observing that all too often the traumatic experiences of women soldiers during the war have not been factored into our expectations of how they should act after the war. Women's stories from Vietnam poignantly reveal how much hope they pinned on har-

Hanoi market, 1996.

monious domestic life as they lived through decades of violence and disruption. In the early years of the postwar era, when new legal and power structures were negotiated, elite women who might have taken the lead in advocating women's rights were often themselves haunted by war. For example, the official conduit for raising women's problems at the national level is the Women's Union, and women attain high position in that organization by dint of extraordinarily patriotic war service. Kim Cuc's story of giving birth in the jungle and then running from bombs, of ten years of harsh living conditions, offers a window for understanding why other powerful figures in the organization might campaign hard for equality in the workplace but focus on the well-being of the family as the main avenue to improve women's lives.

Many of the academic women who courageously research and write about women's issues are also products of war and revolution. These women witnessed the hard lives of their mothers and are grateful for any family happiness they can find. Le Thi Quy, for example, told me once that her willingness to stick her neck out to help women "comes from the heart." Her mother had been ostracized by her own family and married a man she never loved as a way out of the most terrible poverty. She was a fruit peddler who had eight children; twice she delivered a baby right in the marketplace. Similarly, Phan Thanh Hao has watched her mother remain loyal to a difficult man through his imprisonment, illnesses, and flagrant infidelities.

Women like Quy and Hao, who write, carry on research, and advise the government about women's issues, are adamant that the state not forget its promises to women, but at the same time they are deeply devoted to the image of what they term the "complete family" as the bulwark of a stable society. In a recent collection of articles by women on both sides of the Pacific, edited by Kathleen Barry, we can detect what kinds of problems Vietnamese women researchers themselves target and what kinds of solutions they propose to resolve them. Poverty for women is a specter that troubles the authors, because they know that the most vulnerable people in society, the workers least able to compete in the modern market economy, are women. They have found in their studies that women have fewer opportunities for access to loans, education, and cultural life than men. They decry the lack of even the most basic health care for women. Agricultural and forestry workers put in ten and twelve hour days, for example, and their work requires physical stamina, but they are often malnourished and ill from overwork, inadequate sanitation, and contact with insecticides. Women whose work forces them to stand in water for long periods of time are vulnerable to gynecological diseases, and many cannot get even basic treatment. One can sympathize with a researcher who pleads that women's health must be regarded as a state resource, to be guarded and maintained in the interest of all society.

Studies by women demonstrate that laws that outlaw polygamy, protect women's right to choose and divorce a partner, and give women and children rights to common property after divorce are not implemented with sufficient consistency to allow women to count on the legal system for protection. Domestic violence is a problem addressed by some women, as I noted earlier.[6] But abuse on the homefront is not the only worry for women. Le Thi Quy has written about the increase in trafficking in women and children since the open door policy began, and Vietnamese women have become commodities in an international market. Women like Quy view this trade as shameful for all Vietnamese women, a betrayal of everything that they have fought for in the past fifty years, a sign that Vietnam as a nation cannot offer protection to its most vulnerable citizens.[7]

VIETNAMESE WOMEN OF THE WAR GENERATION connect their personal and collective welfare with the security of the nation. Despite the contemporary anxieties expressed in the public arena about the problems of sending women into war, the women I met all insisted that they would take up arms again if the nation was in danger. And they have passed on a powerful legacy to future generations. One night at dinner with Hao and her family, the conversation turned to speculation about an invasion from China at some time in the future. Hao's daughter-in-law, Hanh, a smart, successful businesswoman, mother of two daughters, and daughter of a former militiawoman, said very quietly,

Friendship, 1996.

without a moment's hesitation, "Let them come, we will fight them." She did not mean that she would watch her husband and brothers go to battle while she minded the homefront. For her generation of women, the old adage "When war strikes close to home, even the women must fight" has a concrete meaning, in the history of the nation and in the history of her family.

Hao and I said nothing at the table that night, because we had said it many times before as we worked on this book together: We hope that Hanh's daughters can grow up believing that peace rather than war is the natural state of affairs for Vietnam.

NOTES

INTRODUCTION
Lucky Distance

1. See Alexander B. Woodside, *Vietnam and the Chinese Model: A Comparative Study of Vietnamese and Chinese Government in the First Half of the Nineteenth Century* (Cambridge, MA: Harvard U. Press, 1988).

2. See, for example, Miriam Cooke, *Women and the War Story* (Berkeley: U. of California Press, 1996).

3. Kali Tal, "The Mind at War: Images of Women in Vietnam Novels by Combat Veterans," in *Contemporary Literature,* Vol. 31, 1990, pp. 76–96. See also Linda Dittmar and Gene Michaud, eds., *From Hanoi to Hollywood: The Vietnam War in American Film* (New Brunswick, NJ: Rutgers U. Press, 1990).

4. Susan Brownmiller, *Seeing Vietnam: Encounters of the Road and Heart* (New York: HarperCollins, 1994, p. vii).

5. See, for example, David Chanoff and Doan Van Toai, *Vietnam: A Portrait of Its People at War* (London: Tauris, 1996).

6. The Rosie the Riveter story has been revised to show that American women's postwar lives were fraught with contradictions and that their wartime experiences influenced the ways they raised their daughters. See Sherna Berger Gluck, *Rosie the Riveter Revisited: Women, the War and Social Change* (New York: Meridian, 1988).

7. The effort to bring women into history, to view them as active participants in events, and to assess their impact on official and popular culture is not limited to any single discipline. But for this study, anthropological works on women's narratives and field workers' reflections about the dynamic relationship between women as writers, interpreters, and informants have been especially useful. See, for example, Ruth Behar, *Translated Woman: Crossing the Border with Esperanza's Story* (Boston: Beacon Press, 1993); and Mary Steedly, *Hanging without a Rope: Narrative Experience in Colonial and Post-Colonial Karoland* (Princeton, NJ: Princeton U. Press, 1993).

8. See James C. Scott, *Domination and the Arts of Resistance: Hidden Transcripts* (New Haven: Yale U. Press, 1990); and Gayatri C. Spivak, "Subaltern Studies: Deconstructing Historiography," in *Selected Subaltern Studies,* ed. Ranajit Guha and Gayatri C. Spivak (New York: Oxford U. Press, 1988).

9. A volume of poetry from this archive has been produced, but it contains no women's writings. See *Poems from Captured Documents,* selected and translated

by Thanh T. Nguyen and Bruce Weigl (Boston: U. of Massachusetts Press, 1994). See also one American veteran's story about discovering diaries in a knapsack he took from a Vietnamese soldier in *Kontum Diary: Captured Writings Bring Peace to a Vietnam Veteran,* by Paul Reed and Ted Schwarz (Arlington, TX: Summit Press, 1996).

10. See James Freeman's collection of the oral histories of Vietnamese refugees in California in *Hearts of Sorrow: Vietnamese Lives* (Stanford: Stanford U. Press, 1989).

11. See David Chanoff and Doan Van Toai, *Vietnam: A Portrait of a People at War.*

12. Le Ly Hayslip, with Jay Wurts, *When Heaven and Earth Changed Places* (New York: Penguin Books, 1989). See also Nam Phuong, *Red on Gold* (Claremont, CA: Albatross Books, 1991); Nguyen Thi Thu-Lam, *Fallen Leaves: Memoirs of a Vietnamese Woman from 1940 to 1975* (New Haven: Yale U. Council on Southeast Asia Studies, 1989); Nguyen Thi Dinh, *No Other Road to Take,* trans. Mai Elliot (Ithaca, NY: Cornell U. South East Asia Program, 1976) (originally published in Hanoi as *Khong con duong nao khac.* Nha xuat ban phu nu, 1968) [hereinafter cited as *No Other Road to Take*]; Nguyen Thi Tuyet Mai, *The Rubber Tree: A Memoir of a Vietnamese Woman Who Was an Anti-French Guerrilla, Peace Activist, and Publisher* (New York: McFarland Press, 1994); Cao Ngoc Phuong, *Learning True Love* (Berkeley, CA: Parallax Press, 1993).

13. Lady Borton, *After Sorrow: An American Among the Vietnamese* (New York: Kodansha, 1995).

14. One of the most useful commentaries on oral history is Diane Bell and Shelley Schreiner, eds., *This Is My Story: Perspectives on the Use of Oral Sources* (Geelong, Victoria, Australia: Deakin U., 1990).

15. Letter from Nguyen Minh Thu, Hanoi, August 28, 1997.

16. Ngo Vinh Long, *Vietnamese Women in Society and Revolution, Vol. I* (Cambridge, MA: Vietnamese Resource Center, 1974).

17. Of the rich literature on memory, these works have been of particular use: Susan Rodgers, ed. and trans., *Telling Lives, Telling History: Autobiography and Historical Imagination in Modern Indonesia* (Berkeley: U. of California Press, 1995); Jane Kramer, *The Politics of Memory: Looking for Germany in the New Germany* (New York: Random House, 1996); Jay Winter, *Sites of Memory, Sites of Mourning: The Great War in European Cultural History* (Cambridge: Cambridge U. Press, 1995); and K. W. Taylor and John Whitmore, eds., *Essays into Vietnamese Pasts* (Ithaca, NY: Cornell U. Press, 1995). Benedict Anderson's *Imagined Communities* (New York: Verso, 1983) has informed my notions of tradition, community and the nation-state in Vietnam, although he does not deal with gendered memories and sentiments about the nation.

18. A note on Vietnamese names: In Vietnam, the family name precedes the personal name. For example, Nguyen Ngoc Tuan's family name is Nguyen. But individuals are called by their personal names, and so he is called Mr. Tuan by English speakers. In Vietnam, terms that indicate the age and status relationship between people are used. I would call Tuan "Anh Tuan" to indicate that we are of the same age group and friends. Phan Thanh Hao, whom I would call Madame

Hao in English if I were not on a first-name basis with her, I call "Chi Hao," which literally means "sister Hao." After a great deal of deliberation, Hao and I decided to use the simplest designations possible in this book to avoid confusing Western readers.

PART ONE   Messages

CHAPTER ONE
Through a Hairnet: Mothers, Warriors, and the Nation

1. This information is taken from a briefing by Dr. Nguyen Quoc Dung, Vice Director of the Institute for Military History, in Hanoi, January 1997. Of course, there was an "elephant" in the room with Professor Dung and me, for his narrative was a response to U.S. histories of the war. As U.S. pilots knew all too well, by 1967, the North Vietnamese had developed a sophisticated, powerful antiaircraft defense system.

2. See Jay Winter, *Sites of Memory, Sites of Mourning: The Great War in European Cultural History*. Winter argues that the massive losses from the Great War in Europe precipitated a return to traditional, religious forms of mourning and shows how families and communities created memorials to help them come to terms with the deaths of soldiers whose bodies could not be recovered.

3. From the briefing by Professor Dung and from a publication that he used for his statistics: *Thanh nien xung phong: phuc vu giao thong van tai thoi chong My* by Nguyen Van De (Hanoi: Nha xuat ban giao thong van tai, 1995). A recent newspaper article raises questions about the military's accounting of casualties: Nguyen Tuan, "Volunteer Youth: Issues we need to address" [Thanh nien xung phong—van de can phai xem xet] *Lao Dong,* March 21, 1996.

4. Two books clearly set out the issues. Cynthia Enloe's *Does Khaki Become You? The Militarization of Women's Lives* (London: Pandora, 1988) argues for a feminist approach to militarization, which she views as constructed along gendered lines according to cultural and political imperatives. See Enloe's revised, updated version, *Maneuvers: Militarizing the Lives of Women* (Berkeley: U. of California Press, forthcoming). Jean Elshtain argues against the feminist interpretation of war. See *Women and War* (Chicago: U. of Chicago Press, 1995). A useful survey of the literature on women and war is in Micaela di Leonardo, "Morals, Mothers, and Militarism: Antimilitarism and Feminist Theory," *Feminist Studies,* Vol. 11, Fall 1985, pp. 607–617.

5. Sara Ruddick's work inspires these questions. Ruddick argues that women's maternal instincts lead naturally to women's roles as peacemakers. See *Maternal Thinking: Toward a Politics of Peace* (Boston: Beacon Press, 1989).

6. For a fine study of the role of women in the French resistance, see Margaret Collins Weitz, *Sisters in the Resistance: How Women Fought to Free France, 1940–1945* (New York: John Wiley & Sons, 1995). See also Nora Benallegue,

"Algerian Women in the Struggle for Independence and Reconstruction," *International Social Science Journal,* Vol. 35, 1983, pp. 703–718; Margaret Randall, *Sandino's Daughters: Testimonies of Nicaraguan Women in Struggle* (Vancouver, B.C: New Star Books, 1981); and her updated study, *Sandino's Daughters Revisited: Feminism in Nicaragua* (New Brunswick, NJ: Rutgers U. Press, 1994).

7. The colorful story of the Rani of Jhansi Regiment of the Indian National Army is told in "Nationalism and Feminism in Late Colonial India: The Rani of Jhansi Regiment, 1943–1945," by Carol Hills and Daniel C. Silverman, *Modern Asian Studies,* Vol. 27, 1993, pp. 741–760.

8. K. Jean Cottam, "Soviet Women in Combat in World War II: The Ground Forces and the Navy," *International Journal of Women's Studies,* Vol. 3, 1980, pp. 345–357. Two collections of writings by and about women in war serve as useful comparative references: Shelley Saywell, *Women in War: From World War II to El Salvador* (New York: Penguin Books, 1986); and Dorothy Sheriden, ed., *Wartime Women: An Anthology of Women's Wartime Writing for Mass-Observation 1937–45* (London: Mandarin, 1990).

9. "The Museum of Vietnamese Women," in *Women of Vietnam,* No. 4, 1995, pp. 4–6. See Cynthia Enloe's astute analysis of the politics of the South Vietnam Women's Museum, "Women After Wars: Puzzles and Warnings," in Kathleen Barry, ed., *Vietnam's Women in Transition* (London: Macmillan Press, 1996, pp. 299–315).

10. See Neil L. Jamieson, *Understanding Vietnam* (Berkeley: U. of California Press, 1993, p. 7). This is the single most useful cultural history of modern Vietnam for the nonspecialist and specialist alike.

11. Keith W. Taylor, *The Birth of Vietnam* (Berkeley: U. of California Press, 1983, pp. 1–13). John K. Whitmore cautions against imposing a Chinese model of patriarchal kinship on Vietnam, instead argues for recognizing the Southeast Asian pattern of bilateral social organization and relative high status for women. See "Social Organization and Confucian Thought in Vietnam," *Journal of Southeast Asian Studies,* Vol. 60, 1984, pp. 296–306.

12. Ngo Duc Thinh, "The cult of the female spirits and the Mother Goddess 'Mau,'" In *Vietnamese Studies,* No. 3, 1996, pp. 83–96.

13. See Jennifer Holmgren, *Chinese Colonization of North Vietnam* (Canberra, Australia: Australian National U., 1980).

14. See David Marr, *Vietnamese Tradition on Trial, 1920–1945* (Berkeley: U. of California Press, 1981), for a very useful essay on women's issues in the early nationalist period. The passage is on pp. 200–201. I must note here that many versions of these tales exist, and Marr presents some of the more colorful accounts.

15. *Ibid.,* pp. 198–199.

16. *Ibid.,* pp. 211–212.

17. Tai Van Ta has written about women's rights in the Le Code in "The Status of Women in Traditional Vietnam," *Journal of Asian History,* Vol. 15, 1981, pp. 97–145. For an excellent analysis of women in the French period, see Ngo Vinh Long, *Vietnamese Women in Society and Revolution,* Vol. I.

18. Quoted in *Women in Vietnam*, eds., Mai Thi Tu and Le Thi Nham Tuyet (Hanoi: Foreign Languages Publishing House, 1978, pp. 92–93).

19. In *Ho Chi Minh On Revolution: Selected Writings, 1920–66*, ed., Bernard B. Fall (New York: Praeger, 1967, pp. 13–14). Originally printed in *Le Paria*, August 1, 1922.

20. Marr, *Vietnamese Tradition on Trial*, p. 248.

21. In *Women in Vietnam*, ed. Tu and Tuyet, p. 123.

22. Taken from Marr, *Vietnamese Tradition on Trial*, pp. 244–245.

23. In *Women in Vietnam*, Tu and Tuyet, eds., p. 146.

24. *Women in Vietnam*, Tu and Tuyet, eds., p. 163. Arlene Eisen takes her figures from this source, but the numbers must be considered estimates only. See Eisen, *Women and Revolution in Vietnam* (London, Zed Books, 1984). To see how women can be erased from history, read the account by the then commander-in-chief of the Vietnam People's Army, the famous General Vo Nguyen Giap. In *Dien Bien Phu* (Hanoi: Gioi Publishers, 1994). General Giap gives due respect to the laborers who supported the armies, but does not mention specifically the work of the thousands of women who contributed to the victory.

25. *Vietnamese Studies*, Number 10, special issue on Vietnamese women, Hanoi, 1966, pp. 29; 146 [hereinafter cited as *Vietnamese Studies*, No. 10, 1966].

26. See a translation of *Cuoc Khang Chien Chong My Cuu Nuoc, 1954–75* [Vietnam: The anti-U.S. resistance war for national salvation, 1954–1975: Military Events]. Translation from the Foreign Broadcast Information Service, published by the U.S. Army Military History Institute, July 3, 1982, p. 75. My thanks to Robert Brigham for this document.

27. *Ibid*, p. 91.

28. See "Volunteer Youth: Issues We Need to Address," *Lao Dong*, March 21, 1996.

29. See *Thanh Nien Xung Phung*, pp. 31–33.

30. See Eisen, *Women and Revolution in Vietnam*, Chapter 7, for a useful summary of women's service in the South. Again, Professor Dung is constructing history to respond to American charges that the Communist insurgence in the South was managed and supplied by the North. Instead, he claimed that women's local initiatives sparked the socialist, nationalist resistance of the Viet Cong forces.

31. See her memoir, *No Other Road to Take*.

32. The poet is Luu Trong Lu, and the poem is included in an article by Christine Pelzer White, "Vietnam: War, Socialism, and the Politics of Gender Relations." In Sonia Kruks, Rayna Rapp, and Marilyn B. Young, eds., *Promissory Notes: Women in the Transition to Socialism* (New York: Monthly Review Press, 1989, pp. 172–192).

33. Her story is in *Vietnamese Studies* 10, Hanoi, 1966, pp. 85–110.

34. From *No Other Road to Take*, p. 70.

35. Mary Ann Tetreault makes the point that male admiration for women's war service is double-edged in a useful overview, "Women and Revolution in Vietnam." In Kathleen Barry, ed., *Vietnam's Women in Transition*, pp. 38–57).

CHAPTER TWO
War's People: Through a Women's Lens

1. "Duc Hoan and Feature Films about Hanoi," *Cinematographic Magazine,* Hanoi, 1988.

2. I do not intend here to survey the history of film in Vietnam, only to link one woman's history with her art. For one survey of films made from 1953 to 1983, see Nguyen Tri, "30 Years of the Vietnamese Cinema," *Vietnam Courier,* No. 5, Hanoi, 1983.

3. Jamieson, *Understanding Vietnam,* p. 87.

4. In *Vietnamese Literature,* eds. Nguyen Khac Vien and Huu Ngoc; trans., Mary Cowan et al. (Hanoi: Foreign Languages Publishing, 1979, p. 329).

5. See Marr, *Vietnamese Tradition on Trial,* pp. 154–155.

6. For a useful history of the Vietnamese village at this time, see Hy V. Luong, *Revolution in the Village: Tradition and Transformation in North Vietnam, 1925–1988* (Honolulu: U. of Hawaii Press, 1992).

7. See Le Thi Quy, "Domestic Violence in Vietnam and Efforts to Curb It." In *Vietnam's Women in Transition,* pp. 263–274.

CHAPTER THREE
Broken Promises: The Lives of a Militiawoman

1. This is an appendix of portraits at the end of *Vietnamese Studies,* No. 10, Hanoi, 1966.

2. From *Nu Anh Hung: Luc Luong Vu Trang Nhan Dan* (Hanoi: Nha xuat ban quan doi Nhan Dan, 1994).

3. See *Vietnam Voices: Perspectives on the War Years, 1941–1982.* Compiled by John Clark Pratt (New York: Viking, 1984, pp. 195–200).

4. From Thomas D. Boettcher, *Vietnam, the Valor and the Sorrow: From the Home Front to the Front Lines in Words and Pictures* (Boston: Little Brown, 1985, pp. 232–236).

5. *Vietnam Voices,* p. 196.

6. *Vietnam, The Valor and the Sorrow,* p. 235.

7. *Vietnam Voices,* p. 258.

8. In *Vietnam: The Anti-U.S. Resistance War,* p. 91.

9. Originally published in *Vietnam Courier,* Hanoi, April 15, 1965. Reprinted in *Vietnam Voices,* pp. 200–201.

10. From *Vietnamese Studies,* 10, Hanoi, 1966, pp. 132–140, and *Women in Vietnam,* pp. 252–271.

11. *Women in Vietnam,* p. 265.

12. Gerard Chaliand, *The Peasants of North Vietnam,* trans., Peter Wiles (Baltimore: Penguin Books, 1969).

13. *Ibid.,* p. 178.

14. *Ibid.,* p. 215.

15. *Ibid.*, p. 240. Ironically, when the male soldiers returned home to the villages, they often angrily ejected these women from their hard-won positions and jobs.

16. See Nguyen Van De, *Thanh nien xung phong*, p. 26.

PART TWO   Memories

CHAPTER FOUR
A Bombshell for a Vase: Leaving Home to Save Home

1. See *Thanh Nien Xung Phong*, Ch. 1.

2. In "Volunteer Youth: Issues That Need To Be Addressed."

3. See *Vietnam: A Portrait of its People at War*, p. 53.

4. Quoted in Mark Clodfelter, *The Limits of Air Power: The American Bombing of North Vietnam* (New York: The Free Press, 1989, p. 73).

5. From Phan Thanh Hao's unpublished memoir, *One Among Millions,* manuscript courtesy of the author.

CHAPTER FIVE
Shovels, Hoes, and Guns: Women on the Ho Chi Minh Trail

1. This information is taken from biographical data in *The Other Side of Heaven: Post-War Fiction by Vietnamese and American Writers*, ed. Wayne Karlin, Le Minh Khue and Truong Vu (Willimantic, CT: Curbstone Press, 1995), and from information obtained during an interview with Le Minh Khue conducted in Hanoi in May 1996. Her soon to be published short story about the Ho Chi Minh Trail is not available to me at this time.

2. From the memoir of Nguyen Thuy Kha, who joined the army in 1971 and was assigned to Platoon 3, Company 6, of the Lam Son Army. His memoir is included in a collection of memoirs and reports written by military and civilian personnel who worked or observed events on the Ho Chi Minh Trail during the American War. I have used a translation in manuscript copy taken from the original publication in *Tap chi van nghe quan doi* [Military Literature and Art Review] (Hanoi: Military Publishing House, 1990, courtesy of the William Joiner Center for the Study of War and Social Consequences). When I refer to *Memoirs,* it is to these manuscript translated versions unless I state otherwise. As the preface to the published memoirs declares, they were compiled in part to show the heroic determination of the men and women who worked on the Trail. The editors of the volume describe the entries as a "collection of personal experiences related by people who saw action in the Truong Son range. Moreover, as most of the authors are not professionals, this book should not be regarded as a literary work,

but only as a modest attempt to document for readers just one aspect of the war." These materials cannot be read simply as representations of firsthand wartime re-actions because some were reconstructed from diaries and published after the war. Yet for the historian, they are useful, for one can detect between the lines a sense of immediacy, of tension between seasoned soldiers and journalists and others who did not understand military conditions, and contradictions between higher ups and the rank and file.

3. Memoir by Thep Moi, who identifies himself as a writer for *Truong Son Magazine*. I find no date for his piece, but judging from its content, it was writ-ten from notes taken during the war and a return visit to the Ho Chi Minh Trail soon after 1975.

4. The Vietnamese internal documents usually refer to the Ho Chi Minh Trail as the Truong Son Route, for the mountains that the roads traversed, or in the military records as Line 559, for the military unit that commanded the region. But the name "Ho Chi Minh Trail" [Duong Ho Chi Minh] was not simply an American usage, for in 1959 the road was officially named after Ho Chi Minh when it became a unit of the military on the anniversary of his birth, May 19.

5. In *Vietnam Voices: Perspectives on the War Years, 1941–82*, pp. 240–242.

6. This description of the Trail is taken from the introduction to the *Memoirs*. The term "sapper" is used by Vietnamese translators for *cong binh*. In reality, they were demolitions experts who worked on the roads, combat engineers. The true sappers are defined in the Vietnamese sources as elite combat units that launch se-cret attacks on enemy bases, depots, and other strategic locations. See *Vietnam: The Anti-U.S. Resistance War for National Salvation*, FBIS trans., pp. 94–95. In line with Vietnamese sources, I use the term "sappers" throughout to refer to com-bat engineers.

7. Major General Phan Trong Tue from a diary dated 1965, in *Memoirs*.

8. Thep Moi in *Memoirs*.

9. This is a history of Line 559 compiled from seasonal reports from the field. In the manuscript translation I have used, the reports do not seem to have been edited extensively by postwar revisionists. Problems between the Hanoi officials in charge of resources and commanders in the field, tension about unrealistic ex-pectations from the center in light of conditions on the Trail, and issues of morale among the troops are discussed frankly. I refer to passages from the document ac-cording to the date they were written. A revised, published version is titled *Lich su duong Ho Chi Minh* [A History of the Ho Chi Minh Trail]. Hanoi: Nha xuat ban quan doi, 1995. This translation is used by permission of the William Joiner Center, where it is on file. Hereinafter referred to as *History of Line 559*.

10. In *History of Line 559*.

11. In his memoir.

12. *Ibid*.

13. Reports dated April 1965 to October 1966 in the *History of Line 559*.

14. Reports dated November 1967 to October 1968 in the *History of Line 559*.

15. Memoir of Thep Moi.

16. In his *Memoirs*.

17. In the memoir of Nguyen Sinh, a reporter for the Party newspaper, *Nhan Dan,* January 1969, in *Memoirs*.

18. Memoir of Nguyen Hai Thoai, an engineering student sent out to work on the roads under the direction of the Ministry of Transportation and Communications. His memoir is useful, for he admits his ignorance of conditions on the Trail and offers the reader the perspective of someone involved in the work but an outsider to the culture of the roadbuilders and military personnel.

19. Nguyen Sinh in *Memoirs*.

20. Do Vu, a journalist who traveled with the volunteers during the dry seasons after 1967. In *Memoirs*.

21. See Jonathan Shay, *Achilles in Vietnam: Combat Trauma and the Undoing of Character* (New York: Touchstone, 1995, pp. 51–68).

22. Cited in Phan Trong Tue's memoir.

23. This anonymous forty-year-old composer's diary begins with an entry in December 1965 and ends with one dated June 1996. It is available in manuscript form, courtesy of the William Joiner archives.

24. Memoir of Nguyen Hai Thoai.

25. In the memoir of Trong Khoat.

26. As told to Nguyen Sinh, in *Memoirs*.

27. *Ibid.*

CHAPTER SIX
Only Soldiers: Women and Men in War

1. See Stephanie Gutman, "Sex and the Soldier," *New Republic,* February 24, 1997, pp. 18–22, for one example of the recent media coverage about women in the military. See as well Leisa Meyer, *Creating GI Jane: Sexuality and Power in the Women's Army Corps During World War II* (New York: Columbia U. Press, 1996) and Cynthia Enloe, *The Morning After: Sexual Politics at the End of the Cold War* (Berkeley: U. of California Press, 1993).

2. In Kathryn Marshall, *In the Combat Zone: An Oral History of American Women in Vietnam, 1966–1975* (Boston: Little, Brown, 1987, p. 228).

3. In Shelley Saywell, *Women in War,* p. 145.

4. A translation of this article is included in the materials from the Combined Document Exploitation Center [hereinafter CDEC] on microfilm in the Healey Library at the University of Massachusetts, Boston Campus, through an arrangement with the National Archives and the William Joiner Center on the Study of War and Social Consequences. These 200,000 or so sets of documents contain personal reports, life histories, poetry, newspaper articles, policy statements, and other writings taken from North and South Vietnamese soldiers or other sources

from the period 1966 to 1973 and sent to the CDEC in Saigon. The reels are unindexed and have not yet been properly mined for information.

5. *Ibid.*

6. Phan Trong Tue in *Memoirs.*

7. Duong Trong Dat, *The Maiden Stars* [Nhung ngoi sao con gai] (Ho Chi Minh City, 1985). I have worked from a translation in manuscript form by permission of the author.

8. The Vietnamese title is *Khoang Cach* and the book was published in Hanoi in 1985. I have worked from a manuscript translation courtesy of the author. In the preface to the book, Tran Dang Xuyen writes that the author wrote it to repay a sentimental debt to the linemen, that he wanted to describe the true life stories of ordinary people who had performed no outstanding exploits but simply did their jobs as best they could.

9. Xuan Thieu, "The Tale of the Inn of Two Angels" [Truyen thuyet quan tien]. Published in *Bao van nghe* [Literature and Art], July 1991. I have worked from a manuscript translation, courtesy of Phan Thanh Hao.

10. Bao Ninh, *The Sorrow of War,* trans. by Phan Thanh Hao and Vo Bang Thanh with Katerina Pierce (London: Secker and Warburg, 1993). Originally published as *Than phan cua tinh yeu,* by Nha Xuat Ban Hoi Nha Van, Hanoi, 1991.

11. Duong Thu Huong, *Novel without a Name,* trans. by Phan Huy Duong and Nina McPherson (New York: Penguin Books, 1995).

12. *Ibid.,* p. 49.

CHAPTER SEVEN
Only Women: Maternal Soldiers

1. In the memoirs of a composer, dated 1965–1966; unpublished manuscript.

2. Nguyen Hai Thoi in *Memoirs.*

3. From Major General Phan Trong Tue's memoir.

4. Lynda Van Devanter, *Home Before Morning: The True Story of an Army Nurse in Vietnam* (New York: Warner Books, 1983, p. 117).

5. In *Visions of War, Dreams of Peace,* ed. by Lynda Van Devanter and Joan Furey (New York: Warner Books, 1991, p. 32). Reprinted by permission of the author's family.

6. Nguyen Sinh in *Memoirs.*

7. From the CDEC archives, dated 1966.

8. From the memoir of Trong Khoat, dated 1974, about events in 1967–1968, in *Memoirs.*

9. From the memoir of Dan Hong, recording a journey down the Trail in 1975 in *Memoirs.*

10. From Thep Moi in *Memoirs.*

11. See Cynthia Enloe, *Does Khaki Become You? The Militarization of Women's Lives,* pp. 185–186.

12. From the CDEC archives, dated 1966. Sometimes men adopted a woman's voice in their poetry, so one cannot be certain that this author is indeed a woman. But if not, the point that war blurred gender lines still holds true.

13. From "The Sound of Night," by Cao Tien Le, in *Writing between the Lines*, Kevin Bowen and Bruce Weigl, eds. (Amherst: U. of Massachusetts Press, 1997, pp. 46–50).

14. Adapted from *Glorious Daughters of Vietnam* (Hanoi: Women's Union, 1975).

CHAPTER EIGHT
Picking Up the Pieces: Going Home

1. Firm numbers for Vietnamese casualties and MIAs are not available. These statistics are taken from an interview with a Women's Union representative and they ring true with other reports from Vietnam and the United States. For a reliable account see Marilyn B. Young, *The Vietnam Wars, 1945–1990* (New York: HarperCollins, 1991).

2. See Le Thi Nham Tuyet, "Asking for a Child Practice at Anhiep," in *Some Research on Gender, Family and Environment in Development*, Vol. I. Hanoi: Research Centre for Gender, Family and Environment in Development, 1996, pp. 157–163. This female researcher assumes that society owes women an opportunity to experience motherhood.

3. Nguyen Quang Lap, "The Sound of Harness Bells," in *The Other Side of Heaven*, ed. Wayne Karlin, Le Minh Khue, and Truong Vu (Willimantic, CT: Curbstone Press, 1995, pp. 287–293).

4. For a Vietnamese critique of the medical system and women's health issues, see Ha Thi Phuong Tien, "On the Problem of Health Protection for Female Labourers," in Kathleen Barry, ed. *Vietnam's Women in Transition*, pp. 199–206.

5. See Thai Thi Ngoc Du, "Divorce and its Impact on Women and Families," in *Vietnam's Women in Transition*, pp. 74–86.

6. See Le Thi Quy, "Domestic Violence in Vietnam and Efforts to Curb It," in *Vietnam's Women in Transition*, pp. 263–274.

7. In *Does Khaki Become You?*, p. 84.

8. Ma Van Khang, "Mother and Daughter," from *Vietnam Courier*, No. 11, 1981, originally published as "Me va con," in *Van Nghe*, March 1985. See also the translation in *The Other Side of Heaven*, pp. 340–352.

9. Minh Chuyen, "Meetings at a Pagoda" [Len chua, gap lai], *Van Nghe*, January 4, 1997.

10. In "Women, Marriage, Family and Gender Equality," *Vietnam's Women in Transition*, pp. 61–73.

11. Murray Hiebert, "Single Mothers: Women in Men-Short Vietnam Are Having Children Out of Wedlock." *Far Eastern Economic Review*, Feb. 24, 1994: 60–61.

12. See Le Thi Nham Tuyet, "Asking for a Child Practice at Anhiep Commune."

13. Nguyen Thanh Tam, "Remarks on Women Who Live without Husbands." In *Vietnam's Women in Transition*, pp. 87–92.

14. "Asking for a Child Practice at Anhiep."

15. See Janice Stockard, *Daughters of the Canton Delta: Marriage Patterns and Economic Strategies in South China, 1860–1930* (Stanford: Stanford U. Press, 1989). In the Chinese case, economic independence enabled women to resist marriage.

16. "Asking for a Child Practice at Anhiep."

17. See Le Thi, "Women, Marriage, Family, and Gender Equality," in *Vietnam's Women in Transition*, pp. 61–73.

18. See David Shapiro, "Women's Employment, Education, Fertility, and Family Planning in Vietnam: An Economic Perspective," in *Vietnam's Women in Transition*, pp. 123–143.

19. Recorded by Nguyen Hai Thoai in *Memoirs*.

PART THREE   Meanings

CHAPTER NINE
A Rice Meal Without Rice: The Costs of War

1. Bernard Fall's detailed account, *Hell in a Very Small Place: The Siege of Dien Bien Phu*, notes that the French occupation of the valley totaled 209 days and the actual siege 56 days. The author warns correctly that the recorded data about numbers of support personnel must be considered rough estimates only. I have consulted Marilyn Young, *The Vietnam Wars: 1945–1990*, for more current information. For a Vietnamese account of the siege, see Vo Nguyen Giap, *Dien Bien Phu* (Hanoi, 1994).

2. Bao Ninh, *The Sorrow of War*, pp. 18 and 15. For a fine analysis of the relation between literature and the heroic image of the Vietnamese nation, see Nguyen Ba Chung, "Imagining the Nation," *Boston Review*, Vol. 21, 1996.

3. In *Lao Dong*, March 12 and 14. "The Thickness of Vietnamese Culture" [Be day van ho Vietnam], by Phan Ngoc.

4. *Ibid.*

5. Nhat Lam, "Bua com khong co com."

6. See Ngo Hoang Giang, "Not Just a Habitat" [Khong chi mai nha che than], *Lao Dong*, July 20, 1995.

7. Nguyen The Thinh, "Female Heroes Today" [Nhung anh hung ay, bay gio], *Lao Dong*, December 22, 1994.

8. Thanh Phong, "Twelve young girls, 'live landmarks' from Truong Bon [ve 12 co gai 'coc tieu song' o Truong Bon], *Nhan Dan*, July 27, 1993.

9. Pham Kinh, "Phia sau mot tam hinh," *Lao Dong*, April 1995.

10. *Ibid.*

11. Nguyen Huy Thiep, *The General Retires and Other Stories,* trans. Greg Lockhart (Oxford: Oxford U. Press, 1992). See the discussion of Thiep's work in *The Viet Nam Forum,* No. 14, November, 1994, pp. 7–44, and in Murray Hiebert, *Chasing the Tigers,* pp. 172–173.

12. The author is Vo Thi Hao, and the story was translated into English by Phan Thanh Hao and Sara Bales from the original, "Nguoi sot lai cue rung cuoi," published in 1993. Manuscript translation courtesy of Phan Thanh Hao.

13. See a review by Hue-Tam Ho Tai, "Duong Thu Huong and the Literature of Disenchantment," in *The Vietnam Forum,* No. 14, 1994, pp. 82–91.

14. Hue-Tam Ho Tai, *Radicalism and the Origins of the Vietnamese Revolution,* p. 90.

15. Duc Ban, "The Woman with Her Face Covered" [Nguoi dan ba che mat], *Van Nghe,* March 18, 1996.

EPILOGUE
Women's Worries

1. Linda Basch discussing Cynthia Enloe's work in "Introduction: Rethinking Nationalism and Militarism from a Feminist Perspective." In *Feminism, Nationalism, and Militarism,* ed. Constance Sutton (Arlington, VA: Association for Feminist Anthropology/American Anthropology Association, 1997, p. 5).

2. Ngo Ngoc Boi, "The Blanket of Scraps." Originally published as "Nhong manh von" in 1992 and included in *Literature News: Nine Stories from the Viet Nam Writer's Union Newspaper,* Bao Van Nghe. Selected and translated by Rosemary Nguyen, *Lac Viet* 16, 1997, pp. 96–123. My thanks to Marilyn Young for bringing this story to my attention.

3. See the superb analysis of postwar Europe and Remarque's work in Modris Eksteins, *Rites of Spring: The Great War and the Birth of the Modern Age* (Boston: Houghton Mifflin, 1989).

4. Nguyen Thanh Tam, "Remarks on Women Who Live without Husbands," in *Vietnamese Women in Transition,* p. 87.

5. See Cynthia Enloe, *The Morning After: Sexual Politics at the End of the Cold War* (Berkeley: U. of California, 1993); and "Women after Wars: Puzzles and Warnings," in *Vietnam's Women in Transition,* pp. 299–315. For a succinct critique of women's status in postwar Vietnam, see David Goodkind, "Rising Gender Inequality in Vietnam Since Reunification," *Pacific Affairs,* Vol. 68, Fall 1995, pp. 342–359.

6. Le Thi Quy, "Domestic Violence in Vietnam," *Vietnam's Women in Transition,* pp. 270–271.

7. Le Thi Quy, "The Struggle against the Traffic in Women and Children in Vietnam," unpublished paper, courtesy of the author.

MATERIALS CONSULTED
AND SUGGESTIONS FOR
FURTHER READING

A note about sources: I have included here only those materials that I consulted for this book and that are published and available to American readers. Information from interviews and conversations unless otherwise stated in the text comes from my field work in North Vietnam in spring 1996 and early 1997. Phan Thanh Hao supervised the translations of some of the documents. Others were translated and revised in the United States.

Abu-Lughod, Lila. *Writing Women's Worlds: Bedouin Stories*. Berkeley: U. of California Press, 1993.

Addams, Jane. *Jane Addams on Peace, War, and International Understanding, 1899–1932*. Edited by Allen F. Davis. New York: Garland, 1976.

Alvarez, Sonia. *Engendering Democracy in Brazil: Women's Movements in Transitional Politics*. Princeton, NJ: Princeton U. Press, 1990.

Anderson, Benedict. *Imagined Communities*. New York: Verso, 1983.

Anderson, Karen. *Wartime Women: Sex Roles, Family Relations, and the Status of Women During World War II*. Westport, CT: Greenwood, 1981.

Andors, Phyllis. *The Unfinished Liberation of Chinese Women, 1949–1980*. Bloomington: Indiana U. Press, 1983.

Badran, Margaret. "Competing Agendas: Feminists, Islam and the State in Nineteenth and Twentieth Century Egypt." In Deniz Kandiyoti, ed., *Women, Islam and the State*. Philadelphia: Temple U. Press, 1991.

Baker, Mark. *Nam*. New York: Berkeley Books, 1984.

Balaban, John. *Remembering Heaven's Face: A Conscientious Objector's Moving Memoir of the Vietnam War*. New York: Touchstone, 1992.

Bao Ninh. *The Sorrow of War*. Translated by Phan Thanh Hao and Vo Bang Thanh with Katerina Pierce. London: Secker & Warburg, 1993.

Barry, Kathleen, ed. *Vietnam's Women in Transition*. London: Macmillan, 1996.

Becraft, Carolyn. *Women in the Military, 1980–1990*. Washington, DC: Women's Research and Education Institute, 1991.

————. *Women in the U.S. Armed Services: The War in the Persian Gulf.* Washington, DC: Women's Research and Education Institute, 1991.

Behar, Ruth. *Translated Woman: Crossing the Border with Esperanza's Story.* Boston: Beacon Press, 1993.

Bell, Diane, and Shelley Schreiner, eds. *This Is My Story: Perspectives on the Use of Oral Sources.* Geelong, Victoria, Australia: Deakin U., 1990.

Benallegue, Nora. "Algerian Women in the Struggle for Independence and Reconstruction." *35 International Social Science Journal* (1983): 703–718.

Berkin, Carol, and Clara Lovett, eds. *Women, War and Revolution.* New York: Holmes and Meier, 1980.

Boettcher, Thomas D. *Vietnam: The Valor and the Sorrow.* Boston: Little, Brown & Co., 1985.

Boris, Eilen, and Peter Bardaglio. "The Transformation of Patriarchy: The Historic Role of the State." In Irene Diamond, ed., *Families, Politics, and Public Policy.* New York: Longman Press, 1983.

Borton, Lady. *After Sorrow: An American Among the Vietnamese.* New York: Kodansha, 1995.

Bousquet, Ben, and Colin Douglas. *West Indian Women at War: British Racism in World War II.* London: Lawrence and Wishart, 1991.

Bowen, Kevin, and Bruce Weigl, eds. *Writing Between the Lines.* Amherst, MA: U. of Massachusetts Press, 1997.

Braybon, Gail, and Penny Simmerfield. *Out of the Cage: Women's Experiences in Two World Wars.* London: Pandora, 1987.

Breen, William J. "Black Women and the Great War: Mobilization and Reform in the South." *44 Journal of Southern History* (August 1978): 421–440.

Brownmiller, Susan. *Seeing Vietnam: Encounters of the Road and Heart.* New York: HarperCollins, 1994.

Bui, Diem, with David Chanoff. *In the Jaws of History.* Boston: Houghton Mifflin, 1987.

Butler, Judith, and Joan Scott, eds. *Feminists Theorize the Political.* New York and London: Routledge, 1992.

Butler, Susan. *American Women Writers on Vietnam: Unheard Voices. A Selected Annotated Bibliography.* New York: Garland Press, 1990.

Campbell, D'Ann. *Women at War with America.* Cambridge: Harvard U. Press, 1984.

Cao, Ngoc Phuong. *Learning True Love.* Berkeley: Parallax Press, 1993.

Chaliand, Gerard. *The Peasants of North Vietnam.* London: Penguin, 1969.

Chanoff, David, and Doan Van Toai. *Vietnam: A Portrait of a People at War.* London: Tauris, 1996.

Chatterjee, Partha. "The Nationalist Resolution of the Women's Question." In Kumkum Sangari and Sudesh Vaid, *Recasting Women: Essays in Colonial History.* New Delhi: Kali for Women, 1989.

Chapkis, Wendy, ed. *Loaded Questions: Women in the Military*. Amsterdam: Transnational Institute, 1981.

Charlton, Sue Ellen M. *Women in Third World Development*. Boulder, CO: Westview Press, 1984.

Clodfelter, Mark. *The Limits of Air Power: The American Bombing of North Vietnam*. New York: The Free Press, 1989.

Cock, Jacklyn. *Women and War in South Africa*. London: Open Letter Press, 1992.

Collinson, Helen, ed. *Women and Revolution in Nicaragua*. London: Zed Books, 1990.

Combined Document Exploitation Center (CDEC). Saigon, 1966–1973. On microfilm and uncatalogued at the Joiner Center, U. of Massachusetts at Boston.

Connell, R. W. *Gender and Power*. Stanford: Stanford U. Press, 1988.

Cooke, Miriam. *Women and the War Story*. Berkeley: U. of California Press, 1996.

———, ed., and Roshni Rustomji-Kerns. *Blood into Ink: South Asian and Middle Eastern Women Write War*. Boulder, CO: Westview Press, 1994.

Corbett, Deborah. "Women in Iraq." In *Saddam's Iraq: Revolution or Reaction?* Edited by Committee against Repression and for Democratic Rights in Iraq. London: Zed Books, 1986, 120–135.

Cornum, Rhonda. *She Went to War: The Rhonda Cornum Story*. Novato, CA: Presidio Press, 1992.

Costello, John. *Virtue under Fire: How World War II Changed Our Social and Sexual Attitudes*. Boston: Little, Brown, 1985.

Cottam, K. Jean. "Soviet Women in Combat in World War II: The Ground Forces and the Navy." 3 *International Journal of Women's Studies* (July/August, 1980): 345–357.

Croll, Elisabeth. *Feminism and Socialism in China*. London: Routledge, 1980.

———. *From Heaven to Earth: Images and Experiences of Development in China*. London: Routledge, 1994.

Cuoc Khang Chien Chong My Cuu Nuoc, 1954–75. [Vietnam: The anti-U.S. resistance war for national salvation, 1954–1975: military events.] From FBIS. U.S. Army Military History Institute, July 3, 1982.

Derrida, Jacques. *Writing and Difference*. Trans. Alan Bass. Chicago: U. of Chicago Press, 1978.

Di Leonardo, Micaela. "Morals, Mothers, and Militarism: Anti-Militarism and Feminist Theory." 11 *Feminist Studies* (Fall, 1985): 607–617.

Dietz, Mary G. "Context Is All: Feminism and Theories of Citizenship." 116 *Daedalus* (Fall, 1987).

Dittmar, Linda, and Gene Michaud, eds. *From Hanoi to Hollywood: The Vietnam War in American Film*. New Brunswick, NJ: Rutgers U. Press, 1991.

Duiker, William. *The Rise of Nationalism in Vietnam: 1890–1941*. Ithaca: Cornell U. Press, 1976.

Douglas, Mary. *Purity and Danger: An Analysis of Concepts of Pollution and Taboo.* London: Arc Paperbacks, 1984.

Duong, Thu Huong. *Paradise of the Blind.* Trans. Phan Huy Duong and Nina McPherson. New York: Penguin, 1993.

————. *Novel without a Name.* Trans. Phan Huy Duong and Nina McPherson. New York: Penguin, 1995.

Eksteins, Modris. *Rites of Spring: The Great War and the Birth of the Modern Age.* Boston: Houghton Mifflin, 1989.

Eisen, Arlene. *Women and Revolution in Vietnam.* London: Zed Books, 1984.

Elshtain, Jean Bethke. *Women and War.* Chicago: U. of Chicago Press, 1995.

————, and Sheila Tobias, eds. *Women, Militarism and War: Essays in History, Politics and Social Theory.* Savage, MD: Rowman and Littlefield, 1990.

Enloe, Cynthia. *Bananas, Beaches and Bases: Making Feminist Sense of International Politics.* London: HarperCollins, 1988.

————. *Does Khaki Become You? The Militarization of Women's Lives.* London: Pluto Press, 1983.

————. *Maneuvers: The Militarization of Women's Lives.* Berkeley: U. of California Press, forthcoming.

————. *The Morning After: Sexual Politics at the End of the Cold War.* Berkeley: U. of California Press, 1993.

Fall, Bernard. *Hell in a Very Small Place: The Siege of Dien Bien Phu.* New York: Da Capo, 1966.

————, ed. *Ho Chi Minh on Revolution.* New York: Praeger, 1967.

Fraser, Nancy. *Unruly Practices: Power, Discourse, and Gender in Contemporary Social Theory.* Minneapolis: U. of Minnesota Press, 1989.

Freeman, Mark. *Rewriting the Self: History, Memory, Narrative.* London: Routledge, 1993.

Freeman, James M. *Hearts of Sorrow: Vietnamese Lives.* Stanford: Stanford U. Press, 1989.

Gender and Development in Vietnam. Compiled by Le Thi Nham Tuyet, Le Van Phung, and La Nam Thin. Hanoi: Nha xuat ban khoa hoc xa hoi, 1995.

Gilmartin, Christine, Gail Hershatter, Lisa Rofel, and Tyrene White, eds. *Engendering China: Women, Culture and the State.* Cambridge, MA: Harvard U. Press, 1994.

Gioseffi, Daniela, ed. *Women on War.* New York: Simon & Schuster, 1988.

Gluck, Sherna Berger. *Rosie the Riveter Revisited: Women, the War and Social Change.* New York: Meridian, 1987.

Goldman, Nancy Loring, ed. *Female Soldiers—Combatants or Noncombatants?* Westport, CT: Greenwood, 1982.

Goodkind, Daniel. "Rising Gender Equality in Vietnam Since Reunification." 68 *Pacific Affairs* (Fall 1995): 342–359.

Grant, Rebecca, and Kathleen Newland, eds. *Gender and International Relations.* Bloomington: Indiana U. Press, 1993.

Gutman, Stephanie. "Sex and the Soldier." *The New Republic,* February 24, 1997, pp. 18–22.

Haines, David. "Vietnamese Kinship, Gender Roles, and Societal Diversity: Some Lessons from Survey Research on Refugees." 8 *Vietnam Forum* (1986): 204–217.

Hartsock, Nancy. *Sexuality and Politics: The Barracks Community in Western Political Thought.* New York: Longmans, 1983.

Hayslip, Le Ly. *When Heaven and Earth Changed Places.* New York: Penguin, 1989.

Hendessi, Mandana. *Armed Angels: Women in Iran.* London: Change International Reports, 1990.

Hickey, Gerald. *Free in the Forest: Ethnohistory of the Vietnamese Central Highlands.* New Haven: Yale U. Press, 1982.

———. *Village in Vietnam.* New Haven: Yale U. Press, 1964.

Hiebert, Murray. *Chasing the Tigers: A Portrait of the New Vietnam.* New York: Kondansha, 1996.

———. "Single Mothers: Women in Men-Short Vietnam Are Having Children Out of Wedlock." *Far Eastern Economic Review.* February 24, 1994, pp. 60–61.

Higonnet, Margaret Randolph, et al. *Behind the Lines: Gender and the Two World Wars.* New Haven: Yale U. Press, 1987.

Hills, Carol, and Daniel Silverman. "Nationalism and Feminism in Late Colonial India: The Rani of Jhansi Regiment, 1943–1945." 27 *Modern Asian Studies* (1993): 741–760.

Ho Chi Minh. *Ho Chi Minh on Revolution: Selected Writings, 1920–1966.* Bernard Fall, ed. New York: Praeger, 1967.

Hodgkin, Thomas. *Vietnam: The Revolutionary Path.* London: Macmillan, 1981.

Holmgren, Jennifer. *Chinese Colonization of North Vietnam.* Canberra, Australia: Australian National U., 1980.

Hong-Kingston, Maxine. *The Woman Warrior: Memoirs of a Girlhood Among Ghosts.* New York: Dell, 1976.

Isaksson, Eva, ed. *Women and the Military System.* London: Harvester-Wheatsheaf, 1988.

Jamieson, Neil. *Understanding Vietnam.* Berkeley: U. of California Press, 1993.

Jayawardena, Kumari. *Feminism and Nationalism in the Third World.* London: Zed Press, 1986.

Jeffords, Susan. *The Remasculinization of America: Gender and the Vietnam War.* Bloomington: Indiana U. Press, 1989.

Johnson, Kay Ann. *Women, the Family, and Peasant Revolution in China.* Chicago: U. of Chicago Press, 1983.

Karlin, Wayne, Le Minh Khue, and Truong Vu, eds. *The Other Side of Heaven: Postwar Fiction by Vietnamese and American Writers*. Willimantic, CT: Curbstone Press, 1995.

Karnow, Stanley. *Vietnam: A History*. London: Penguin, 1983.

Kerber, Linda K. "May All Our Citizens Be Soldiers and All Our Soldiers Citizens: The Ambiguities of Female Citizenship in the New Nation." In *Women, Militarism, and War: Essays in History, Politics and Social Theory,* ed. by Jean Bethke Elshtain and Sheila Tobias. Savage, MD: Rowan and Littlefield, 1990, 89–104.

Kolko, Gabriel. *Anatomy of a War: Vietnam, the United States and the Modern Historical Experience*. New York: New Press, 1994 ed.

Koonz, Claudia. *Mothers in the Fatherland*. New York: St. Martin's Press, 1987.

Kramer, Jane. *The Politics of Memory: Looking for Germany in the New Germany*. New York: Random House, 1996.

Kruks, Sonia, Rayna Rapp, and Marilyn B. Young, eds. *Promissory Notes: Women in the Transition to Socialism*. New York: Monthly Review Press, 1989.

Larson, Wendy W. *Shallow Graves: Two Women and Vietnam*. New York, Random House, 1986.

Lavie, Smadar. *The Poetics of Military Occupation: Mzeina Allegories of Bedouin Identity under Israeli and Egyptian Rule*. Berkeley: U. of California Press, 1990.

Lich Su Duong Ho Chi Minh. Hanoi: Nha xuat ban quan doi, 1995.

Linde, Charlotte. *Life Stories: The Creation of Coherence*. New York: Oxford U. Press, 1993.

Lockhart, Gary, trans. *The General Retires and Other Stories*. Oxford: Oxford U. Press, 1992.

Luong, Hy. V. *Revolution in the Village: Tradition and Transformation in North Vietnam 1928–1988*. Honolulu: U. of Hawaii Press, 1992.

MacKinnon, Catherine. *Towards a Feminist Theory of the State*. Cambridge, MA: Harvard U. Press, 1989.

Mai, Thi Tu, and Le Thi Nham Tuyet, eds. *Women in Vietnam*. Hanoi: Foreign Languages Publishing House, 1978.

McDonald, Sharon, Pat Holden, and Shirley Ardener, eds. *Images of Women in Peace and War: Cross-Cultural and Historical Perspectives*. Madison: U. of Wisconsin Press, 1988.

Marr, David. *Vietnamese Anticolonialism, 1885–1925*. Berkeley: U. of California Press, 1971.

———. *Vietnamese Tradition on Trial, 1920–1945*. Berkeley: U. of California Press, 1981.

———, and Christine White, eds. *Postwar Vietnam: Dilemmas in Social Development*. Ithaca, NY: Cornell U. Press, 1988.

Marshall, Kathryn. *In the Combat Zone.* Boston: Little, Brown, 1987.

Mernissi, Fatima. *Doing Daily Battle: Interviews with Moroccan Women.* London: Women's Press, 1987.

Meyer, Leisa. *Creating G.I. Jane: Sexuality and Power in the Women's Army Corps During World War II.* New York: Columbia U. Press, 1996.

Mohanty, Chandra Talpade, et al. *Third World Women and the Politics of Feminism.* Bloomington: Indiana U. Press, 1991.

Momsen, Janet, and Vivian Kinnaird, eds. *Different Places, Different Voices: Gender and Development in Africa, Asia and Latin America.* London: Routledge, 1993.

Nakahara, Michiko. "Forgotten Victims: Asian and Women Workers on the Thai-Burma Railway." 23 AMPO: *Japan-Asian Quarterly Review* (1991): 21–25.

Nam, Phuong. *Red on Gold.* Claremont, CA: Albatross Books, 1991.

Ngo, Duc Thinh. "The Cult of the Female Spirits and the Mother Goddess 'Mau.'" 3 *Vietnamese Studies* (1996): 1–13.

Ngo, Thao. *Nguyen Thi-Nguyen Ngoc Tan.* 4 vols. Hanoi: Nha xuat ban san khau, 1996.

———. *Nhu Cuoc Doi.* Hanoi: Nha xuat ban san khau, 1997.

Ngo, Vinh Long. *Vietnamese Women in Society and Revolution.* Vol. I. Cambridge, MA: Vietnamese Resource Center, 1974.

Nguyen, Ba Chung. "Imagining the Nation." 21 *Boston Review* (1996).

Nguyen, Khac Vien, and Huu Ngoc. *Vietnamese Literature: Historical Background and Texts,* trans. Mary Cowan, et al. Hanoi: Foreign Languages Publishing House, 1979.

Nguyen, Rosemary, trans. *Literature News. Nine Stories from the Vietnam Writer's Union Newspaper.* 16 *Lac Viet,* 1997.

Nguyen, Thanh T., and Bruce Weigl, eds. and trans. *Poems from Captured Documents.* Boston: U. of Massachusetts Press, 1994.

Nguyen, Thi Dinh. *No Other Road to Take.* Trans. Mai V. Elliott. Ithaca: Cornell U. South East Asia Program, 1976. Originally published in Vietnamese in Hanoi, 1968.

Nguyen, Thi Thu-Lam. *Fallen Leaves: Memoirs of a Vietnamese Woman from 1940 to 1975.* New Haven: Yale U. Council on Southeast Asia Studies, 1989.

Nguyen, Thi Tuyet Mai. *The Rubber Tree: A Memoir of a Vietnamese Woman Who Was an Anti-French Guerrilla, Peace Activist, and Publisher.* New York: McFarland Press, 1994.

Nguyen, Van De. *Thanh nien xung phong: phuc vu giao thong van tai thoi chong My.* Hanoi: Nha xuat ban giao thong van tai, 1995.

Nora, Pierre, and Jacques Le Goff. *Constructing the Past: Essays in Historical Methodology.* Cambridge, England: Cambridge U. Press, 1985.

Nu Anh Hung: Luc Luong Vu Trang Nhan Dan. Hanoi: Nha xuat ban quan doi nhan dan, 1994.

Ong, Aihwa. "Colonialism and Modernity: Feminist Re-Presentations of Women in Non-Western Societies." 3–4 *Inscriptions* (1988): 79–93.

Parker, Andrew, Mary Russo, et al., eds. *Nationalism and Sexualities*. New York: Routledge, 1992.

Personal Narratives Group. *Interpreting Women's Lives: Feminist Theory and Personal Narratives*. Bloomington: Indiana U. Press, 1989.

Peterson, Spike, ed. *Gendered States: Feminist (Re)visions of International Relations Theory*. Boulder, CO: Lynne Rienner, 1992.

Phan, Thi Nhu Bang. *Ta Thi Kieu. An Heroic Girl of Ben Tre*. South Vietnam: Liberation Editions, 1966.

Pike, Douglas. *Viet Cong: The Organization and Techniques of the National Liberation Front in Vietnam*. Cambridge, MA: MIT Press, 1966.

Prados, John, and Ray W. Stubbe. *Valley of Decision: The Siege of Khe Sanh*. Boston: Houghton Mifflin, 1991.

Pratt, John, comp. *Vietnam Voices: Perspectives on the War Years, 1941–1982*. New York: Viking, 1984.

Radner, Joan N. *Feminist Messages: Coding in Women's Folk Culture*. Urbana: U. of Illinois Press, 1993.

Randall, Margaret. *Sandino's Daughters: Testimonies of Nicaraguan Women in Struggle*. Vancouver, B.C.: New Star Books, 1981.

———. *Sandino's Daughters Revisited: Feminism in Nicaragua*. New Brunswick, NJ: Rutgers U. Press, 1994.

Reed, Paul, and Ted Schwarz. *Kontum Diary: Captured Writings Bring Peace to a Vietnam Veteran*. Arlington, TX: Summit Press, 1996.

Remarque, Erich Maria. *All Quiet on the Western Front*. Trans. A. W. Wheen. Boston: Little Brown, 1929.

Rodgers, Susan, ed. and trans. *Telling Lives, Telling History: Autobiography and Historical Imagination in Modern Indonesia*. Berkeley: U. of California Press, 1995.

Ruddick, Sara. *Maternal Thinking: Toward a Politics of Peace*. Boston: Beacon Press, 1989.

Russo, Valeria, Lorenza Sebesta, and Elizabetta Addis, eds. *Women at War: Images of Women Soldiers*. London: Macmillan, 1993.

Samuels, Raphael, ed. *Patriotism: The Making and Unmaking of National Identity*. 3 vols. London: Routledge, 1989.

Sanararian, Elizabeth. *The Women's Rights Movement in Iran*. New York: Praeger, 1982.

Saywell, Shelley. *Women in War: From World War II to El Salvador*. New York: Penguin, 1986.

Scott, James C. *Domination and the Arts of Resistance: Hidden Transcripts*. New Haven: Yale U. Press, 1990.

Scott, Joan W. *Gender and the Politics of History*. New York: Columbia U. Press, 1988.

————. "The Evidence of Experience." 7 *Critical Inquiry* (1991).

Sen, Gita, and Caren Grown. *Development, Crises, and Alternative Visions: Third World Women's Perspectives*. New York: Monthly Review Press, 1987.

Shay, Jonathan. *Achilles in Vietnam: Combat Trauma and the Undoing of Character*. New York: Touchstone, 1995.

Sheridan, Dorothy. *Wartime Women*. London: Mandarin, 1990.

Spivak, Gayatri C. "Subaltern Studies: Deconstructing Historiography." In *Selected Subaltern Studies*, ed. Ranajit Guha and Gayatri C. Spivak. New York: Oxford U. Press, 1988.

Statistics on Vietnamese Women, 1985–1994 [So lieu ve phu nu Viet Nam]. Hanoi: Statistical Publishing House, 1995.

Staunton, Irene, ed. *Mothers of the Revolution: The War Experiences of Thirty Zimbabwean Women*. Bloomington: Indiana U. Press, 1990.

Steedly, Mary. *Hanging without a Rope: Narrative Experience in Colonial and Post-Colonial Karoland*. Princeton: Princeton U. Press, 1993.

Steitz, Barbara J. "From Home to Street: Women and Revolution in Nicaragua." In *Women Transforming Politics*, ed. by Jill M. Bystdzienski. Bloomington: Indiana U. Press, 1992, 162–174.

Stiehm, Judith Hicks. *Arms and the Enlisted Woman*. Philadelphia: Temple U. Press, 1989.

Stockard, Janice. *Daughters of the Canton Delta: Marriage Patterns and Economic Strategies in South China, 1860–1930*. Stanford: Stanford U. Press, 1989.

Stone, Anne J., ed. *Women in the Military: International Perspectives*. Washington, DC: Women's Research and Education Institute, 1992.

Summerfield, Penny. *Women Workers in the Second World War*. New York: Routledge, 1989.

Sutton, Constance R., ed. *Feminism, Nationalism, and Militarism*. New York: Association of Feminist Anthropologists and International Women's Anthropological Conference, 1995. Washington, DC: American Anthropological Association.

Sylvester, Christine. *Feminist Theory and International Politics in a Postmodern Era*. Cambridge: Cambridge U. Press, forthcoming.

Ta, Van Tai. "The Status of Women in Traditional Vietnam." 15 *Journal of Asian History* (1981): 97–145.

Tai, Hue-Tam Ho. *Radicalism and the Origins of the Vietnamese Revolution*. Cambridge, MA: Harvard U. Press, 1992.

————. "Duong Thu Huong and the Literature of Disenchantment." 14 *Vietnam Forum* (1994): 82–91.

Tal, Kali. "The Mind at War: Images of Women in Vietnam Novels by Combat Veterans." 31 *Contemporary Literature* (1990).

Tanaka, Stefan. "Imagining History: Inscribing Belief in the Nation." 53 *The Journal of Asian Studies* (1993).

Taylor, Keith W. *The Birth of Vietnam.* Berkeley: U. of California Press, 1984.

————, and John K. Whitmore, eds. *Essays into Vietnamese Pasts.* Ithaca, New York: Cornell U. Southeast Asia Program, 1995.

Terry, Wallace. *Bloods: An Oral History of the Vietnam War by Black Veterans.* New York: Ballantine Books, 1984.

Tetreault, Mary Ann, ed. *Women and Revolution in Africa, Asia, and the New World.* Columbia, SC: U. of South Carolina Press, 1994.

Tickner, J. Ann. *Gender in International Relations.* New York: Columbia U. Press, 1992.

Tsing, Anna L. *In the Realm of the Diamond Queen.* Princeton: Princeton U. Press, 1993.

Truong, Nhu Tang. *A Vietcong Memoir: An Inside Account of the Vietnam War and Its Aftermath.* New York: Harcourt Brace, 1985.

Turner, Victor, and Edward Bruner. *The Anthropology of Experience.* Urbana: U. of Illinois Press, 1986.

Van Devanter, Lynda. *Home Before Morning.* New York: Warner, 1983.

————, and Joan A. Furey. *Visions of War, Dreams of Peace.* New York: Warner, 1991.

The Vietnam Forum: A Review of Vietnamese Culture and Society. New Haven: Yale U. Council for Southeast Asia Studies.

Vietnam: The Anti-U.S. Resistance War for National Salvation 1954–1975. Military Events [Cuoc khang chien chong my cuu nuoc 1954–1975]. FBIS trans., June, 1982.

"Vietnamese Women." 10 *Vietnamese Studies.* Hanoi: Xunhasaba, 1966.

Visweswaran, Kamala. "Defining Feminist Ethnography." 3 *Inscriptions* (1988): 27–44.

Vo, Nguyen Giap. *Dien Bien Phu.* Fifth ed. Hanoi: Gioi Publishers, 1994.

Watson, Lawrence, and Maria-Barbara Watson-Franke. *Interpreting Life Histories.* New Brunswick, NJ: Rutgers U. Press, 1985.

Weitz, Margaret Collins. *Sisters in Resistance: How Women Fought to Free France, 1940–1945.* New York: John Wiley & Sons, 1995.

White, Christine Pelzer, "Vietnam: War Socialism and the Politics of Gender Relations." In *Promissory Notes: Women in the Transition to Socialism.* Sonia Kruks, Rayna Rapp, and Marilyn B. Young, eds. New York: Monthly Review Press, 1989.

Whitmore, John K. "Social Organization and Confucian Thought in Vietnam." 60 *Journal of Southeast Asia Studies* (1984): 296–306.

Wiegersma, Nancy. *Vietnam—Peasant Land, Peasant Revolution: Patriarchy and Collectivity in the Rural Economy.* New York: St. Martin's Press, 1988.

Winter, Jay. *Sites of Memory, Sites of Mourning: The Great War in European Cultural History.* Cambridge, England: Cambridge U. Press, 1995.

Woodside, B. Alexander. *Community and Revolution in Modern Vietnam.* Boston: Houghton Mifflin, 1976.

————. *Vietnam and the Chinese Model: A Comparative Study of Vietnamese and Chinese Government in the First Half of the Nineteenth Century.* Cambridge, MA: Harvard U. Press, 1988 (originally, 1971).

Yalom, Marilyn. *Blood Sisters: The French Revolution in Women's Memory.* New York: Basic Books, 1993.

Young, Marilyn. *The Vietnam Wars, 1945–1990.* New York: HarperCollins, 1991.

Yuval-Davis, Nira, and Floya Anthias, eds. *Woman, Nation, State.* London: Macmillan, 1989.

INDEX